MAGIC AND ENGLISH ROMANTICISM

MAGIC AND ENGLISH ROMANTICISM

ANYA TAYLOR

THE
UNIVERSITY OF GEORGIA PRESS
ATHENS

Set in 12 on 12½ point Mergenthaler Garamond type
Printed in the United States of America

Library of Congress Cataloging in Publication Data

Taylor, Anya.
    Magic and English romanticism.

    1. English poetry—19th century—History and
criticism.   2. Romanticism—England.   3. Magic
in literature.   I. Title
PR590.T38   821'.7'09   78–5590
          ISBN 0–8203–0453–0

Chapter 4 is based on an article that appeared in the
spring 1972 issue of the *Wordsworth Circle*. Grateful
acknowledgement is given to the editor of the journal for permission to use that material here.

FOR MARK, ANDREW, AND NICHOLAS

Contents

Acknowledgments

Since the time when I first began seeing references to magic and formal adaptations of magical spells in romantic poetry, and trying to understand why magic should appear so often, I have incurred many debts both to generous scholars and to the books they have written. Above all, I am indebted to Thomas McFarland, whose important book *Coleridge and the Pantheist Tradition* taught me to see the cohesiveness and "reticulation" of the many strands of Coleridge's thought, and it showed me an inimitable grace and precision of scholarship. Professor McFarland directed my research when this book was in its rudimentary form as a dissertation, and since then he has read and criticized the many intermediate forms it has taken. Professor Allen Mandelbaum has helped me time and again, reading several versions and bolstering morale with his kindness and attentiveness. Professor Howard O. Brogan also read and reread the book as it changed under the pressure of his meticulous suggestions; Professor Paul Magnuson offered helpful suggestions toward a broadening of view; and Professor Charles I. Patterson, Jr., his demonic energy working benevolently to root out errors, advised me in sharpening my interpretations. Whatever strengths this book possesses belong to these people; its weaknesses are, of course, my own.

There are four other teachers and friends who have helped on early versions of this book and suggested by their own studies on either magic or poetic theory areas where I could pursue my investigations: Professor Coleman O. Parsons, authority on magic and witchcraft in Scott, offered helpful comments and encouragement; Professor John Hollander allowed me to work on spells long ago in his seminar on the lyric and gave advice thereafter; Professor Helaine Newstead taught me to see the importance of magic in medieval romance; and Professor Joseph Campbell inspired me as an undergraduate to see the connections between primitive and sophisticated myths and to dare to combine ideas from different disciplines.

With so much help from others, this book comes as an anticlimax. But there are still others, close to the hearth and heart, to thank: my husband Mark, always judicious, cheerful, and ready with the right word, and our sons Andrew and Nicholas, whose "magic years" coincided with my own. It is to these three, as a small tribute to their joyful and sustaining companionship, that I dedicate this book.

A. T.

Introduction

In the concluding chapters of *Religion and the Decline of Magic*
Keith Thomas explains why magic ceased at the end of the
seventeenth century to be a moving force in European
thought. The major reason was "the triumph of the mechanical philosophy," which "involved the rejection both of scholastic Aristoteleanism and of that neoplatonic theory which had
threatened to take its place. With the collapse of the micro-
cosm theory went the destruction of the whole intellectual
basis of astrology, chiromancy, alchemy, physiognomy, astral
magic, and their associates."[1] A new spirit of independence
together with practical improvements in controlling an unpredictable environment combined to render visitations of
spirits and efforts to control them virtually preposterous.
The incidence of witches, possessions, enthusiasms, black
and white magic, astrological consultations, and alchemical
laboratories fell off toward the end of a century that had begun
with science and magic "advancing side by side" and corroborating each other's ventures into the unknown.

It is one of the triumphs of late seventeenth- and early
eighteenth-century thought to have eradicated superstition, to
have *écrasé l'infâme* and the subsidiary beliefs which nurtured it,
and to have encouraged the establishment of clear and distinct
ideas and the discarding of a priori opinions, unsubstantiated
prejudices, and other idols that are impervious to proof. In the
light of Voltaire's ridicule of religion or Diderot's biological
fancies or Hume's irrefutable statements on the natural history
of religion—devastating in the very title ascribing to religion
an organic development—one can hardly take seriously the
alchemical transmutations of Thomas Vaughan, the sober
elucidations of the provenance of spirits by Ralph Cudworth,
and the benighted superstitions of Henry More. Although

magic and alchemy had contributed at the beginning of the seventeenth century an atmosphere stimulating to the discoveries of heliocentrism, the infinity of worlds, and the circulations of the blood,[2] by the end of the seventeenth century these Neoplatonic, hermetic, and animistic ways of thinking had been eroded, if not obliterated, by science.

Yet seventy years later, in the face of clear philosophical and scientific refutation, and of less clear but even more pungent mockeries of spiritualistic beliefs, there is a revival of interest in these phenomena beginning with Gray and Collins and gathering momentum with Coleridge and Shelley. For intelligent heirs of the Enlightenment such as Coleridge and Shelley, what possible meaning could there be in these outdated modes of thinking—primitive, credulous, and anxious, as obsolete as earth goddesses, witches, and spells to cure gout? What, in other words, might justify a study of magic in romanticism, a movement that begins a full century after the sure decline of magic as it affected religious belief and that arises in part from extreme skepticism?

Is there in the romantic movement a regressive irrational impulse? In spite of decades of critical labor to disprove such irrationality, to fend off the charges that the romantics inspired the will to power, rampant individualism, the end of the spirit of community, and the growth of ambitious nations, to dissociate the humanistic English romantics from their dynamic (and often sinister) German contemporaries, is there some aspect of romantic work that may be considered atavistic?

There is an irrational and regressive aspect to romanticism, but it arises for humanistic reasons. The arguments of Locke for the origin of ideas in nature, of Hume against connective cause, even Hartley's more aesthetic analogies of vibrations with musical chords shaking the medullary substance, provoke a restless feeling that something is missing, or being denied, as if the insistence on scientific proof, on visible substance, is too simple. The urge—occasionally manifested by poets from Gray to Shelley—to look backward and find some unprovable powers arises from a desire to affirm the existence of spirit, of imagination, and of freedom in the face of exclusively physical hypotheses. Where the unpredictable exists, there the human being can assert his humanness apart from all other organisms that are observed and measured. This desire to see in the human animal some element that is unknowable, mysterious, or occult leads many romantic thinkers to suspend their disbelief, to turn back beyond the experimental scientists to the Cambridge Platonists, to the magi of the Renaissance, to Norse and Celtic myths, and to the Alexandrian philosophy of the first and second centuries, seeking metaphors for poetry.

There have been many speculations on the zeitgeist that appears around the middle of the eighteenth century, with some critics calling it the insistence of horror or of vision, others calling it a longing for the unpredictable, the distant, the vital, the turbulent, or the powerful. This spirit is a response to emptinesses and inadequacies in the contemporary thought that had aimed for rational observable proof.[3] Magic and alchemy, in presuming to deviate from the fixed laws observed and catalogued by science, break into the predictions of science, disturb the set order of material substances, and hint at unexamined shadowy truths. In these areas that remain unknown a spiritual freedom may still exist. An extreme form of this position is voiced by Dostoevsky's Underground Man who seeks to deny by the unpredictability of his acts that two plus two equals four.

An analogy to such a return to the irrational is described by Gershom Scholem in his writing on mystical revivals in Judaism. Scholem postulates a rhythm of alternation from rational to irrational faith, and he suggests that a private, ecstatic, emotional stage of belief often follows a strictly formulated stage as a reaction against the way doctrine blocks the worshipper from large areas of feeling. Scholem calls this mystical stage romantic.[4] A similar reaction follows the empirical materialist formulations of eighteenth-century philosophers who fenced in the area of experience accessible to the senses and discouraged as unknowable a view beyond the fence. While Hume, for one, did recognize a shadowy area of unknown and incomprehensible force, he preferred not to examine it, recommending that we learn as much as we can about this life and not draw inferences about an area that we cannot know clearly.

One of the subjects of inquiry in which eighteenth-century philosophical explanations were least satisfactory was language. A section on "Words" seems to have been obligatory in studies of the mind from Locke on. Locke himself in the third book of his *Essay Concerning Human Understanding* speculates "how great a dependence our words have on common sensible ideas, and how those which are made use of to stand for actions and notions quite removed from sense, have their rise from thence, and from obvious sensible ideas are transferred to more abstruse signification." This process proves to him the principle that he has already argued—namely "how nature, even in the naming of things, unawares suggested to men the originals and principles of all their knowledge." [5] Like Locke, David Hartley is also mechanical, though he acknowledges that "it is difficult to explain words to the bottom by words." He declares that "since words may be compared to the letters used in algebra, language itself may be termed one species of algebra." [6] Seeing words to be as transparent as ciphers, he pronounces the aim of philosophy to be to decipher the mysteries of nature, imagined to be susceptible of numerical resolution. With a similar avidity for a scientific reduction of this hitherto mysterious theme, Joseph Priestley in his *Theory of Language and Universal Grammar* hopes to render the subject as inductively clear as his other voluminous studies of gas, combustion, electricity, and light. The workings of language seemed to him potentially as orderly as those of oxygen. Such optimism, as Hans Aarsleff describes it in *The Study of Language in England 1780–1860*, assumed that language, like all other material substances, was penetrable by science if the scientist were only attentive to the evidence of his senses, an optimism that reached its high point in Condillac's *Traité de la formation méchanique des langues, et des principes physiques de l'étymologie.*[7] Explanations of words as the names of sensations are pursued throughout the century, until in the writings of Lord Monboddo, James Harris, Rousseau, von Humboldt, and Herder a new awareness of the subject's nonmechanical elements occurs.

While the late eighteenth-century poet may have felt timid about disputing the materialists' theories of matter or mind, however essentially fanciful these descriptions of association and sensation may have been, he was less timid about disputing the mechanical theory of language, for the poet knows that the description is partial and that Hartley is wrong when he says that words are as simple as numbers. On the grounds of language the late-eighteenth-century poets thus can begin to dispute the philosophers, for they feel that here, if not in the description of the mind itself, the philosophers are intuitively wrong. In reaction to the inadequacies of these philosophical analyses of language the poets and imaginative thinkers of the late eighteenth century occasionally turn to metaphors of magic, for magic assumes that words are not themselves material but partake of spirit and that words have an inscrutable power to influence matter, particularly when arranged in mysteriously rhythmic ways and when impelled by ecstatic possessed states of mind. In turning to these metaphors, they return to an ancient tradition.

So ancient is the tradition that language is magical that merely listing bibliography would exceed the limits of this book. I can only indicate the areas which the enlightened philosophers believed were too murky for scientific concern. In keeping with the many allusions to the power of language in antiquity—the chorus of *Agamemnon* chanting "there surges within me / singing magic / grown to my life and power"; Odysseus shielding from the Cyclops the knowledge of his name and hence the control of his person—there was a pervasive belief that charms, or *epôdai*, could heal the body and the soul, that from Homer through the pre-Socratic philosophers and orphic initiates conjurations were therapeutic and could alter the life of men.[8] Plato's views on this matter are conflicting. On the one hand he records Socrates' belief in *Charmides* 157b that "the cure of the soul . . . has to be effected by the use of certain charms, and these charms are fair words, and by them temperance is implanted in the soul." Faith in the healing of the whole person through language put Plato in the ancient tradition of the therapy of the word, which Aristotle disputed. On the other hand the conclusion of the *Cratylus* contradicts the assumptions of *Charmides*. In it Socrates decides that words have in the end no power over things or ideas, which persist below the shifting names given to them without affecting their essence. According to this aspect of his thought, Plato tries to divert his fellow citizens from the hypnosis of the oral tradition, from dependence on words, spells, and nonliterate education, and from the fabulous sorcerers, seers, and witches who bound their susceptible souls.[9]

Plato's conflicting thoughts are not resolved, and we know that *res-verba* relations became only more intricate in late antiquity, when Plato's dilemma merged with Egyptian and Babylonian theurgy in Alexandria. The spells from the hermetic books, collected by A. J. M. Festugière, operated on the assumption that the names of things intimately belong to them and participate in their nature, and that the more the sorcerer can enunciate about the object under consideration, particularly about its hitherto secret, sometimes obscene, nature, the more power over its aspects the sorcerer will gain. Synonyms and terms in apposition are therefore abundant, and descriptions are elaborate, so that no aspect may escape mutation into a word, and hence absorption into the sorcerer's field of perception. Here, for example, is part of a very long spell: "I invoke you, ye holy ones . . . mighty arch-daimons . . . earth-dwellers, haunters of sky-depths, nook-infesting, murk-enwrapped, scanning the mysteries, guardians of secrets . . . ;

terror-strangling, panic-striking, spindle-turning; snow-scatterers, rain-wafters, spirits of air; fire tongues of summer-sun, tempest-tossing lords of fate." [10] The spell becomes a meeting place for the substance of the thing being magnetized into the field of the incantation and for the understanding of the sorcerer who is beaming its force into the language, trying to encompass all possibly related aspects, to notice what was hidden, and by noticing it in words to prevent any aspect from slipping outside his ken. The spell is a field of force drawing the thing into its power, aspect by aspect, name by name; because of this predatory intent, it is no wonder that the spell is often spoken of later as a web, with the victim caught in threads of words that leave him no room to breathe. (See, for example, Shelley's *Witch of Atlas* for this conflation of images.) He is caught, held, absorbed into the being of his enchanter, having entered through the medium of words into his mind.

The spell thus accomplishes a transference of material substance into spiritual ether, a refinement of the original being, and an enlargement of the sorcerer's spirit for having been added to from without, for having contained a thing as represented in its name, and in the names of its attributes. Some of the literature of the Alexandrian period concerns questions on the relationship of spells to their content and to their inventors' spirits, and possibly even the allegorical readings of Greek and Old Testament texts, popular in the period and beautifully elucidated by Don Cameron Allen in *Mysteriously Meant*,[11] are in part motivated by a desire to explore all the possible layers of meaning in a text so that the meanings will be absorbed, through the potent primary layer of meaning, into the mind. This layer of the actual words on the page will fold within it the others, and will unfold, once absorbed, into quadruple power. Having learned from the fourth book of Plotinus's *Enneads* about the powers of songs to join the passionate spirit of the singer with the hidden life of the object of the song and to tap through this conjunction the vital music of the universe that links all things, Porphyry, Jamblichus, Proclus, and, later, Psellus continue to praise the magician's intensive spirit as it projects its energy through language onto the substantial world and into the realm of invisible demons. This whole period of spiritual ferment, as E. R. Dodds shows in his *Pagan and Christian in an Age of Anxiety*, synthesizes oriental and Greek speculations on the interaction among things, the names of these things, the sounds of the names heard in the air, the rhythms of these sounds together, and the minds that contain the sounds.[12]

The relationship of words to things continues to perturb the early fathers, particularly Origen and Augustine, by prompting speculations on the gradations in verbal effectiveness: how, they wonder, can the spells of Orpheus, Moses, Amphion, Hermes, and of human poets be differentiated from God's utterance of the first spell: "Let there be Light"? Origen struggles against Celsus's charge that Christ was a mere magician no different from Simon Magus or other magicians in the Old Testament; in the midst of making his major distinction—that Christ works his miracles for the good of others rather than for his own glorification—he illuminates certain areas of word magic. To Celsus's point that it makes no difference what names one calls the gods, Origen answers "that a profound and obscure question is raised by this subject, that concerning the nature of names. The problem is whether, as Aristotle thinks, names were given by arbitrary determination; or as the Stoics hold, by nature; the first utterances being imitations of the things described and becoming their names . . . ; or whether, as Epicurus teaches . . . names were given by nature, the first men having burst out with certain sounds descriptive of the objects." Origen advocates a study to "show the nature of powerful names, some of which are used by the Egyptian wise men, or the learned men among the Persian magi, or the Brahmans, or Samanaeans among the Indian philosophers, and so on according to each nation"; then we could "establish that so-called magic is not, as the followers of

Epicurus and Aristotle think, utterly incoherent, but as the experts in these things prove, is a consistent system, which has principles known to very few." [13] Believing that wise men like the magi know how to communicate with demons, Origen explains that the words of charms and spells must be in strict order and that these words cannot be translated without losing their potency.

Similarly convinced of the efficacy of incantations in theurgic practice, and well-read in neoplatonic theories of language, Augustine works to distinguish between human words in time and the divine Word in Eternity, and his speculations have received intensive commentary. [14] From an acknowledgment of the power of sorcerers and enchanters both in scripture and in the *Aeneid*, Augustine concludes, "how much more able is God to do those things which to skeptics are incredible, but to His power easy" (*The City of God*, 21:6). In his footsteps Florentine Neoplatonists such as Pico della Mirandola, Marsilio Ficino, and Lazarelli returned in the fifteenth century to the fountainhead whence Augustine himself had drunk, and fortified their hopes for the effectiveness of songs by studying Plotinus. What Plotinus had recommended in theory, the Neoplatonists practiced in fact—astral songs for influencing the cosmic and political scene, as Frances Yates and D. P. Walker have demonstrated. Walker shows that "Lazarelli holds a magical theory of language, that he believes that words have a real, not conventional connexion with things, and can exert power over them. . . . Moreover, the word is not merely like a quality of the thing it designates, such as its colour or weight; it is, or exactly represents, its essence or substance. A formula of words, therefore, may not only be an adequate substitute for the thing denoted, but may even be more powerful." [15]

Continuing the tradition of believing that magic is a consistent system of powerful names intimately but mysteriously connected to their referents, Henry Cornelius Agrippa speaks at length in *Three Books of Occult Philosophy* of the secret powers

of words. Though he does not himself compose incantations as
Ficino had, he recommends the kinds that work best and
suggests the reasons why they work: "Words carry with them
not only the conception of the mind but also the virtue of the
speaker . . . and this oftentimes with so great a power that
often they change not only the hearers but also other bodies
and things that have no life." Not only is the spell the nexus of
speaker, hearer, and thing, but it derives its power from God's
own language. "Voice and words have efficacy in magical
works because that in which nature first exerciseth magical
efficacy is the voice of God." Because God created with language, in the first spell that Augustine also analyzes, the words
for things occur by analogy in the mind through a sort of
divine birth. "The Platonists," he speculates, "say that in this
very voice, or word, or name framed, with its article, that the
power of the thing, as it were some kind of life, lies under the
form of signification. First, conceived in the mind, as it were
through certain seeds of things, then by voices or words, as a
birth brought forth; and lastly, kept in writings." Sentences
have more power than single words, he believes, because they
are capable of conveying truths. Examples of powerful sentences are "verses, enchantments, imprecations, deprecations,
orations, invocations, obtestations, adjurations, conjurations
and such like." The verses he particularly has in mind are
orphic hymns, for "such like verses made according to the Rule
of the Stars, full of signification and meaning, and opportunely
pronounced with vehement affection and by the violence of the
imagination, do confer a great power in the enchanter, and
sometimes transfers it upon the thing enchanted." To be
powerful the enchanter's verses must be imbued with spirit,
"warm, breathing, living, bringing with it motion, affection,
and signification." Agrippa concludes this part of his discussion with words that seem to influence important elements of
romantic poetic theory: "and therefore, magicians enchanting
things are wont to blow and breathe upon them the words of
the verse, or to breathe in the virtue with the spirit, that so the

whole virtue of the soul be directed to the thing enchanted, being disposed for the receiving of said virtue."[16] Words, holding within them the potency of the real things they name, reach out to these things and change them, impelled by the passionate spirit of the speaker. Within this ancient tradition, though perhaps without a direct knowledge of it (though Yates argues that Berowne in *Love's Labour's Lost* is Giordano Bruno and others have argued that Prospero is modeled on the magician John Dee), Shakespeare makes his heroes and heroines susceptible to charming words and unchains spirits with spelling charms.[17] And Robert Greene's Friar Bacon shouts in his disputation, "I tell thee, German, magic haunts the ground."

Nevertheless it seems that the ascription of magical power to the imagination, as opposed to the words it impels, begins in the Renaissance with the question "Why are some words more effective than others?" (or "Why are some people's words more effective than others'?"). Plotinus's magician is more sensitive and attuned to the natural vibrations than others, but the extension of the magical effect of his songs backward to the power that charges them has not begun. When the mind itself begins to be probed for sources of this effectiveness, it too is described as having magical power. Following on from such an extension of magical quality to the imagination of the magic-maker, the image is applied to the act of imaging certain fantastic shapes, of creating distorted figures out of nothing, or out of parts of observed phenomena, of creating "parti-coloured births" (as Giovanni Batista Porta phrases it, alluding perhaps to Laban's cattle spotted by contagious magic). The application of the magical image widens to pertain not just to the transformation of things by combinations of names but to the forms ultimately composed out of language by a visionary (or maddened) imagination, which becomes a "magic organ" (Edward Young's term) rather than an inert receptacle of fading sensations. The interest in the power of the imagination in turn projects the image even further back into

yet deeper places; Jacob Boehme, probing the nature of the
shadowy force of creativity, which he called *magia*, writes of
the potentiality of the will seen as both God and the mother of
Eternity. This seventeenth-century German shoemaker whose
visions of a vital dialectical universe influenced Blake, and
whose emphasis on the mysteries of the spirit helped keep
Coleridge from despair, calls God's creativity as it implodes in
vortices of fire a divine *magia*: "Magic is the mother of eternity,
of the being of all beings; for it creates itself and is understood
as desire." Boehme's utterances are cryptic, but he implies that
his magic is self-making and self-reflexive. It is everything
originative, a creative power that works imaginatively on
nothingness.[18] Boehme's vision of magic as will, desire,
imagination, indeed, all creativity, influences the important
German philosopher Franz von Baader.[19] The use of magic as a
term for describing the way language works is pushed by such
a process of extension ever deeper into the sources of power,
until it ends by describing everything about the mind's effect
on the outside world that is not yet understood.

The Renaissance use of images of magic is additionally
complicated in the seventeenth century by a preference for
alchemical imagery, as a promise of a wished change in substance (rather than an intensification through fervor of a given
substance) and as an image for the soul's sublimation, and also
by a conflation of God's word with the human word where
God's word, the Logos, overshadows all human efforts and
makes them blasphemous. It seems significant that the
seventeenth-century poets, including Donne, Vaughan, and
Herbert, used alchemical imagery to describe erotic or
spiritual sublimation, while the romantic poets tended to
prefer images and forms of magic (except that Shelley and
Keats merge the two kinds together) to impel their words. The
difference points to a difference in aims: the seventeenth-
century poets thought of themselves as still tentatively in-
heriting the possibility of transmuting and purifying their
substance, while the romantics were worried about their

ability to speak, sing, or write at all, after the philosophers of the preceding age had reduced this ability to a material sequence of fluids in association. They were no longer worried, however, about blasphemy through separate speech, and they individually usurped the voices that God had previously monopolized.

When we glimpse the complex and ancient tradition of the word-thing relationship, the pronouncements on language by Locke, Hartley, and other empirical philosophers seem even more confining that they seemed intuitively, especially if we imagine that the intuition belongs to a gifted poet searching the philosophers for an understanding of the effectiveness of his words. Such a poet would find in their statements nothing corresponding to his own inner sense of the density of the relationships; he would find ideas far too clear and distinct to be true.

At the end of the 1600s magic declines as a compelling system of belief that had persisted at the edges of Christianity; a century later, however, in the face of scientific arguments against its existence, it reemerges as a way of thinking about art and the psychology of creativity, when the complexity of these processes needs to be reaffirmed. Together with other topics that presume to derive from the realm of mysterious force, magic serves as a metaphor for the irrational powers of language, and of the sources of language in will and will-lessness, in energy and indolence, and in imagination and perception. For romantics who believed with Coleridge that "words are the living products of the living mind and could not be a due medium between the thing and the mind unless they partook of both," and that "the word was not to convey merely what a certain thing is, but the very passion and all the circumstances which were conceived as constituting the perception of the thing by the person who used the word,"[20] the metaphor of magic seemed usefully to ramify through many of the related areas of their concern, as well as to indicate that the power of language goes far beyond the naming of facts.

Like other persistent metaphors, this one does not demand belief, but it gives evidence of emotional, if not intellectual, receptivity to the ideas surrounding it. While the writers between 1720 and 1830 who often think in terms of magic and enchantment are not surreptitious magicians as were many of those of the seventeenth and late nineteenth centuries, they do seem to believe that language, with the weight of the magical tradition behind it, can change the way men think. That such possibilities were hesitantly being rediscovered in the years between 1720 and 1775 can be seen in a few examples of changing use of the metaphor.

1 • An Eighteenth-Century Metaphor

In mid-eighteenth-century England numerous writers began to explore ways of coming to terms with the world. They investigated mythologies in search of a universal principle lying behind all renderings of the divine in fable;[1] they considered the folklore of the wild Celtic regions of Great Britain and invested its superstitions with new truth; they admired the possessed ecstasies of the savages as reported to them by missionaries and settlers; they became curious about the mysteries and ancient language of the Hindus, as if hoping to find in the East a new source of old wisdom;[2] they perceived in bacchic and Eleusinian mysteries not madness but vision, and looked with awe at the raptures of mystics.[3] They began to read the romances of the medieval past in a newly tolerant way, digging into what they called England's "enchanted ground";[4] they admired the plays of Shakespeare and of other Elizabethan and Jacobean dramatists for fantastic elements, praising the miraculous transformations of the supernatural comedies; they read *The Faerie Queene* and "L'Allegro" and "Il Penseroso" with a new intuition that the supernatural was a demonic background for the psyche;[5] they began to cultivate terror in the hopes that it would release hidden energies in the self.[6]

Such pursuits describe the perimeters of this age of sensibility from 1750 to 1798. But they do not explain the core of dissatisfaction which drove writers like James Thomson (1700–1748), Thomas Gray (1716–1771), William Collins (1721–1759), Richard Hurd (1720–1808), Edward Young (1683–1765), and Maurice Morgann (1726–1802) to seek reality in unreason, even in frenzy. Northrop Frye sees this as an age when "the qualities of subconscious association take the lead, and poetry becomes hypnotically repetitive, oracular, incantatory, dream-like, and in the original sense of the word, charming."[7] Some intuition that the universe is alive, that unconscious attentiveness will allow the life to well up in the isolated, formerly rational, individual, and that it will rise in charms or incantations that can break down all rational barriers led these writers to think of poetry in a new way. They submit enthusiastically to being overwhelmed by oracles or invaded by powerful voices, hoping thereby to reach a revitalized center of force.

If they could demonstrate that nature responded to songs and spells, they could disprove materialistic views of nature, and disprove those prevailing theories that claimed that men were merely parts of a continuum of matter. They could prove that not only they but nature herself had depths and mysterious sources of energy that the proponents of Hume and Voltaire scoffed at. If they could show that the depths and forces respond to incantations by virtue of a sympathy that exists between the spirits of nature and the spirit in man, they could banish the arguments of rationalists, whom Coleridge would later call the Cadmuses of French literature, and who, by relying on the evidence of their senses, denied life to the spirit.

Confidence in the value of passionate irrational sources of power can be seen developing in the increased use of metaphors of magic to describe the various mysteries of art. Like the well-known change from metaphors of mirrors to metaphors of lamps, the change from a negative to a positive use of metaphors of magic helps to describe the change from mimetic to expressive theories of art. As we know, the magician is believed to be able to change the things of the world through his projection of energies from within him by incantation; in his ecstatic state he is aware of forces within himself in sympathy with outside forces. Through this awareness he is thought to have the power to banish sickness, to conjure beings, to summon spirits, to make people fall in love, to make people unaccountably drop dead, to make objects change their appearances to correspond to his will. The world is subject to his desire: he can imagine something and compel it to be. Metaphors involving such belief must lead to an increase of faith in the power of men who are sensitive and attuned to nature and of interest in the language such men use to achieve their desires.

Because it puts emphasis on the effectiveness of words, the metaphor of magic was particularly useful in giving these writers a sense of their own importance. If a poet said, for example, that the world takes on life by the power of these whirling words, he would not only be affirming the potential vitality of a world otherwise thought to be fixed, but he would also be setting himself at the center of such changes and making the changes depend on his continued speech. He would also call attention to the fact that he was speaking, and thus to the texture and rhythm of his words. He would force the hearer to be conscious of what he was doing, to admire him, and to fear him, even when the hearer generally disbelieved his claim. The metaphor of magic, unlike other prevalent metaphors for expressive theories of art, not only conveyed a living spiritual power hidden behind merely visible things, but it also provided a means of controlling and of talking about power in mysterious terms. It was natural that poets should begin imagining that their words were the incantations that might rouse an inert nature.

Since it includes spontaneity, suddenness, and supernatural origin in its range of associations, magic may be a more appropriate metaphor for the way the imagination works than the lamp. One of M. H. Abrams's best examples of the use of the lamp to explain how the eye illuminates the surrounding world is at heart a metaphor of magic. "Our senses," Abrams quotes from Young's "Night Thoughts,"

> Give taste to fruits; and harmony to groves;
> Their radiant beams to gold, and gold's bright fire . . .
> Our senses, as our reason, are divine
> And half create the wondrous world they see.
> But for the magic organ's powerful charm

Earth were a rude, uncolour'd chaos still.
Objects are th'occasion; ours th'exploit . . .
Man makes the matchless image, man admires.[8]

Here the magic of the eye and its powerful charm are at least as important as the eye's luminosity; the luminosity comes from within. Trying to learn the source of the lamp's light and the extent of its influence, the poet is thrown back on magic; for science cannot explain these workings of the imagination, the unknowable element that must be relegated to an occult and shadowy sphere.

The importance of this new recognition of power as it appears in a palpable change of metaphor has long been recognized in continental literature. Goethe's youthful readings of Paracelsus, Agrippa, and other figures in the tradition, Wieland's enthusiasm for the fairy tradition of magic learned from Shakespeare, Novalis's intricate theories of magical idealism, Hamann's cultivation of magic to redeem the mysteriousness of Christianity and to refute the mechanistic philosophy, and even Kant's late studies of Zoroaster have been seen as central to the development of continental romanticism as a distinctive movement. Auguste Viatte and Jacques Roos have discussed the phenomenon of an occult revival in France,[9] and critics on Baudelaire and his contemporaries have often emphasized their theories of magical symbolism. But in England, despite the influence of Milton's hermetic "Penseroso," such changes have for the most part been ignored.

The development of a new attitude toward art and the source of art can be seen by examining a series of texts. From part 4 of *The Dunciad* to *The Castle of Indolence* to the odes of Collins and Gray, to the criticism of Edward Young, Richard Hurd, and Maurice Morgann there are indications of a gradual change reflecting the assimilation of Renaissance lore, of Shakespeare, of romance, and of the threat of materialistic theories of nature.

Pope's mockery of magic in *Dunciad* 4 accords with Milton's hostility to magic in *Comus*, with Spenser's castigation of the bewitchments of Archimago, with Chaucer's skepticism in the Canon Yeoman's Tale, and with Dante's damnation of the magician Michael Scot for distorting reality. Pope conforms to the traditional view that magic is a heresy because it distorts reality and sets up men as the source of change, rather than relying on the divine order. It leads other men astray, and induces them to see things wrongly. In the *Dunciad* Pope introduces his magus or wizard at the end of book 4, just as the Queen of Dullness has taught men to ignore Plain Experience (l. 466), Common Sense (l. 467), and the evidence of Nature; to "Make God Man's Image, Man the final Cause" (l. 478), and to "See all in *Self*, and but for Self be born" (l. 480). The satiric speaker rages at the Goddess,

> Then take them all, oh take them to thy breast!
> Thy *Magus*, Goddess! shall perform the rest.
>
> (ll. 515–16)

Warburton's notes inform us that "here beginneth the celebration of the *greater Mysteries* of the Goddess, which the Poet in his Invocation ver. 5. promised to sing."

> With that, a WIZARD OLD his *Cup* extends;
> Which whoso tastes forgets his former friends,
> Sire, Ancestors, Himself. One casts his eyes
> Up to a Star, and like Endymion dies:
> A *Feather* shooting from another's head,
> Extracts his brain, and Principle is fled,
> Lost is his God, his Country, ev'ry thing . . .
>
> (ll. 517–23)

The Magus, inaugurating the rule of Dullness, administers the magic potion of self-love, which brings chaos to society. The potion releases not vision but self-involved imbecility, and under its spell "Art after Art goes out, and all is Night" (l. 640). Bewitched by "Medea's strain" and by "Hermes' wand" (two kinds of magical power which Shelley will pray for at the end of his "Alastor"), the values of the universe are turned upside down by what Pope calls "the uncreating word" (l.

654). To Pope magic is humbug, ignorance, egotism, and benightedness; it turns us into little more than animals, obscuring our reason and debasing our senses, giving us a false idea of the relation between words and visible things. It creates a chaos in which neither art nor true religion nor civility may thrive. Magic is a metaphor for the darkness that engulfs our brave efforts to carve from chaos a coherent civilization.

Many elements of Pope's criticism are included in *Castle of Indolence*, together with elements borrowed from *Comus*. But Thomson's attitude toward magic becomes ambivalent when he suggests that magic releases visions that would otherwise be repressed. The Castle of Indolence is a sanatorium for would-be writers and artists; it is hosted by a wizard who lulls his guests into dream. Under his enchantments the various artists have visions but cannot discipline themselves to give these visions shape; they drift in the enchanted groves, their sinews unstrung, listening to lyres and to aeolian harps. Thomson thus agrees with Pope that a dreaming chaos is debilitating, and he also agrees with Milton's view in *Comus* that magic distorts the divinely ordered world to undermine moral life. Magic plays intellectual tricks with what should appear as simple truth, divinely clear: magic is arrogant, willful, heretical power; it is made by hags, witches, and their malformed progeny, who know they have no place in the orderly part of the forest, and must jealously try to subvert the innocents roaming there.

The view of magic here shared by Thomson and Milton is that magic is antihuman, unconscious, and debilitating rather than conscious, human, and assertive. This magic inheres in nature. When men succumb to it, they turn into natural beings; they are bestialized, losing their distinctly human identities. Thomson's view is ambivalent because he believes that magic releases vision, partly through music, partly through idleness and its accompanying dreams; but like Milton he knows that magic saps the will as Circe's magic had done. Magic paralyzes the artists in the Castle of Indolence not by actually turning them into beasts but by confining them to their imaginations.

The tradition of magic as an escape from time is brought to a significant focus in Thomson's poem. In *The Tempest* magic suspends time and regular, usually inalterable, process; it defies natural laws. This aspect of the tradition will reappear in Shelley's *Prometheus Unbound* 3 and 4 when time is suspended: we enter a world of timeless Permanence through the power of magical songs. But the release out of temporality and sequence is not always seen as beneficial: in *The Castle of Indolence* as in *Comus* the illusion of freedom from time is firmly denied. Milton shows that the only timelessness is the permanent will to virtue founded in God; anarchic sensuous magic leads to the opposite of what it claims, for it is founded in lies.

Rather than allowing men into a world of suspended realities, it binds them into an entirely different timelessness—the timelessness of beasts. Keats recognizes this unchangingness in "Ode to a Nightingale" when he cries: "Thou wast not born for death, immortal Bird!" Finally he knows that the nightingale's song is permanent only because all birds, and the songs they sing, are the same through the centuries. No hungry generations tread them down because each generation is indistinguishable from the preceding one. Animal life is unconscious, and when Comus magically turns his victims into beasts he makes them changeless not by raising them into permanent forms but by brutalizing them (the more so because they think wrongly that they are still human). This is the dehumanizing magic that Andrew Marvell's Soul laments, the magic that binds the soul in a corporeal form. It is this constraining, Circean, brutalizing magic that Thomson claims for the wizard of the Castle of Indolence. Enchanted by sense and mere animal life, the would-be poets in this eighteenth-century Magic Mountain cannot create their poems. The wizard's magic has the fluidity and insubstantiality of dream and unrealized wish, because it is beyond all rational measurements of time, as are nature's repetitive cycles.

This is the magic in nature against which Plotinus had long ago warned the potential magician.

If magic is timeless, formless, and dreamy in Thomson's *Castle*, it is spontaneous, wild, and powerful in William Collins's "Ode on the Popular Superstitions of the Highlands, considered as a subject of Poetry." Collins's ode appeared in 1749, a year after Thomson's *Castle;* it was Collins's last poem before madness silenced him. This ode embraces the chaos which Pope feared, and the poet imagines that submersion in the magic of nature, when joined with a releasing of powerful psychic energy, will result in great poetry. Collins urges upon his friend John Home new subjects and new ways of being. He implores Home to quit the artificial life of London coffeehouses and submit to the savagery of his native land, "whose every vale shall prompt the poet." "'Tis Fancy's land to which thou sett'st thy feet." Where wizards leap insanely under the influence of herbs and chant their crazed spells, "themes of simple, sure effect" will add "new conquests to the Muse's boundless reign." Collins tries to convince Home that Scotland is a rugged tribal country where oral poetry has been passed from father to son, where strange lays about death rites, internecine wars, struggles with sea monsters, and ghostly visitations harrow the soul. In this imaginary Scotland reality is laid bare. In such an elemental world it would be possible to write; influenced by surrounding frenzy, the poet could release his own. As Collins shows in his "Ode on the Passions," he believes that the feelings of "exalting, trembling, raging, fainting" are necessary for poetic composition; a "mind possessed" is the common element between wizard and poet if the poet can only recognize this kinship.

In Collins we see a trend toward the belief that better poems come from unreason than from reason, perhaps in obedience to Plato's formulation in the *Ion.* He also sets the trend for finding in Scotland a tradition of holy madness linked with magical power. With him Scotland became the locale of the primitive, for it refused to be corrupted by continental rules. Its archaic verse-forms and violent superstitions suggested to many romantics after Collins an unexplored physical and spiritual realm for poetry. For example Robert Burns's fidelity to Ayrshire life led him to fill his poems with popular superstitions; Scott, known as "The Wizard of the North," made abundant use of magical rhymes and themes in the spells of Meg Merilies and in his longer lays. Wild Scotland became for Coleridge and Wordsworth, too, what the Germanic past was for Grimm and other German folklorists. Scotland, providing both the themes of unreason and its forms (the ballad, the rune, and the charm), was ancient and popular at once. When the eighteenth century tired of the Thames, it directed its sights toward the northern borders where the Anglo-Saxon and the Celtic past was vivid. These rich superstitions of the Highlands afforded primitive material in England's own domain.

In this tribal land passions erupt in raw form, inducing the newly crazed contemporary poet to participate in a lost ancient bardic tradition:

> At every pause before thy mind possessed,
>   Old Runic Bards shall seem to rise around,
> With uncouth lyres, in many coloured vest,
>   Their matted hair with boughs fantastic crowned;
> Whether thou biddest the well-taught hind repeat
>   The choral dirge that mourns some chieftain brave,
> When every shrieking made her bosom beat,
>   And strewed with choicest herbs his scented grave.
>
>   (ll. 40–47)

Collins plunges into the psyche, as poets from Rimbaud to Ginsberg have since done. Collins's model for creative dislocation is the "gifted wizard seer," who shares his function with the "runic bard." A visionary who "commands the viewless forms of air," the wizard attains by his immediate contact with life and death an ideal of "divine excess":

> 'Tis thine to sing how framing hideous spells,
>   In Sky's lone isle, the gifted wizard seer,
>   Lodged in the wintry cave with fate's fell spear,

> Or in the depth of Uist's dark forest dwells:
>   How they, whose sight such dreary dreams engross,
> With their own visions oft astonished droop,
>   When, o'er the watery strath of quaggy moss,
> They see the gliding ghosts unbodied troop;
>   Or, if in sports, or on the festive green,
> Their destin'd glance some fated youth descry,
>   Who now, perhaps, in lusty vigor seen,
> And rosy health, shall soon lamented die.
> For them the viewless forms of air obey;
>   Their bidding heed, and at their beck repair:
> They know what spirit brews the stormful day,
>   And heartless, oft like moody madness, stare
> To see the phantom train their secret work prepare.
>
> (ll. 53–70)

Wizards see fate and death; they see the supernatural center of storms. They understand that spirits lurk behind events, and in trying to control these "viewless forms of air," their visions and their own powers drive them mad.

If the poet dares to visit the primitive communities at the barbaric edges of the earth and to submerge himself in their customs he can make his language work with the power of the wizards' spells. Under this influence, and stripped of civilized veneer, the poet takes on magical power:

> These, too, thou'lt sing! for well thy magic muse,
> Can to the topmost heaven for grandeur soar.
>
> (ll. 87–88)

Furthermore there is nothing trivial, false, or local about the subjects of wizardry and poetic madness. They partake of the deepest truths. Being improbable and invisible, these themes are all the more truly imaginative than conventional themes, as *Macbeth* proves. Native Scottish themes, "daring to depart from sober truth, are still to nature true." Collins thus makes a distinction between sober truth—visible verifiable fact—and a new imaginative passionate truth, faithful to our most disturbing inner nature and bodied forth in magical figures.

Collins is thus more optimistic about the effect of magical metaphors on poetry than is Thomson. Thomson fears that release will debilitate the poet, leading him to wander undisciplined in a dream world; but Collins sees different possibilities. He thinks that release will lead the poet back to his essential inner primitivism, and he believes that from this formerly subdued side of the self, true poetry will erupt. At the base of their disagreement lies the same disagreement about the definition of magic that has divided others: Thomson believes that magic inheres in nature and draws men down to the level of organic or bestial life; Collins believes that magic is a power unleashed from the depth of a "mind possessed," particularly in wild circumstances where men tap the powers hidden in nature as well as in themselves.

When nature begins to reveal her living power, deeper and more vital, perhaps, than man's, she ceases to be circean and becomes instead a source of energy. To embrace this alien magic is not to lose one's will to dreamy indolence but to discover new sources of strength. While Collins finds vitalizing sources in remote magical areas, Thomas Gray finds the sources of poetry in the depths of nature. For him magic does not lie far off in time and space among savages but deep under the earth's surface: Gray's bard makes a daring plunge into the core of reality which permanently roils in the earth's center. Rather than escaping from the duties that ordinary time imposes, he is a bold adventurer in the manner of Beowulf descending into the ocean to wrestle with Grendel's mother.

At the end of his fastidious poetic career Thomas Gray boldly probes the mysterious. The author of the serene "Elegy Written in a Country Churchyard" was an anguished soul capable of shouting out the meters of "The Bard" and "The Descent of Odin" in all their enthusiasm. "The Descent of Odin" is filled with invocations, incantations, spells, charms, and all manner of magical ravings that attempt to link the magic hidden within the depths of nature and the magic which the poet-magician desires to impose upon this nature. For his spells Gray has adapted the meter of *Macbeth*'s hags, as Coleridge, Shelley, and Byron will do later; the nature into which Odin shouts his spells swirls with a wild inchoate vitality, reminiscent of Boehme's fiery cosmos.

Into the roaring depths Odin the Norse magician bellows the spells that are to impose his will on nature, and the rival magic in the depths of nature answers him:

> Facing to the northern clime
> Thrice he traced the runic rhyme,
> Thrice pronounc'd in accents dread
> The thrilling verse, that wakes the Dead,
> Till from out the hollow ground
> Slowly breath'd a sullen sound.   (ll. 21–26)

In response to his threefold incantation the dead awaken and the ground begins to speak. Odin gains access to the center of nature, and the prophetess lurking below answers him in incantatory tones:

> What call unknown, what charms presume
> To break the quiet of the tomb?   (ll. 27–28)

The magician is full of desire for hidden truths:

> Prophetess, my spell obey,
> Once again arise and say,
> Who th'Avenger of his guilt,
> By whom shall Hoder's blood be split.   (ll. 59–62)

The center of nature is not only the tomb of the dead but the womb of history, for below ground Odin is able to learn the future. In "The Fatal Sisters" dark beings like the weird sisters intone their spells over the loom of the future. An incantatory meter permits them to summon events to come, "to weave the crimson web of war":

> Horror covers all the heath,
> Clouds of carnage blot the sun.
> Sisters, weave the web of death,
> Sisters, cease. The work is done.

In "The Bard" Gray seeks hidden knowledge in the underworld where the dead voice the perennial power of nature. In death the Welsh bards massacred by Edward I have turned into prophetic wizards, "avengers of their native land." These bards, "whose magic song / Made huge Plinlimmon bow his cloud-top'd head" in previous ages, now weave the fabric of the future:

> Weave the warp and weave the woof,
> The winding-sheet of Edward's race.

They mutter to one another in the underworld:

> Now, Brothers, bending o'er th'accursed loom
> Stamp we our vengeance deep, and ratify his doom.

Frenzied by visions, the bard makes the plunge "deep in the roaring tide . . . to endless night." In these and other poems Gray assumes that the source of wisdom and energy is below ground. He assumes that owing to courage and skill with arcane spells, the magician, wizard, or bard can delve into the deep, retrieving wisdom and delivering men from the mysteries to come. His own magical spells summon these mysteries and become the poems he had originally sought in the depths.

Gray is one of the first to interpret nature as chthonian. Perhaps under the influence of Boehme's visions of a deep will and a living ground, or of Giordano Bruno's theories of dark polarities, romantics beginning with Gray anticipate the concern with unreleased sexual, psychic, and cosmic energy that Freud, Jung, and Reich explore in our century. In different ways they envision this energy hidden like oil in the earth's core, ready to gush when tapped by one who knows its secret power.

The realization that nature was a source of energy when coupled with a latent energy in men led to a reinterpretation of English literature. Now raised to the first rank were those works that explored this hidden nature. This reinterpretation in turn led to a new evaluation of originality and genius, as articulated by Richard Hurd, Edward Young, and Maurice Morgann.

In his *Letters on Chivalry and Romance* Hurd praises the realm of magical fabling in literature and advocates a return to earlier English material, consisting largely of witches, demons, incantations, and fairies. "May there be something in Gothic Romance peculiarly suited to the view of a genius, and to the ends of poetry? And may not the philosophic moderns [namely, the Augustans] have gone too far, in their perpetual ridicule and contempt of it?" In praising the English gothic, Hurd anticipates the atavism of Chatterton and Macpherson, who wished to return to the days when poetic language embodied power. England's "native woodnotes wild" were not so much a product of an untainted era as of a peculiarly English genius, thought to be essentially marvelous and defiant of rules. Hurd makes a leap from the gothic era with its legendary beliefs to the prevalence of legend and fantasy in great English poetry. He goes so far as to suggest that all genuine poetry is marvelous, and he blames the neoclassicists for forgetting this truth, and losing sight of the sources of poetic power: "A poet, they say, must follow nature; and by nature we are to suppose can only be meant the known and experienced course of affairs in this world. Whereas the poet has a world of his own, where experience has less to do, than consistent imagination. He had, besides, a supernatural world to range in. He had Gods, and Fairies, and Witches at his command." [10] This marvelous world, Hurd believed, was the province of poets, for poets have inherently magical and wonder-working natures: "This is the poetic world; all is marvelous and extraordinary; yet not *unnatural* in one sense, as it agrees to the conceptions that are readily entertained of these magical and wonderworking natures." Spenser and Shakespeare and the writers of gothic romance who preceded them have natures that correspond to and arouse the marvelous world. To recapture the poetic genius of the great age of English literature, contemporary poets must first resurrect the gothic fantasies that nurtured Renaissance poetry: "What we have lost is a world of fine fabling, a charmèd spirit"; to contemplate this world is to stand upon "enchanted ground." The gothic for Hurd, the Celtic and Norse for Gray, the Scottish for Collins were essentially magical eras and places, where poets penetrated the heart of nature.

Whether they deal with subjects which will revitalize English poetry by their very mention or with shamanistic dislocations of the mind modeled on the early English bards, Gray and Collins obey the strictures of Hurd to explore the wild and dark sides of their genius through magical incantation. Collins's assertion that invisible and fantastic themes are as true to a mysterious inner nature as visible and rational themes is taken up with verve by Edward Young and Maurice Morgann. Young and Morgann pronounce vigorously that the fabulous—so long associated with Shakespeare and Spenser—is the true realm of the creative imagination.

In *The Conjectures on Original Composition* (1759) Young boldly identifies originality with magical summoning: "Imitators only give us a sort of Duplicate of what we had, possibly much better before; increasing the mere drug of books while all that makes them valuable, knowledge and Genius, are at a stand. The pen of an Original writer, like Armida's wand, out of a barren waste calls a blooming spring." [11] Tasso's Armida, the daughter of a Persian magician in *Jerusalem Delivered*, represents the lure of the exotic east, a pagan danger to the Christian knights. Yet Young turns these temptations into virtues. Armida's wand creates where there were no visible materials to work with; her spring arises by magical means. The idea of the wand as pen emerges even more clearly a few pages later: "An Original, by being as excellent as new, adds admiration to surprise; then are we at the writer's mercy; on the strong wind of his imagination, we are snatched from Britain to Italy, from climate to climate, from pleasure to pleasure, we have no home, no thought, of our own, till the magician drops his pen. And then falling down into ourselves, we awake to flat realities, lamenting the changes, like a beggar who dreamt himself a prince." The imagination not only transforms the material it describes, metamorphosing a desert into a spring, but it also transforms and transports the reader who is caught in the spell of fictive illusion. The magician's imaginings arise from a world of dream where disbelief is willingly suspended, not from the waking realities of the beggar or of the barren waste.

Young compares the poet's creative process to merely mechanical and associative creation: "Genius is a Master workman, learning is but an Instrument. . . . Nor is it strange; for what, for the most part, mean we by genius, but the power of accomplishing great things without the means generally reputed necessary to that end? A genius differs from a good understanding as a magician from a good architect: that raises his structure by means invisible; this by the skillful uses of common tools. Hence genius has ever been supposed to partake of something divine." The power of genius is like a magician's in being instantaneous and whole; it does not juggle a mass of little things according to rules or laboriously erect a structure. Instead the methods of the genius are invisible and magical, as effortless as God's own creativity. Both magical and vegetable (or organic) vitality are opposed to deliberate skill and are thus related. As the magician of Young's last passage is contrasted with the architect, so the vital root of genius is contrasted here with mechanics: "An Original may be said to be of a *vegetable* nature; it rises spontaneously from the vital root of genius; it *grows*; it is not *made:* Imitations are often a sort of Manufacture wrought up by those Mechanics, Art and Labour, out of pre-existent materials not their own." This conception of art as a magical power arising through a magical process follows the familiar lines of organic criticism. Both praise the transformation and origination of wholes, not the coordination of preexistent parts; both are related by analogy to divine creation. Young describes the magical genius, who is here almost a genie, as the god overtaking the man from within: "Contract full intimacy with the Stranger within thee—Let thy Genius rise (if a Genius thou hast) as the Sun from Chaos; and if I should then say, like an Indian, worship it, (though too bold) yet should I say little more than my second rule enjoins, (viz.) Reverence thyself." Young has replaced Christianity with an eclectic worship of a human power rising powerfully from within; the Original, creating ex nihilo as God did at the beginning of the world, has magical power.

It is against this sort of passionate inspired criticism that Joshua Reynolds levels his complaints at the beginning of his discourse 6 (1774). He sneers at critics who, like the ignorant inhabitants of eastern countries, claim that the "ruins of stately edifices" were "built by magicians." "The untaught mind finds a vast gulf between its own powers, and those works of complicated art, which it is utterly unable to fathom; and it supposes that such a voice can be passed only by supernatural powers." [12] He warms to his satire, becoming increasingly scornful: "And as for artists themselves, it is by no means their interest to undeceive such judges, however conscious they may be of the very natural means by which their extraordinary powers were acquired." Those who do not realize that "it is by being conversant with the inventions of others that we learn to invent" are ashamed to admit that they imitate: "To derive all from native power, to owe nothing to another, is the praise which men who do not much think on what they are saying bestow sometimes upon others, and sometimes on themselves; and their imaginary dignity is naturally heightened by a supercilious censure of the low, the barren, the grovelling, the servile imitator." The real artist is one who realizes that "the mind is but a barren soil; a soil which is soon exhausted, and will produce no crop, or only one, unless it be continually fertilized and enriched by foreign matter." The real artist knows, says Reynolds, that "nothing can come of nothing," that the mind does not create by supernatural origination, as

Young imagines. But Reynolds seems to have been fighting a losing battle even against his own changing opinions, as evidenced twelve years later in discourse 13, where he proclaims that art is art because it deviates from nature, leading the artist to be called divine.

In his famous essay on Falstaff, Maurice Morgann, more even than Young, found everything that Shakespeare touched turned to gold. He believed that Shakespeare had penetrated the core of protean nature and that his creations were essentially true because they were fabulous. Shakespeare is for Morgann a Prospero who summons up grandiose imaginary worlds. Proclaiming Shakespeare "this great Magician, this daring *practicer of arts inhibited*," Morgann believes that even Aristotle would agree that Shakespeare's magical creation went far beyond what Morgann thought to be the "naturalness" of the Greek dramatists. He imagines Aristotle's words:

Convinced, I see that a more compendious *nature* may be obtained; a nature of *effects* only, to which neither the relations of place, or continuity of time, are always essential. Nature, condescending to the faculties and apprehensions of man, has drawn through human life a regular chain of visible causes and effects: But Poetry delights in surprize, conceals her steps, seizes at once upon the heart, and obtains the Sublime of things without betraying the rounds of her ascent: True Poesy is *magic*, not *nature*; an effect from causes hidden or unknown.[13]

Humbled by the supremacy of Shakespeare over Sophocles, the imaginary Aristotle goes on to praise the mystery of Shakespearean construction, so much more subtle than the obvious, predictable machinations of nature: "To the Magician I prescribed no laws; his law and his power are one; his power is his law. Him, who neither imitates, nor is within the reach of imitation, no precedent can or ought to bind, no limits to contain. If his end is obtained, who shall question his course? Means, whether apparent or hidden, are justified in Poesy by success; but then most perfect and most admirable when most concealed.—But whither am I going!" After his fanciful impersonation of Aristotle, Morgann hastens back to the character of Falstaff, but not before dropping a footnote to a vast and fertile digression. With the example of Shakespeare before him, Morgann becomes rapturous speculating that all of poetry may be magic. His excitement may be sensed as he explores these uncharted seas:

These observations have brought me so near to the regions of Poetic *magic* (using the word here in its strict and proper sense, and not loosely as in the *text*), that, tho' they lie not directly in my course, I yet may be allowed in this place to point the reader that way. A felt propriety, or truth of art, from an unseen, tho' supposed adequate cause, we call *nature*. A like feeling of propriety and truth, supposed without a cause, or as seeming to be derived from causes inadequate, fantastic, and absurd,—such as wands, circles, incantations, and so forth,—we call by the general name *magic*, including all the train of superstition, witches, ghosts, fairies, and the rest.—Reason is confined to the line of visible existence; our *passions* and our *fancy* extend far beyond into the *obscure;* but however lawless their operations may seem, the images they so wildly form have yet a relation to truth, and are the shadows at least, however fantastic, of *reality*.

Magic embodies the passions, otherwise unimaginably hidden in the depths of our being. Magic is not limited to external representations of observable truths or to a provable sequence of natural causation; it penetrates to that obscure region where reason loses its way because it finds no clearly marked signs.

Morgann links imagination to magic, believing that passion moves from abstraction to the creation of objects giving imaginary form to the abstraction. The natural process of creation which Morgann thinks is magical exists on two levels: "Extravagant as all this appears, it has its laws so precise that we are sensible both of a local and temporary and of an universal magic; the first derived from the general nature of the human mind, influenced by particular habits, institutions, and climate; and the latter from the same general nature abstracted from those considerations." The perfect examples of the two kinds of magic appear in Shakespeare—the first

Macbeth; the second, lasting and universal, *The Tempest.* Morgann concludes: "The whole play of the *Tempest* is of so high and superior a nature that *Dryden,* who had attempted to imitate in vain, might well exclaim that '*Shakespeare's magic* could not copied be, / Within that circle none durst walk but *He.*'" Genius is magical because its causes cannot be analyzed or reproduced; the passions in general can be described as magical also, as a way of probing the unknown within ourselves. In Morgann's opinion Shakespeare more than any other genius realized the potentialities of magic for interpreting this kind of "fantastic" inner "reality."

Morgann's discovery of the magical nature of art is far removed from the neoclassical horror of magic. Morgann's writings summarize and go beyond the work of his contemporaries. He comprehends Gray's desire to plunge into nature, and Collins's desire to bare his passions in the manner of the primitive wizard. He understands Hurd's magical nationalism and Young's belief that original genius in general follows magical processes. But Morgann also goes on, where Coleridge pursues him, to suggest areas of the irrational will from which poetry springs, to adumbrate Coleridge's interest in the symbol as a natural need of the mind, and to hint at the magical power of the imagination. Magic is deeply imbedded in nature; it is part of England's past and thus a criterion of Englishness; it is also universal in primitive belief, erupting spontaneously from the unconscious.

When we juxtapose Pope's line that under the spell of the Magus "Art after Art goes out, and all is night" and Morgann's statement that "true Poesy is *Magic,* not *nature,*" we perceive the changing attitude toward magic has coincided with, and perhaps even partially inspired, a reassessment of the essence of art, a discovery that art is no longer a representation of a rational order but stands as an expression of passion, unknown irrational power, the outpouring of a fantastic, hidden, vital reality. This transformation in attitude indicates the complexion of some of the dissatisfactions and yearnings of this period.

It was a period that could ravage the Middle Ages, the Renaissance, folklore, orientalism, and even the study of language in a search for the primitive within the self—part of the great drive to counteract the tyranny of rationality.

In England the writers whom we have examined seemed to intuit the need for a renewal of magical metaphors before they actually learned about the complex theories of the Renaissance. In England many of the texts of Plotinus, Jamblichus, Proclus, Ficino, Pico, Bruno, and Boehme mentioned in the introduction were translated at the end of the eighteenth century, coincidentally with the poetic use of such metaphors. This coincidence may have been symptomatic of a general climate of interest. Bishop Berkeley's *Siris* (1744) opened up the world of the hermetic books, of Plotinus's *Enneads*, of Proclus, Jamblichus, and Ficino, in his flight from tar-water to the *scintilla spirituosa*; Ralph Cudworth's *True Intellectual System of the Universe* provided a compendium of ancient mysteries; Thomas Taylor's translations and commentaries on Plotinus, on the mystical initiations, on hymns of Orpheus, on Proclus's *Theological Elements*, and discussions of the Chaldean oracles, began to appear in 1787; William Law's translations of Jakob Boehme became available in 1764; available since 1727, though a potboiler, had been Daniel Defoe's remarkably sympathetic description of Renaissance theory, *The Compleat System of Magick: or The History of the Black Art*, where he defined magic as "truly science" as Pico and Paracelsus had defined it before him.[14] The material seems to have become so popular that Sir Walter Scott recapitulated it in his richly documented *Letters on Demonology and Witchcraft*,[15] and even William Godwin repeated it in his late *Lives of the Necromancers* (1835), which he had been compiling, as Mary Shelley knew, for many years. By 1801 a full compendium of Renaissance magical theory existed in Francis Barrett's *Magus, or The Celestial Intelligencer*. Barrett, a London occultist who may have been known to Blake's circle, paraphrases much of Agrippa, writing that

The instrument of enchanters is a pure, living, breathing spirit of the blood, whereby we bind or attract, those things which we desire or delight in. . . . Indeed, the virtues of man's words are so great, that when pronounced with a fervent constancy of mind, they are able to subject Nature. . . . Almost all charms are impotent without words because words are the speech of the speaker and the image of the thing signified or spoken of; therefore, whatever wonderful effect is intended, let the same be performed with the addition of the operator; for words are a kind of occult vehicle of the soul; therefore all the forcible power of the spirit ought to be breathed out with vehemency, and an arduous and intense desire.[16]

Barrett's words prove that the substance of Agrippa had not been lost in the intervening two centuries; Agrippa's advice that an enchanter requires vitality of spirit and an understanding of the symbolic nature of words was still current, and available to poets anxious to write in an occult vehicle.

Many important preromantic figures had nothing to do with the subject as a metaphor for their art or as a model for their rhythms. Crabbe, Cowper, and Smart never mention it; and Blake, because of his desire to escape the manacles of form, purposely rejected it. But a strange assortment of writers did find the metaphor useful since it expanded the terrain of the "je ne sais quoi," giving room for mystery and inscrutable power. In its very vagueness the metaphor encompasses mysteries of origination, cause and effect, change, influence, potency, vibrancy, and newness that are inexplicable in rational terms. It explains these mysteries by refusing to explain them. Thus it allowed poets and critics to believe in the power of nature's inherent magic and the power of man's verbal magic without having to feel embarrassed, since this vacillation is built into the theory. It also provides a shorthand answer to questions that neither psychology nor literary criticism has yet answered—questions about the effect of sounds on natural things and about the possibility of controlling men by calculated incantation.

Poets and critics in this era let the meanings of the word

magic ramify and thus permit speculation, never finally resolved, about the relation of the poet to the dynamic, changing, and animate universe around him. If there was a prevailing sense that reason was limited, it was metaphors like those of magic that bridged the void between the poet and the vast, often orgiastic, universe beyond him. Magic preserved the essence of the mystery, but gave it a name for the poet to conjure with. If it did not conclusively answer any questions, at the very least the interest in magic and related supernatural phenomena was responsible for forging some unusual verses in poets otherwise laboring in a worn-out mode.

The purpose that it served in not resolving questions was to relieve anxiety about conventional verse. In their anxiety to break out of neoclassical forms, to align their imaginations with radical mysteries which they sensed must exist somewhere, though they did not know where, these poets and critics resemble some of the prophets of our own day, desperately seeking to find a new ground of meaning. They seem to proclaim, like Norman O. Brown in 1968, "What our time needs is mystery; what our time needs is magic." [17]

As they groped toward some freedom that they knew they did not have, but that they knew enough to wish for, they sought power—not restraint, not morality—and sought it both in nature and themselves. The underlying disagreement as to whether magical power inheres in natural things or arises in things only when men exercise on them the magical power of their words extends into literature as a disagreement between the respective powers of things and words. With Gray, Young, and Morgann the balance tips clearly in favor of a magic imposed by men through words, though mention is still made of the magic of nature right along with that of words. Recognizing this shift in emphasis, we must consider poetic elements which link poetic aims to magic.

2 • *Magical Language and Poetic Analogy*

If mid-eighteenth-century writers like Thomson, Collins, Hurd, Young, and Morgann were responsible for reviving magical metaphors to express their new understanding of the relation between nature and mind, there were still other, more technical, reasons for turning to these metaphors. One of these was a widespread curiosity about the origin and development of language, arising in reaction to materialistic theories. James Beattie's *Theory of Language*, Lord Monboddo's *Of the Origin and Progress of Language*, Rousseau's *Essay on the Origin of Languages*, and Herder's *Essay on the Origin of Language* are only a few of the many books on language appearing at this time; and while they often disagree with each other on crucial issues, together they indicate a general climate of concern that fostered the development of semantics. Semantics was invented by romantics, according to Stephen Ullman, for they had "an intense and catholic interest in words, ranging from the archaic to the exotic, and including the dialects of the countryside and the slang of the underworld. Even more important, they were fascinated by the strange and mysterious potencies of words." [1] In view of the complex interplay developing at this time between nature and mind as complementary, sometimes hostile, powers, it is no wonder that the effect of potent words on things should be studied and that this study should lead to experiments in a poetry of spells and to a concentration on those elements of poetry that have always seemed to work in magical ways.

On the level of practical poetics, the question of language's power is no less urgent and is no less susceptible to magical interpretation than it is on a theoretical level. The poet, confronting his words and aiming to combine them into images, similes, metaphors, and symbols in an ascending order of fusion, questions the effectiveness of his combinations. Even if Homer and Nora Chadwick may overstate the case in calling spells the first poems,[2] the myth of the poem as incantation nevertheless seems to arise quite spontaneously for each individual poet. William Butler Yeats voices an age-old truism when he asks in his essay "Magic": "Have not poetry and music arisen, as it seems, out of the sounds the enchanters made to help to enchant, to charm, to bind with a spell themselves and the passers-by? These very words, a chief part of all praises of music or poetry, still cry to us their origin."[3] From Aeschylus to Mallarmé poets have hoped that their words possessed the power to make the things they described resemble their descriptions, or at least to absorb some of their newly assigned qualities. In the etymology of charm from *carmen*, of enchant from *cantare*, of spell from *spel* (Anglo-Saxon "tale"), the literary possibilities in magic come to the surface. Do words render things or invent them? If they invent them, do they do so by casting light on them or by creating them?

The magician accomplishes what every speaker accomplishes, but to a greater extent: he imagines a system in language that substitutes for what we might normally call the real system, if we suppose one to be there. To understand the notion that the magician simply exaggerates the normal activity of language, we should look at what is usually thought to underlie magic.

In magical theory the magician, acknowledging no transcendent principle, acts directly on the vital energies circulating through nature. He aims to change nature. Lacking the humility common to both the scientist and the priest, he refuses to recognize laws beyond his power, whole systems of reality separate from and resistant to his categories. "Magic embodies the valuable truth that the external world can in fact be changed by man's subjective attitude toward it," writes George Thomson in considering the magical origins of Greek drama and the solipsism of the magical illusion.[4]

The magician pretends to affect the world through the

medium of inspired language. His words have, he imagines, a palpable energy which vitalizes the things beyond his mind, and these words achieve potency by mysteriously combining his own powers, nature's powers, and a presumably physiological power compressed into the sound, the sign, or the idea of each individual word and of these individual words in a rhythmical interrelation. "The magician's breath is regarded as the medium by which the magical force is carried," explains Bronislaw Malinowski; "the voice generates the power of magic."[5] The mind is the center from which magical sympathies radiate, and words are the spokes along which the energies proceed outward to invigorate the world of things.

Like the ordinary speaker, but more intensely, the magician in naming things calls them into being or, more accurately, recognizes them standing above those things that he has not named. By getting a name, a thing becomes more insistently itself (it becomes a rose, instead of a blur of redness, softness, sweetness, smallness, and multifoliateness); by being thought of, it enters into a mental world (the mind where it lives conceived) at the same time that it becomes more distinct in the physical world (by being seen and named, thus set off as something distinct from the air, ground, grass, and spring).

Although the magician surpasses the ordinary speaker in glorifying language, the process is essentially similar, as many commentators have remarked. For example Kenneth Burke explains that "the magical decree is implicit in all language; for the mere act of naming an object or situation decrees that it is to be singled out as such-and-such rather than as something-other."[6] In *Language and Myth* Ernst Cassirer seems to agree that magic is inherent in the act of naming things, observing that "the potency of the real thing is contained in the name—this is one of the fundamental assumptions of the myth-making consciousness itself."[7] Martin Heidegger in *On the Way to Language* is moved by one of Stefan George's poems to think that "Only where the word for the thing has been found is the thing a thing. Only thus *is* it . . . no thing *is* where the word, that is, the name is lacking. The word alone gives being to the thing."[8] The very existence of things is dependent on the names that language gives them. Being vanishes in the absence of words.

By presuming to interpret the universe in the light of its exclusive system of relationships seen as names and names in syntactical combinations, magic encloses the magician in an inner universe. Because of the very limitations that the naming of a thing imposes, the magician can no longer see the world except in the terms that he has set. Like all of us he interprets as a sign of power what is in truth a sign of his own isolation, and thus is able by language to bewitch himself into thinking himself powerful. Magic is a kind of potent solipsism, "potent," because it is "enabling"; it is "founded on the notion that, by creating the illusion that you control reality, you can actually control it."[9]

Freud has judged this state of mind unrealistic, but in coining the term *omnipotence of thought* to describe the solipsism and subjectivity of magic, he shows the connection between magic and art: "Only in one field has the omnipotence of thought been retained in our own civilization, namely in art. In art alone it still happens that man, consumed by his wishes, produces something similar to the gratification of these wishes, and this playing, thanks to artistic illusion, calls for the effects as if it were something real. We rightly speak of the magic of art and compare the artist with the magician."[10] Unfortunately Freud goes on to link both art and magic with psychosis, believing that, as the church did in banning magic, to invent an alternative reality is to betray the reality to which we owe allegiance. Out of touch with reality, possessed by fabulous visions, the shaman, the neoplatonic magician, or the magical poet seems to participate in an unnatural world, which he superimposes onto reality. His belief in "the omnipotence of thought" leads him to believe that his imaginings are as real as the fact of the external world.

Owing to these fundamental assumptions about the power

of language and mind in magical theories however sophisticated or primitive, the study of magic seems to be conducive to outbursts of poetry. In the Renaissance and the romantic periods, particularly, with the resurgence of belief in the power of the mind to change the existing state of things, we find simultaneously a reawakening of interest in magic and of faith in the poetic imagination. Soaring egos that engulf their surroundings and effulgent and original fabling seem to be contemporaneous, for in these periods imaginative fables are interchangeable with reality, and serve to enhance the glory of the fablers. Similarly a belief in a flexible, dynamic, and even animate universe, accessible to change from various directions, seems to coincide with the questionings of mimetic definitions of art, for the outside world can be changed by the expression of an inner and subjective truth. As the certainty of a static world order diminishes, the possibility of metamorphosis increases; *phantastike* forms are as likely as *eikastike* ones. The magician's power to transform inert things with his words becomes the model for the poet's nonmimetic fabling, and magic comes to describe the enchanted world created by the imagination, as opposed to the artifice and convention and mimesis supposed to be typical of neoclassical art. Thus it seems to be a historical fact that a concern with the possibilities of magic increases the hope for poetry, and the hope for poetry seems to increase the likelihood that poetry will be produced, particularly a poetry rich in metaphor, analogy, transferences, transformations, metamorphoses, and symbols.

Certain aspects of the assigning of names, the discovery of analogy, and the development of symbol seem inherently magical, even when they appear in eras when magic itself is unimportant. Let us examine the magical aspect of poetry before considering the specific use of metaphors about magic in the poetry of Coleridge, Byron, and Shelley.

One of the central features of magical language, correlative with the magician's omnipotence of thought and with the thing's dependence on its name, is a belief that a simultaneous realization of events in the mind and in the world outside is possible. The magician believes that he can transcend successiveness, that he is not tied to the diurnal tedium that ordinary men endure. Instead of submitting to the customary sequences of one thing after another, he leaps out of successiveness into simultaneity. Things happen for him all at once, quick as a wink, often punctuated with the word *lo*, signalling a sudden miraculous appearance.

This simultaneity or synchronicity in time (paralleled by proximity in space) occurs first in the arrangements of words. In response to them and to their expression of desire and fear, time and space are thought to collapse on each other. Freud, again, has perceived this clearly: "Objects as such are overshadowed by the idea representing them; what takes place in the latter must also happen in the former, and the relations which exist between ideas are also postulated as to things. As thought does not recognize distances and easily brings together in one act of consciousness things spatially and temporally far removed, the magic world also puts itself above spatial distance by telepathy, and treats a past association as if it were a present one."[11] The patterns that thought takes in language are assumed to apply to the things that language names; thus things depend on the transformations that grammar imposes.

Jung's term *synchronicity*, which helps him to explain how the archetypal symbol is an agent for the retrieval of past time, is available to us not only for studying Proust, Joyce, Mann, and Woolf but also for studying the romantics. For them suddenness, explosion, and revolution were instinctive modes of thought. The romantic magician shouts "Arise!," "Now!," "Come." He expects an instantaneous response and gets one, insofar as he has imagined it. It is significant that Jung's interest in synchronicity developed as he studied Paracelsus and alchemy, and these studies led him, as they led others before him, to a concern with a magically unified sensibility ignoring the distinctions between now and then, here and there, I and it, the inner and the outer. The seemingly superficial limits between thoughts and things are cancelled in the words that unite them. At the drop of a hat things seem to rearrange themselves at the behest of words.

The Old French word for magic is *gramayre*, and this allusion to our "grammar," however tenuous, reminds us of the protean powers of linguistic structures, whereby we change the aspects of things by the order in which we perceive them and by the actions that we subsequently take on the evidence of these arrangements. Our emphasis of first and last, here and there, now and later, is expressed in syntax, but it bears no necessary relation to the outside sequence. Each of these temporal or atemporal observations is a spell that we cast on things which continue to plod along in their own inscrutable time.

Such a magical simultaneity can be seen in the greater romantic lyric, where the thing observed is both inside and outside at the same time; and observation and meditation, seeing and thinking, are one. That simultaneity can likewise be seen in the poem which calls for itself and unfolds in that call, with no gap in time between the wish and its realization. The poet imagines so clearly what he wants that the imagined vision turns into his desire. Keats's "lo!" erases time; it accomplishes what all Keats's torments at the passing of time could not do. The spontaneity often attributed to the composition of the romantic poem arises rather from the careful cultivation of techniques of synchronicity, for the poem telescopes the time between the command and a response from the outer world.

If time is no barrier, then space, as Freud showed, is certainly not either. For likenesses of parts, as in homeopathic medicine where pointed leaves are thought to cure stabbing pain, are available across distance through memory. Believing that likeness and analogy correspond throughout nature, setting up recurrent patterns which allow one thing to affect another, the magician is liberated from place as from time. He is, as Keats imagines Endymion to be, "full alchemiz'd, and free of space," once the lunar imagination begins to work its enchantment. Perhaps more than Keats, however, it is Coleridge who specialized in these magical condensations and evaporations of time and space, as we shall see, pointing the way to the playing with time in the modern novel. The perception of analogous things merging across time and space is not unique to magical ways of perceiving. Yet it so pervades magical thought that it has become a distinguishing characteristic of it. Frazer's clarification of the differences between contagious and sympathetic magic permits us to see that this way of thinking is characteristically poetic too. [12] When in sonnet 73 Shakespeare establishes the likeness among five processes of aging—trees, ruined buildings, days, fires, and men,—he does in his complex way what a magician would do in a simple way: that is, to see the universe everywhere alive with reflections of himself and reminders of his kinship with that organic whole. In the face of these analogies different kinds of magicians would react differently: whereas the primitive magician would try to exploit these resemblances in the belief that if he could stop the fire from dying, the man, too, would live, the neoplatonic magician would stop short at such pragmatism. He would rest at the summoned vision of universal correspondences.

"That analogies can be made," Hazard Adams says in his introductory remarks to *Blake and Yeats*, "that there are such things as metaphors, suggests that there is some sort of unity in our diverse world; and if our symbolical world is literally the real world, then a metaphor becomes not simply, imaginatively true, but literally true—or at least the line between literal and imaginative truth is erased." [13] In making analogies in wider and wider arcs across the known reality, we confer on it a coherent interrelated unity that it did not possess previously.

In pointing out the similarities between two things, the magician or the poet has two major choices. He either finds organic resemblances already in nature as in the Shakespeare sonnet above, or he unearths resemblances not previously visible. In other words the analogies may be magical because they *are* natural, or else they may be magical because they are *not* natural, corresponding to the problem we found in chapter 1 to lie at the heart of magical theory. They either reveal the magic in nature as "Lycidas" does, for instance, when vegetable nature forecasts in its seasonal recurrence the ressurrection of Edward King and all men, or they impose similarities otherwise hidden. In the first instance it is nature itself which is full of sympathies and correspondences reassuring us of its vitality. In the second instance, to be elaborated later, the poet is the one who yokes together things thought to be incongruous, thus showing that whatever resemblances they have exist in his mind alone. Accordingly, in the first instance, the poet is the passive looker-on, longing to participate in a life not his own; in the second he is the active organizer and conveyor of life to a nature inert without his words.[14]

At least three poetic techniques seem to draw their effectiveness from the philosophy of magic, which they in turn reinforce. Metaphor, personification, and symbol have as their common principle the transference of identity through analogy. All depend upon a recognition of analogies between nature and human life, and the poet aims to exploit these analogies to enhance one or the other analogue. The sympathies operate across time and space, through visible and invisible resemblances, through the similarities between past and present, through the coincidence of dream or idea with some slight fact of observed reality. As events happen in similar or contiguous situations, just so in the magical view they will come to pass for the situation at hand. By appealing to parallel events, the magician brings to bear the force of precedent; he pairs the spiritual energies behind a certainty with those that should activate an uncertainty. Allusions as well as physical resemblances accomplish this pairing. As Malinowski discovered, "mythical allusions . . . when uttered unchain the powers of the past and cast them into the future."[15] The importance of such coincidence for the magical view is not limited to primitive thinking: the omens in physical and historical resemblance, in contiguity, and in synchronicity are dreaded or welcomed in civilized life; and certainly these principles of beneficent or maleficent likeness abound in poetic thinking.

That magical analogies impel incantations is clearly illustrated in the Cheremis charm that Thomas Sebeok examines. Sebeok uses this text to suggest that charms hold "the ingredients of poetry." [16] Conversely poems are in turn often composed of elements of charms. In translation the charm reads:

> As the appletree blossoms forth,
> Just so let this wound heal!
> .   .   .   .   .   .
> When water can blossom forth,
> Only then overcome me.

In the first couplet the magician appeals to the certainty of an appletree's blossoming to assure the healing of the wound, as if by relating healing to a natural organic process, the wound would "understand" that it had no choice but to heal in the same way that the seemingly blighted winter tree has no choice in spring but to blossom. Here, then, the tree is to be an example to the wound, which is to mimic the tree's restoration.

In the second couplet, however, the magician appeals to an impossibility instead of to a certainty, and reverses the direction of the magical commands. The magician links the fate of the wound's infection with the fate of water, and he devises a riddling formula (reminiscent of those in Grimm's fairy tales) according to which the patient's death would be as impossible as the blossoming of water.

In each case the direct commands are preceded by parallel natural situations which govern the effectiveness of the commands by emphasizing the analogies and sympathies in the animate universe. The first stresses the similarity of manner ("As the appletree blossoms"); the second, the temporal conjunction ("When water"). The symmetries of the charm itself correspond to the symmetries in nature and the lives of men. One action infects another; events are not separate and discrete, but are transmuted by those juxtapositions that language half-creates.

Metaphor, personification, and symbol are types of analogy that are both poetical and magical. Metaphor, discovering previously unnoticed congruities, tries to use the resemblances of two things to bring them together. Paralleling each other (and thereby lighting each other up) the "extremes" of a metaphor are able to define an area of fear or desire which has yet no known language to express it.[17] In the spell this illumination is intended to be not merely enlightening for the reader but to be instructive to the parts of the metaphor themselves: they are to learn each other's ways.

On a larger scale than the verbal metaphor the two "extremes" of a double plot serve likewise to extend each other's meanings, working on those principles of correspondence so basic to the theory of magic. William Empson in *Some Versions of Pastoral* suggests that the whole idea of double plots is magical in much the same way that metaphor itself is magical. From the example of Shakespeare's *Troilus and Cressida* he ventures: "The two parts make a mutual comparison that illuminates both parties ('love and war are alike') and their large-scale indefinite juxtaposition seems to encourage primitive ways of thought ('Cressida will bring Troy bad luck because she is bad'). This power of suggestion is the strength of the double plot; once you take the two parts to correspond, any character may take on *mana* because he seems to cause what he corresponds to or be the Logos of what he symbolizes."[18] Juxtaposed for the purpose of casting light on each other, the two plots, like the two extremes of the metaphor "love is war," extend each other's meanings and the range in which each can operate. A new sphere of power opens up for each, and at the same time they affect each other by magical influence.

Not only do the "extremes" of a metaphor define an area of

unknown and invisible "reality," but the vehicle of the metaphor extends the identity of the tenor and, by distributing it, annihilates its solidity. The identity of the thing in question begins to belong to other things and to partake of them. In this distribution of attribute and name, substance is scattered, and things seem to pass from one resemblance to another. Love is a rose; anger is a tree. In each exchange love becomes more roselike, anger more treelike, and the real nature of these emotions (whatever that may be) is falsified, because it is changed. Ever more protean, these inexplicable emotions begin magically to assume new shapes, to conquer new areas of possible meaning. As they are metamorphosed by their metaphorical names, they participate in the nature of other things, and in turn animate these other things. Accordingly the words of a poetic metaphor change the substances of feelings or things by identifying them with other things. Like the magical universe the poetic one is full of participations, sympathies, and transformations. In both worlds the magical word enacts its rearrangements in defiance of discrete identities, and by applying new names it betrays these identities.

The magician also personifies the natural world, for it appears to respond to human lamentation or joy in a truly remarkable way. The pathetic fallacy then may also be thought to have its source in magical ways of thinking. The magician who sees the weather as dreary and depressing when his mood is such is confirmed by his believing in magical sympathies. Trees that seem to weep when he does become emblems of his sorrow and effigies of it. A field of daffodils seems to laugh and to dance in a joyous analogy to his mood; or owls hoot and mastiffs stir when he himself senses the presence of evil. The pathetic fallacy is sympathetic in the magical sense; the poet organizes the animate nature around him, and he is the axis of its multiple sympathies.

Action symbolically represented in the spell is intended to release the emotion surrounding future action. The magical words become the symbol of an action that is anticipated. To explain the use of symbols in magical thinking, Malinowski gives the example of the savage "whistling for the wind," since whistling relieves the anxiety of waiting for the wind to rise and since in the gust of whistling the breath simulates the very wind that it wants.[19] In *Coral Gardens and Their Magic* Malinowski examines spells that by their symbolic action organize the life of the planting culture. The words stand for realities that they initiate: "the magical word," he says, "is coeval with that aspect of reality which it has to influence."[20] The magician, for example, enacts in advance the harvesting of the crop that is as yet not even sown. Similarly, when he elucidates a long Panamanian spell for childbirth, Claude Lévi-Strauss insists on the importance of the symbol for magic. The words of the spell concretize a chaotic event. The spell is the "coalescence and precipitation of diffuse states."[21] For Lévi-Strauss the symbol is not so much aesthetic as psychologically therapeutic: "The shaman provides the sick woman with a language, by means of which unexpressed, and otherwise inexpressible psychic states can be immediately expressed."[22] The spell, then, clarifies a series of actions and rehearses them on a symbolic level. The symbolic action of magic, like the symbol of poetry, embodies an outside "reality" that is vague and complex; it concentrates the diffuseness, and, in doing so, draws that diffuseness into the area of the comprehensible. "It always partakes of the reality which it renders intelligible," explains Coleridge himself; "and while it enunciates the whole, abides itself as a living part in that unity of which it is the representative."[23] As the "visible sign for something invisible" or "the outward sign of an inward state," the symbol is also the present sign of a future state, and as such it is an augury as well as an instruction—a symbol and a signal.[24]

The symbolic action of the primitive spell is best illustrated in one of the "predatory" spells collected by C. M. Bowra in *Primitive Song.* The magician constructs a hunting spell which will accomplish the deed in advance. To be caught, the animal

must first be caught in the mind's snare. Because of this
practical purpose, these spells are precise, perceptive, shrewd;
they frequently imitate not only the hunter's own projected
action but even the sounds of his prey. The spells are full of
sharp images and phonetic effects that aim to reproduce the
presence of the prey not in remembrance, but (by a strange
telescoping of time) in advance. To this symbolic action the
real hunt is an anticlimax:

> You belly full of rock-flint,
> Great-toed one, who with your feathers say *tsa-tsa*,
> Who eat the heart of melons,
> Give me one of your feathers.

> Ostrich, rising and flying,
> Long-necked and big-toed,
> Belly full of rock-flint, great bird,
> Wide-mouthed male ostrich,
> Flying, running, great bird,
> Give me one of your tail-feathers.

> Ostrich, with dusty flank,
> Running great bird, fluttering feathers here and there,
> Belly that says *khou-khou*,
> Running, walking male ostrich,
> Give me one of your tail-feathers.

> Male ostrich, looking up,
> Belly that says *khari, khari*,
> Ostrich, whose bowels alone are not fit to eat,
> Give me one of your leg-bones, ostrich!

> He who has two bones, which say *hui-hui*,
> Male ostrich who has wonderful marrow,
> Who with his face says *gou-gou*,
> Might I possess you, my ostrich! [25]

The magician seeks directly to enchant the ostrich. He seems
to watch closely, as if circling around, ever more familiar and
intimate, ever more possessive. At first the ostrich is discovered pillaging melons, fluttering feathers. Then, startled
by the observer, it races away; the pace of the verse accelerates;

the magician-hunter seems to be near enough to see its mouth wide in outrage; then, in stanza three, the bird is in a frenzy, losing feathers, covered with dust; and the magician, hearing its rocky stomach growling, emboldens his requests. As the magician anticipates his victory, his praise of the bird becomes more culinary. He has mentally transformed the great beast into food by shifting the refrain, closing in on details, escalating his demands. Imagery, refrains, onomatopoeia, direct address, and the anticipation of precise future action substitute for a series of real actions. The spell as a whole with all its poetic effects determines the outcome of the hunt. It stands as a proof that the hunt will succeed. It symbolizes and organizes a proposed actuality.

There are limits to the kinship imagined by poets to exist between magic and poetry, however. Even after seeing the essentially magical quality of analogies, parallel plots, metaphors that exchange corresponding aspects, symbols that serve as prognostications, and images that capture the essential nature of the thing, we can certainly object to any broad application of magical theory to poetry. Most notably poetry differs from magical verse because each poem is a unique occurrence. It does not recur. It is not rigidly formulaic; it arises out of a specific individual personality (even though artfully designed) rather than being a traditional construct aiming to work automatically on the universe.

More specific objections should be made to the attribution of magical qualities to individual poetic elements. Metaphor in most sophisticated verse does not permit a complete submergence of the thing to be compared and the thing it is compared to, the tenor and the vehicle. The vehicle does not really abolish the tenor's true nature, for we usually recognize a tension between the two, the presence of an aloof consciousness deliberately making the analogy, thereby reminding us that this analogy is a fiction and that therefore no occult powers can truly pass from one side to the other, or from the name to the thing, or from the inside to the outside. Instead a poet does the comparing, and he is proud of his skill. Blake's "Poison Tree" seems a good example of the transference of identities between the tree and love—and between then the tree and hate. The tree becomes an effigy of feelings, giving substance within it to the furious rages of insubstantial emotion. But while the tree is an effigy in a magical sense, the metaphor is not truly an identity, but rather a hypothesis, a tentative way of working with these complex emotions, and a representation of parts of them only. There is always a distance between tenor and vehicle, always a sense that the love may have other aspects and that the poet is trying out images to fit those aspects.

Transference of identity through metaphor seems to be true for the famous last stanza of Yeats's "Among School Children." In the metaphor *labour is blossoming*, labor seems at first glance to have no other life; it is a large abstract word absorbing many unspecified meanings (work, growth, and child-bearing); it gets its real specific life from "blossoming" and becomes as effortless as the productions of spring. But then even this identity is undercut by the next word, *or*, where again we learn that the assigning of these vehicles is only contingent and hypothetical, for blossoming could as easily be dancing; and dancing and blossoming, despite the ease and grace and wholeness characteristic of both their movements, are not the same. The possibility that blossoming equals labor is further scattered in the next three lines in which Yeats enumerates the kinds of activities which could be construed as labor—soul work, the work of becoming beautiful, the attainment of wisdom. All these elaborations of the tenor prove that it has more of a reality than is shown fully in its vehicle blossoming, and that blossoming, with its later call for the tree's indivisibility of past, present, and future (or of body, heart, and soul), is only a shot in the dark, one of several valiant efforts to describe the complex state of the unity of the self, and the impossibility of separating transcendent ideas of it from the body out of which these ideas grew. Yeats is advocating unity, but not creating it in the identities of his metaphors; they are always apart, and while the lines are enchanting in their sound, the tenor has not been transformed into a vehicle, but has kept its distance because of its complexity. Yet some transference has taken place nevertheless. Labor hardly exists for us (except in line 4, blear-eyed wisdom out of midnight oil) outside of the soul-making of the chestnut tree. And if labor could always have the unity of pattern, motion, body, and idea of that peculiar art form (the dance) which only exists in the enactment, we would truly be self-delighting. Tree and dance stand for us as ideals of labor. Thus in a future world, where we have attained unity of being, labor and blossoming will indeed be an identity, and both will be identical to the dance. Thus the analogy is hypothetical *now*, but when all is arranged, either by the gyres of history or by the phases of the moon or the soul, the parallel will cease being hypothetical and its parts will become identical *then*. In other words tenor and vehicle should become one, but in an imperfect divided world they are not. We are urged to try to make them one, and the first stage of this persuasion is to make us think of them in connection with each other as tentatively one.

Certainly, given the infinite multiplicity of kinds of metaphors (as indicated in Christine Brooke-Rose's *Grammar of Metaphor*), we cannot look at one example and draw conclusions about identity or tension in metaphor. If we were to look at T. S. Eliot's famous simile—"the evening is spread out against the sky / Like a patient etherised upon a table"—we would decide in favor of disjunction. Here a shock of dissimilarity startles us into attending to the poem; the anesthesia forms part of a consciously elaborate design of numbness, and also becomes a projection of the narrator. We have to strain all the facts of existence to imagine an evening (which has no existence in space unless it be as a flat purple sky) as a body on an operating table, and the effort defeats us. The difficulty of imagining the two as one forces us to ascribe this simile to the mind of the impotent, numb, and passive speaker, who is revealing his own problems exactly by his creation of a simile which has no bearing on the outer scene. That the tenor is in no danger of merging with the vehicle is an emblem of Prufrock's own isolation from things outside of his mind. Even the names he assigns to things do not correspond. In this example, then, the tension between tenor and vehicle cannot be used to prove that metaphors never achieve identity because this tension is part of characterization. It indicates a spiritual sickness which prevents the character from discovering any healing identity between his own concepts and the world beyond the periphery of his consciousness. Prufrock would be a different "person" if the magical power of metaphor and of assigning names worked for him.

It can be safely said, however, that sometimes metaphors do attempt to establish an identity between tenor and vehicle, even when they record its failure or its postponement to an ideal future. Yeats's "Lovers' Song," like Sebeok's Cheremis charm, shows influences and processes moving from one parallel to another, and in Coleridge's "Rime of the Ancient Mariner" and Shelley's *Prometheus Unbound* 4 these magical identities and transformations not only occur but become subjects of the poems.

When images or metaphors become symbols, they begin to perform more strictly magical feats, becoming the thing they signify and at the same time remaining themselves in the remarkable prestidigitation most aptly described by Coleridge. The magical nature of symbols has received much attention from anthropologists, who have found that symbols, or "molecules of rituals" with "great semantic richness," are multivalent, spreading their significance in the direction of the shaman, his patients (or victims), the universe at large, past events and present ones.[26] To see this multivalence at work in the symbol we can look at Wordsworth's "Strange Fits of Passion I Have Known." When Wordsworth's lover allows the moon's fate to substitute for Lucy's, a superstitious terror flashes through him as he watches the moon drop. The moon *is* Lucy; the image of the moon is dying in Lucy's stead, but also preceding Lucy, since Lucy's fate is paired to the moon's. Thus Wordsworth's poem is both effigy and prophecy, and the lover is accordingly filled with dread. But even in this strangely primitive poem, we are reminded that we are in the realm of possibility, not in the realm of tribal certainties. We become aware of a speaker thinking up possibilities which might very well come true, and we are aware, also, that this speaker is telling us something about the intensity of his feeling, and the love he feels turns him into a primitive believer in omens and magic, effigies and prophecies. While the identity of Lucy with her symbol the moon shows Wordsworth using the symbol as a magical center, he is also revealing that love itself is magical, for the lover perceives magical significance in everything that concerns the loved one.

In short, then, our sense that a poet's consciousness is coming between the extremes of a metaphor or is telling us something about the general nature of his symbol makes us question that a magical transference or interpenetration is taking place, and it keeps us from suspending our disbelief and succumbing to the magical changes supposedly occurring in the poem. Veering from gullibility to skepticism and back again, we are kept in a pleasurable anxiety.

Our literary distance breaks down when we are faced with the distinctive meter of the primitive spell, adapted in varying degrees by Renaissance, mid-eighteenth-century, and romantic poets. This meter, demonstrated in spells by Shakespeare, Jonson, Dryden, Gray, Coleridge, Shelley, Byron, and Beddoes, makes irrelevant whatever transferences may or may not have been occurring in the metaphors of the poem. It does not really matter whether the parts of an analogy have power over each other or not, for this pounding senseless meter asks us to forget all questions about meaning.

In discussing the lyric in *Anatomy of Criticism*, Northrop Frye presents two useful categories, rooting kinds of poetry either in sound or in sight, in babble or doodle, or in charm or riddle. The charm is the *Ur*-form for all poems that emphasize sound for sound's sake, beginning with the child's meaningless babble. Frye suggests that the power of the charm may have physiological origins: "The radical of *melos* is *charm:* the hypnotic incantation that, through its pulsing dance rhythm, appeals to involuntary physical response, and is hence not far from the sense of magic, or physically compelling power. The etymological descent of charm from *carmen*, song, may be noted. Actual charms have a quality that is imitated in popular literature by work songs of various kinds, especially lullabies, where the drowsy sleep-inducing repetition shows the underlying oracular or dream pattern very clearly." [27] Frye does not limit this magical power to the charm, but instead suggests that at bottom both *melos* and *opsis* are magical: "Just as the charm is not far from a sense of magical compulsion, so the curiously wrought object, whether sword-hilt or illuminated manuscript, is not far from a sense of enchantment or magical imprisonment." [28]

The original forms, frequently exploited by romantics who felt compelled to return to origins, seem to arise from a time in the childhoods of self and race when a unity of head and heart, of rational and irrational, was assumed to have existed. The charm may for this reason have seemed to them the perfect vehicle for fleeing the eighteenth century and returning to a romantic universal poetry combining the naive and the sentimental.

The notion that the spell or charm is an original form from an imaginary time when the mind and the body were one helps to explain a paradox—that the much praised omnipotence of thought is embodied in mindless forms. Rationality operates through the medium of irrationality. But with the myth of the charm as an *Ur*-form, the romantics are enabled to return to primitive, childish, and therefore presumably unified sensibilities. Seeing the spell as primal poetry, they hoped to gain power through irrationality and the occult correspondences which seem to arise in its sounds.

Irrationality rules the spell from the creative process which overtakes the magician to the weirdness of the lines themselves to the hypnosis of the hearer. In composing his spell the magician sets aside reason to permit an invasion of what seems to be supernatural energy. He anticipates a similar response in his hearers, who should relinquish their critical faculties under the impact of the spell's rhythm, until they find themselves in a subdued and malleable state—a "willing suspension."

In bewitching its audience the spell is intended to release irrational feelings, both tribal and infantile, group-oriented and prelogical. Hypnotic sound, heavy-handed and repetitive, approaches nonsense and pulverizes meaning. Like the riddle, the nonsense rhyme, and the nursery rhyme, the original nonliterary spell clings to its primitive character, its maker fearing to release a new and untried effect by changing established formulae. As poems to be chanted, spells emphasize words as sounds more than words as meanings, intended to reach us (like Eliot's "auditory imagination") at some level below reasoned discourse. Since the poet claims to have retrieved these sounds from a dark dreamlike irrationality, they are to touch us there also, eroding the boundaries between fact and fancy, meaning and nonsense, sense and sound.[29]

The general irrationality of the *Ur*-form of the spell is increased by the way the elements are packed together. The spell is thought to gain power by omitting connections, measuring its potency by its density. Potency measured by density is a principle that applies to the repetition of poetic elements on all levels: density of analogy, of allusion, of meter, of imperatives, and of names, all contributing to a compulsive tone. The densities of sound and correspondence frequently override a clear statement of meaning and seem to hypnotize the reader not to expect one. In the magical spell these repeated poetic elements are so exaggerated that they seem to exist for their own sakes, overwhelming the hearer with sound. Such density is common to primitive spells collected by Malinowski and Bowra, to Anglo-Saxon spells, to folkloric spells collected in the romantic era from Scotland and Germany. In order to create an aural experience so sensory that the hearer must abandon his private will, commands are mesmeric, lists of magical ingredients seem endless; the hearer is lulled by alliterations and subjected to a meter as visceral as a drumbeat.

The meter of the spell is notoriously dense. When this meter reemerges in consciously written poetry we may suspect that the poet is pretending to evoke supernatural powers or accomplish certain transformations. The meter of the magical spell makes blatant the recurrence on which meter as a whole depends. Individual words pound and shout, creating an unsophisticated emphatic meter which might well be called "isochronic." (Even Wimsatt and Beardsley in their attacks on linguistic analysis of isochronism concede that it may apply to primitive verse.[30]) Repeated parts of words (assonantal, alliterative, and rhyming) force the listener to attend to their sound and disregard their sense. A free-for-all of emphasis ensues, pitched stridently, like a series of exclamations.

The alliteration and repetition recall the spell's origins: in England, the accentual four-stress tradition to which the spell is still tied. Here, for example, an Anglo-Saxon spell against a wen displays the constant spell elements:

> Wenne, wenne, wenchichenne,
> Hēr ne scealt þū timbrien, ne nenne tūn habben,
> ac þū scealt north eonene tō þan nihgan berhge,
> Þer þū hauest ermig ēnne broþer.
> Hē þē sceal legge lēaf et hēafde.
> Under fōt wolues, under ueþer earnes,
> under earnes clēa, ā þū geweornie.[31]

An Old High German spell betrays a similarly heavy-handed meter:

> Eiris sazan idisi, sazan hera duoder,
> Suma hapt heptidun, suma heri lezidun,
> suma clubodun, umbi cuoniouuidi.
> insprinc haptabandun, inuar uigandun.[32]

It is not difficult to recognize in the Anglo-Saxon spell the origin of the spells of the weird sisters in *Macbeth*. The background is germanic, not latinate. These spells, too, repeat whole words, parts of words, and an emphatic four-stress meter, tying in these aural resources with resources of analogy, metaphor, symbol, personification, image, and foreshortened time and space—the repertoire of sympathetic magic as it deals with the unknown or approximates its voice:

> Fillet of a fenny snake,
> In the cauldron boil and bake;
> Eye of newt, and toe of frog,
> Wool of bat, and tongue of dog,
> Adder's fork, and blind-worm's sting,
> Lizard's leg, and howlet's wing,
> For a charm of powerful trouble,
> Like a hell-broth boil and bubble.[33]

In the Anglo-Saxon, German, and Shakespearean spells, the association of incantation, dancing, motion, and music may account to some extent for the unabashed repetitions and may also suggest a larger, more physiological aspect of the magician's power over his audience's collective intelligence, like a snake charmer charming a snake. Indolent and empassioned, involuntary and voluntary, the spell rouses its hearers to action.

The meter of the spells in *Macbeth* expresses the dark powers of the underworld rather than the promethean aspirations of *The Tempest*. The wild and whirling words are as compelling as a nightmare; for the dark powers administer "the insane root that takes the reason prisoner." Thus in *Macbeth* the heavily accented meter and the repetition of words and whole phrases serve the submerged forces of evil that rise to the surface in the action. On the other hand Shakespeare brings magic into the rational sphere in *The Tempest* and the rhythms change accordingly, keeping all the while their close relationship to music and motion. In *The Tempest* Shakespeare follows the alternative tradition of the Italian Renaissance magicians. *Macbeth* and

The Tempest present the yin and yang of magical possibilities, the dark side and the bright.

In his "Magic in *The Tempest*" Hardin Craig explains Prospero's rationality: "A master magician leads a spiritual existence in the realm of a limited ideal existence. . . . Ideas are the only examples of perfection, but they are only ideas (or dreams). . . . Prospero operates through Ariel by means of the agency of mind. Since Ariel's powers are music, poetry, and spectacle as well as fear and terror, he can do whatever mind can do and that is everything that can be conceived." [34] Prospero's spells are appropriately rational and yet forever illusory. While *Macbeth* explores the subconscious aspects of magic—a kind of black magic that forces rationality to yield—*The Tempest* explores the heretical aspects of white magic, in which the magician plays at being God, exercising complete control of the action. Prospero's spells are more syntactical but no less authoritative than the witches'; for in each play the spells (whether from the unconscious atavistic depths or from the conscious arrogant reason) instigate the events that make up the play.

The meter characteristic of spells in *Macbeth* is modified in such imitations as Ben Jonson's magical *Masque of Queenes*. The voice of malevolent irrationality seems to become less threatening in such examples as this:

> The Owle is abroad, the Bat, and the Toade,
> And so is the Cat-a-Mountaine:
> And Ant, and the Mole sit both in a hole
> And Frog peepes out o' the fountayne. [35]

The expert modulation of assonance and of alliteration, the manipulation of quantity and pause, are testimony that control supersedes madness; and in the decorative stanzas of Campion, Dryden, and Gay not dread but elegance enchants:

> Choose the darkest part o' the grove,
> Such as ghosts at noon-day love.
> Dig a trench, and dig it nigh
> Where the bones of Laius lie;

> Altars raised of turf or stone,
> Will th'infernal pow'rs have none.
> Answer me, if this be done?
>   'Tis done.[36]

In this "spell" Dryden is loyal to the truncated trochaic line that Shakespeare perfected, but he makes it unswervingly regular without any of the sudden breaks that occur in *Macbeth*. Here, then, the peculiar spell-sound of foregrounded commands, heavily-accented four-beat (or three-beat) meter, heavy alliteration, and frequent repetitions—the heritage of the Anglo-Saxon and Germanic magicians—fades into the urbane iambics of the Restoration. It becomes a playful variation of the poet's customary voice. The constant spell-meter thus undergoes some variation in the neoclassical period, but with Coleridge on occasion it returns abruptly to its original form, based on his careful investigation of Copper Indian primitive magic, of Shakespeare's supernatural plays, and of the physiological effects of meter.

When the meter of the spell eases up and becomes discursive, losing rime-packed, end-stopped, and refrain-filled lines, as in "Kubla Khan" or "Ode to the West Wind," it may no longer sound like a spell, but only because the meaning of "incantatory" has changed. Coleridge, Shelley, and Byron still think that they are writing spells and call their poems fancifully "spells," but they have substituted a circling and swaying syntax for pounding meter, believing that their flexible lines will be as potent as the rigid lines of the primitive, and believing that within these circling lines spatial and temporal analogies will be able to work their contagions.

Poets such as Coleridge, Shelley, and Byron seem to have emphasized the magical powers of metaphor, symbol, personification, and rhythm outlined for poetry in general in this chapter, and they seem to have minimized those qualities that differentiate poems from spells. We have seen that poems differ from spells in the recognition that tenor and vehicle will never be fused into an identity but will always keep tension between them; in the refusal to be an entirely closed and self-referential system, an artifact of inherited power; in the persistence of meaning and the rejection of weirdness and gibberish; and in the underlying belief that the poetic utterance is individual, instead of rigidly determined by past successes and failures. These factors separate poems from spells as they are found in magical situations. But the romantics were trying to tap that very irrationality that we find alien and to embody it in their poetry. The spell promised them just what they were seeking in the quest to revitalize the spirit. It promised a return to the original voice of savage man; it promised an obliteration of rationalistic convention; it promised through the fusions occurring in metaphor and symbol a direct interchange between the mind's concept of a thing and the thing's physical body beyond; it promised, finally, the difficult combination of rational power with irrational energy—"omnipotence of thought" achieved through mindlessness. It promised all this, and the promise alone was enough to make poetry change. Poetry did change, and it changed in part under the influence of reviving theories of magical language and the hope these held out for what words could do.

3 • Coleridge and the Magical Power of the Imagination

Deeply knowledgeable about the Renaissance, steeped in the problems of his immediate predecessors of the late eighteenth century, and capable of seeing the philosophical significance of these problems in the context of European thought as well as their practical application to poetic technique, Samuel Taylor Coleridge was a pivotal figure in the tradition that art is a kind of magic. This tradition was important to him because it contributed to solving the larger problem of the revitalization of spirit. Coleridge tried to revitalize spirit by proving that men were supernatural rather than natural beings, whose greater than natural powers separated them from the continuum of things.

He considered the revitalization of spirit in his writings on literature, aesthetics, psychology, philosophy, and theology and in his poetry. He consulted Unitarians, empiricists, Cambridge Platonists, Neoplatonists, German idealists, and many others to help him develop his thoughts. Without subscribing for long to any one doctrine, he used whatever would help him, quoting, disputing, and discarding, seeking at different times in his life through these various approaches to free the spirit from "the blind idiot called Nature," even as he persistently and precisely observed the natural scene.

Intimately tied to his efforts to prove the supernatural life of the spirit was his theory of the magical power of the imagination, a theory which has often bewildered Coleridge's readers. This theory, confusingly presented in the twelfth and thirteenth chapters of the *Biographia Literaria* as the climax of the first half of the book and the preparation for the second, is subsidiary to his larger theory of the supernatural self and is dependent upon it. For the notion that men are supernatural extends to their having power through passionate language to transform the nature from which they are separating themselves. Coleridge's discovery of the miracle of the self arises in connection with his readings of magical texts; the definitions of the imagination in the *Biographia* depend on that discovery; and the discussions of supernatural literature in the late literary lectures and of Plotinus, Neoplatonists, and occultists in the late *Philosophical Lectures* help to explain these earlier definitions. I will discuss magical themes and meters in the poetry in the next chapter, after a theoretical basis for their use has been established.

Coleridge often claims that he had read Plotinus, Jamblichus, Ficino, Bruno, Boehme, and Pico della Mirandola when he was still at Christ's Hospital as a charity boy. Charles Lamb corroborates this claim in his description of Coleridge "in the day-spring of [his] fancies," when Coleridge, "Logician, Metaphysician, Bard!," lectured to the passersby who stood in the Cloisters, "intranced with admiration," while he unfolded the mysteries of Jamblichus or Plotinus, each passerby weighing "the disproportion between the *speech* and the *garb* of the young Mirandula."[1] In the *Biographia* Coleridge spends many pages expressing his gratitude to these writers. He credits Plato and his followers and Boehme and Law with helping him feel how "human nature itself fought up against [the] willful resignation of intellect" and how the powers of the mind preexist the experience of perception. They helped to teach him, he recalls, that "we learn all things indeed by occasion of experience; but the very facts so learnt force us inward on the antecedents, that must be pre-supposed in order to render experience itself possible."[2] In chapter 9 of the *Biographia* he confesses that from these writings he learned to refute the Lockean presupposition that "*nihil in intellectu quod non prius in sensu*" by adding the "qualifying '*praeter ipsum intellectum.*'" The famous passage at the beginning of chapter 9 describes these debts: "The early study of Plato and Plotinus, with the commentaries and the *Theologia Platonica* of the illustrious Florentine [Ficino]; of Proclus and Gemisthius Pletho; and at a later period of the *De immenso et innumerabili*, and the *De la causa, principio et uno* of the philosopher of Nola [Bruno], who could boast of a Sir Philip Sidney and Fulke Greville among his patrons, and whom the idolators of Rome burnt as an atheist in the year 1600; had all contributed to prepare my mind for the reception and welcoming of the *Cogito quia sum, et sum quia cogito*; a philosophy of seeming hardihood, but certainly the most ancient and therefore presumptively the most natural" (pp. 94–95).

Despite these exuberant claims and his belief that these philosophies are natural or intuitive, several commentators have argued that there is no proof of these readings since Coleridge's own statements are after the fact, Charles Lamb's reminiscences are filtered through Coleridge's memories, and the allusions in the poetry, as tracked down by John Livingston Lowes, John Beer, and others, are ambiguous. These sources and other heterodox approaches full of curious and rhapsodic imagery, however, were amply summarized and quoted in secondary sources such as Cudworth's *True Intellectual System*, Mosheim's *Ecclesiastical History*, Berkeley's late dialogues, in Gibbon's *Decline and Fall of the Roman Empire* and in Augustine's *Confessions* 8, and *The City of God*. In order for Coleridge to glimpse the vast aspirations and stimulating vistas of these writers there was no need for him to have read every word of the originals or to have preserved studious notes of his excited youthful skimming or to have kept his library receipts or proofs of purchase. For a young enthusiast and apologist, who cannot be accused of having small Latin and less Greek, these compendia were enough: he sought images and intuitions and sometimes caught them on the wing. Indeed, if he did not read the Neoplatonists themselves as early as he claims, even skeptics grant that he may have done so by 1797.

Coleridge's feeling for these heterodox sources, however and whenever studied, was so persistent that even in 1810 he could seriously recommend to new clergymen a postgraduate year of reading the Neoplatonists so as to understand better the workings of the creative mind. In notebook entries 3934 and 3935 he explains that "one excellence of the Doctrine of Plato, or of the Plotino-platonic Philosophy, is that it never suffers, much less causes or even occasions, its Disciples to forget themselves, lost and scattered in sensible Objects disjoined or *as* disjoined from themselves." This philosophy "rouses" the Soul "to acts and energies of creative Thought." "No man worthy the name of man can read the many extracts from Proclus, Porphyry, Plotinus, &c, . . . without an ahndung, an inward omening, of a system congruous with his nature, & thence attracting it." Unlike modern "Anti-philosophy" this philosophy excites and wakens "tremulous feeling" in the heart, "as if it heard or began to *glimpse* something which had once belonged to it, its Lord or its Beloved—even as a man recovering gradually from an alienation of the Senses or the Judgments on beginning to recollect the countenances of his Wife, Mother, Children, or Betrothed."[3]

Although this philosophy lies close to the springs of our spirit and heals it from any alienation the heart may have experienced, Coleridge implies that between his youthful reading and his acknowledgment of indebtedness a period intervened during which he was ashamed of his interest. "Why need I be afraid? Say rather how dare I be ashamed of the Teutonic theosophist, Jacob Behmen?" Boehme's writings, and those of the other mystics whom Coleridge read, "acted in no slight degree to prevent my mind from being imprisoned within the outline of any single dogmatic system. They contributed to keep alive the heart in the head; gave me an indistinct, yet stirring and working presentment, that all the products of the mere reflective faculty partook of death, and were the rattling twigs and sprays into which a sap was yet to be propelled from some root to which I had not penetrated, if they were to afford my soul either food or shelter. If they were too often a moving cloud of smoke to me by day, yet they were always a pillar of fire throughout the night, during my wanderings through the wilderness of doubt, and enabled me to skirt, without crossing, the sandy deserts of utter disbelief." Coleridge continues to acknowledge his debts to such writings as he fends off charges of plagiarism, claiming that whatever coincidence existed between his own thinking and Schelling's was owing to their "equal obligations to the polar logic and dynamic philosophy of Giordano Bruno" and to "that same affectionate reverence for the labours of Behmen and other mystics which I had formed at a much earlier period" (pp. 95, 98, 103). Coleridge suggests, then, that he absorbed these works on mysticism and the occult before his first fascination with Hartley's associationist psychology in his second year at Cambridge and that these works had helped to form his intuitions about the powers of the mind.

Coleridge's early letters and notebooks reveal an early involvement with abstruse studies. Even in the "Lectures on Revealed Religion" (1795), in the full flush of his concentration on Hartley, he hints at some dissatisfaction with associationist mechanisms when he says that "in length of Time by the magic power of association we transfer our attachment from the Reward to the action rewarded and our fears and hatred from the Punishment to the Vice Punished."[4] By the use of this image he implies that however clearly Hartley seems to have described the widening circles of association accreting one to another by means of vibrations, the process is still so incomprehensible and wonderful that it seems to work by magic. Hartley's psychology is inadequate in helping him prove the supernatural life of the spirit, and so the mystics and magicians again become important to him in 1796 when they lead him like a pillar of fire through the deserts of skepticism and teach him to see the "acts and energies of creative Thought."

This time is crucial to the twenty-four-year-old Coleridge because he is trying to disprove atheism. The development of his refutations occurs in a sequence of vivacious letters to his brother George, to Thomas Poole, to Josiah Wade, and to John Thelwall between 1794 and late 1796.[5] These letters show him in various ways struggling to reconcile the skepticism of his head with the credulity of his heart and his coming more and more bravely to oppose Thelwall's denial of our supernatural life. To his brother George, Coleridge confesses having had "too much Vanity to be altogether a Christian— too much tenderness of Nature to be utterly an Infidel. My head took pleasure in the levities of Voltaire, my heart tremblingly alive to the feelings of Humanity," loved Jesus. During this period when he was preaching frequently to Unitarian congregations, his "faith was made up of the Evangelists and the Deistic Philosophy—a kind of *religious Twilight*" (letter 44, March 30, 1794). He begins to emerge from the twilight later in 1794 after he has met atheists such as Thomas Holcroft, Erasmus Darwin, and William Godwin. He experiences "the fierceness and dogmatism" of Holcroft, the flippant ignorance of Erasmus Darwin on religious subjects, and the immorality of Godwin; Coleridge ardently opposes atheism because he feels that it produces bad men and confirms them in their badness. "Believe me, Thelwall! It is not Atheism that has prejudiced me against Godwin; but Godwin who has perhaps prejudiced me against Atheism" (June 22, 1796). He writes angrily to Wade (January 27, 1796) of Erasmus Darwin: "All at once he makes up his mind on such important subjects as whether we be the outcasts of a blind idiot called Nature, or the children of an all-wise and infinitely good God; whether we spend a few miserable years on this earth, and then sink into a clod of the valley, or only endure the anxieties of mortal life in order to fit us for the enjoyment of immortal happiness?" Coleridge studies hard to escape from the blind idiot called Nature. He plans to read "Chemistry and Anatomy . . . all the works of Semler and Michaelis, the German theologians, and of Kant" (to Poole, May 5, 1795), and he does read "Bishop Taylor, Old Baxter, David Hartley and the Bishop of Cloyne [Berkeley]" (to Poole, November 1, 1796) in order to support his early intuition that "some homeborn Feeling is the center of the Ball, that rolling on thro' Life, collects and assimilates every congenial Affection" (to Southey, July, 1794), that there is, in other words, a spiritual center independent of nature's imprint and which has a tenacity of its own.

He is now emboldened to defy the skeptical Thelwall, announcing that "I am *deep* in all out of the way books, whether of the monkish times, or of the puritanical aera—I have read & digested most of the Historical Writers—; but I do not like History. Metaphysics, & Poetry, & 'Facts of Mind'—(i.e. Accounts of all the strange phantasms that ever possessed your philosophy-dreamers from Tauth [Thoth] the Egyptian to Taylor, the English Pagan) are my darling Studies." He asks Thelwall to order for him "Iamblichus, Proclus, Porphyrius, &c, Plotini Opera, a Ficino" and says that he is about to read Dupuis's *Origine de tous les cultes, or Religion universelle* (November 19, 1796). Though he called himself a necessitarian and claimed to disbelieve in guilt, innocent of the feelings that would soon overwhelm him (to Thelwall, May 13, 1796), his readings about "Facts of Mind" in these "darling studies" help him to prove his ardent hope that men are not clods of dirt affected by blind cause.

When Thelwall objects to the mysticism of his researches, Coleridge begins to speculate on the possible existence of the soul (December 17, 1796):

Next as to "mystical"—Now that the thinking part of Man, i.e. the Soul, existed previously to its appearance in its present body, may be very wild philosophy; but it is very intelligible poetry, inasmuch as Soul is an orthodox word in all our poets; they mean by "Soul" a being inhabiting our body & playing upon it, like a Musician inclosed in an Organ whose keys were placed inwards.—Now this opinion I do not hold—not that I am a Materialist; but because I am a Berkeleian—Yet as you who are not a Christian wished you were, that we might meet in Heaven, so I, who do not believe in this descending, & incarcerated Soul, yet said, if my Baby had died before I had seen him, I should have *struggled* to believe it.

He wants to believe in soul, for "[my] philosophical opinions are blended with or deduced from my feelings." He wants to believe, and the feeling makes him believe that there is something to believe in.

On the last day of 1796, as his "Ode to the Departing Year" is being published, Coleridge is able to tell Thelwall that he has found a solution, grounded in his intuition of self: "Well, true or false, Heaven is a less gloomy idea than Annihilation! Dr. Beddoes, & Dr. Darwin think that Life is utterly inexplicable, writing as Materialists—You, I understand, have adopted the idea that it is the result of organized matter acted on by external Stimuli. As likely as any other system; but you *assume* the thing to be proved. And I, tho' last not least, I do not know what to think about it—on the whole, I have rather made up my mind that I am a mere apparition—a naked spirit!—and that Life is I myself I which is a mighty clear account of it." Though through his complex tone he slightly apologizes to Thelwall, Coleridge nevertheless dares to speak to Thelwall about the miracle of the self that will inform many of his later remarks and lead eventually to the *Biographia*'s grounding in the infinite I AM.

His statement that "Life is I myself I" anticipates his famous statement to Thelwall: "My mind feels as if it ached to behold something *great*—something One & Indivisible" (October 14, 1797). It will be elaborated in the agonized formulations of the 1810 *Friend* when he writes ("The Meaning of Existence") that in saying with wonder "It is," "thou wilt have felt the presence of a mystery," and feel such awe that "the very words 'there is nothing! or—There was a time, when there was nothing!' are self-contradictory. There is that within us which repels the proposition with as full and instantaneous a light, as if it bore evidence against the fact in the right of its own eternity." [6] Through an imaginative intuition of the wonder of our own being, we refute the rational and sensual understand-

ing of a surrounding nothingness, and we come through
higher reason to know that "not to be, then, is impossible: to
be, incomprehensible." Such intuited wonder underlies the
arguments of the *Statesman's Manual* (1816) in which "men of
Reason" are shown to "feel the presence of a mystery" which
"fixes the spirit in awe and wonder," for "that which we find in
ourselves is (gradu mutato) the substance and the life of all our
knowledge."[7] Like Plotinus's miraculous air-sylph, which
feels a spiritual freedom far beyond the evidence of its caterpil-
lar's senses and grows wings on the evidence of this intuition
(*Biographia*, 1.167), Coleridge's spirit gives him a feeling that
it belongs to a great, expanded, supersensuous world, which
his senses do not begin to perceive. In the 1801 letters to
Wedgwood, he begins to give ratiocinative form to his feelings, which by 1797 were only feelings.

The notebooks of this crucial period show him similarly
involved in quoting as many sources as possible to help him
"introduce a dissection of Atheism—particularly the God-
winian System of Pride" (entry 174, 1795–96). He quotes
Plotinus on revelation, Michael Psellus on the Chaldean
oracles, Jeremy Taylor on glimpses of heaven and unusual
visitations (entry 186), and Ralph Cudworth repeatedly on the
incorporeality of soul; for Cudworth, as Kathleen Coburn
states, "evidently (along with Andrew Baxter) helped to release Coleridge from associationism and necessitarianism"
(note to entry 203). Coleridge discovers in these affirmations of
the inscutable life of the soul the refutation of materialism; for
as he notes later (entry 920, February–May 1801), "Materialists unwilling to admit the mysterious of our nature make it all
mysterious—nothing mysterious in nerves, eyes, &c: but that
nerves think &c! Stir up the sediment into the transparent
water, & so make all opaque." By 1801 the exploration of the
spirit's powers evident in the poetry is further elaborated in the
letters against Locke and the notes on Bruno (entry 928),
Proclus (appendix B, volume 1), and Hermes Trismegistus
(entry 879), but the poetic intuitions precede the rational

presentation of them. Indeed a childish wish may underlie them all: in *Table Talk* (June 10, 1832) Coleridge recalls his efforts as a small boy to cure a cramp by reciting a charm. He was already investigating the influence of "the potent voice" on actual experience: "then repeating this charm with the acts configurative thereupon prescribed, I can safely affirm, that I do not remember an instance, in which the cramp did not go away in a few seconds." [8]

Possibly Boehme and the Neoplatonists kept alive in Coleridge the belief in the mind's autonomous power, in its deeply rooted and unknowable life, in short, in its miraculousness, as demonstrated most remarkably in the free, self-conscious, originating being, as he felt himself to be at his best. When he finds that we begin with the I am I and end in God, he implies that the feeling of one's own imaginative power, one's own omnipotence of thought, precedes a recognition of the divine as an all-pervading I AM. The readings described in the letters and notebooks between 1796 and 1797 served as a middle ground in Coleridge's thoughts between materialism and idealism and as a middle ground in his own personal development. They kept him in touch with the possibility of soul, spirit, and freedom. Coleridge's renewed absorption in his "darling studies" after a period of skepticism coincides remarkably with the beginning of his poetic annus mirabilis; he compares himself with Augustine, who was spiritually rescued by reading "certain Platonic philosophers" (*Biographia*, p. 137).

Coleridge's theory of the mysteriousness of spirit and its modes of self-expression is elusively presented in the *Biographia*. The same sequence we have seen in the letters to Thelwall where he discovers the miracle of the self can be seen almost twenty years later in the *Biographia*, in which he labors to prove the spiritual freedom of the self before he can come to his definition of the imagination. When he discovers with the help of his studies that each self is a miracle, he sees that the miraculous I AM creates in a mysterious way which could be called magical. In the *Biographia* he works to define spirit so that it will be disconnected from things by definition, in that a spirit is a subject that contemplates itself as its own object. Once he has shown men to be spirits, he can go on to imply that their freest operations owe no allegiance to time and space and that they work as if by magic.

His theory of the miraculous self is elaborated from chapter 9 to chapter 14. Boehme and Bruno kept alive his sense of the mystery and complexity of the self and led him to believe that "human nature itself fought up against the willful resignation of intellect." He relies on an original intuitive feeling that "all the organs of spirit are framed for a correspondent world of spirit" (p. 167), and he comes to recognize, with help from Schelling, "that on the IMMEDIATE which dwells in every man, and on the original intuition, or absolute affirmation of it, (which is likewise in every man, but does not in every man rise into consciousness), all the *certainty* of our knowledge depends" (p. 168). Beginning with this radical knowledge of a divine I AM within each man, Coleridge works to evade the problems of which came first, the perceiver or the thing perceived, and boldly starts with the I AM, which in the act of knowledge unites the subjective and the objective. In this self all opposites converge. In the affirmation of "the absolute self, great eternal I AM, then the principle of being, and of knowledge, of idea and of reality; the ground of existence, and the ground of the knowledge of existence, are absolutely identical" (p. 183). Such a oneness within the self-experiencing I AM implies the similar workings of an eternal I AM. The human spirit, echoing the God who said I AM that I AM, can take as his credo also "*Sum quia sum;* I am, because I affirm myself to be; I affirm myself to be, because I am." Thus including within itself its subject and its object, the spirit suffices to itself, like a snake with its tail in its mouth.

Coleridge's discovery here, rooted in his exclamation to Thelwall in 1796 that "Life is I myself I," and allied to his later aphorisms in *Aids to Reflection*, is further elaborated in chapter

12, theses 7 and 8, again with help from Schelling. These theses proclaim that "if then I know myself only through myself, it is contradictory to require any other predicate of self, but that of self-consciousness. . . . Herein consists the essence of a spirit, that it is self-representative." Through dense reasonings Coleridge arrives at the conclusion that "the self-conscious spirit therefore is a will; and freedom must be assumed as a *ground* of philosophy, and can never be deduced from it" (pp. 184–85). Like the air-sylph Coleridge establishes the soul's freedom as the originating fact that needs no arguing. Such freedom from the bounds of matter, time, and mortality will lead him to see the spirit's creative acts as akin to the magician's.

Throughout the central chapters of the *Biographia* Coleridge lays the groundwork for his theory of the imagination by establishing this radical freedom of the self. In the same way that his avowal of self as the basis of his belief in spirit led to his poems' being released, so here the establishment of the freedom of the self as a concept permits him to move to the definitions of the imagination. From this recognition of the mysterious power of the self, Coleridge moves to the triumphant analogy which soon becomes the basis for his definitions: "We begin with the I KNOW MYSELF, in order to end with the absolute I AM. We proceed from the SELF, in order to lose and find all self in GOD" (p. 186). This I AM, first felt to be the immediate root of all one's consciousness, becomes the root of all things and beings and stands as the proof, when intuitions are elaborated by reason, that a divine I AM, parallel to our own, exists. By virtue of this analogy, which traditionally sees the human word animating nature as the divine word had animated the dark waters, Coleridge can turn to the primary imagination, the I AM, intertwined with the secondary, each being the condition of the other.

Though a full definition is postponed once again by an imaginary letter to himself and a promise of future essays on the supernatural in poetry, at the end of chapter 13 Coleridge proclaims: "The imagination then I consider either as primary, or secondary. The primary IMAGINATION I hold to be the living Power and prime Agent of all human Perception, and as a repetition in the finite mind of the eternal act of creation in the infinite I AM. The secondary IMAGINATION I consider as an echo of the former, co-existing with the conscious will, yet still as identical with the primary in the *kind* of its agency, and differing only in *degree* and in the *mode* of its operation. It dissolves, diffuses, dissipates, in order to re-create; or where this process is rendered impossible, yet still at all events, it struggles to idealize and to unify. It is essentially *vital*, even as all objects (*as* objects) are essentially fixed and dead" (p. 202). The primary imagination here is not God but our inherent ability to perceive ourselves as selves, as wholly wonderful, continually renewing ourselves in a manner comparable to God's self-contemplation. The secondary imagination works as a result of the continual working of the primary imagination, again perceiving wholeness, but now acting in its vitalizing perception of persons, situations, or fates beyond ourselves, giving them life, as our wonder at ourselves likewise affirms our own being. By the primary imagination we continually re-create ourselves as grounded in the divine self which is an analogy of us; by the secondary we re-create other beings which similarly become miraculous.

At the end of the following chapter Coleridge returns to the subject, saying that the poet "diffuses a tone and spirit of unity, that blends and (as it were) *fuses*, each into each, by that synthetic and magical power, to which we have exclusively appropriated the name of imagination." He does not explain why he chooses the terms *synthetic* and *magical*, but he seems to see them as self-evident. He goes on to explain that this synthetic and magical power is "first put in action by the will and understanding, and retained under their irremissive, though gentle and unnoticed, controul" and that this power "reveals itself in the balance or reconciliation of opposite or discordant qualities; of sameness with difference; of the general

with the concrete" (2:12). Adapting Sir John Davies's description of the inscrutable metamorphoses worked by the soul,
Coleridge suggests that the imagination likewise "turns /
Bodies to spirit by sublimation strange / As fire converts to
fire the things it burns, / As we our food into our nature
change." In the imagery of alchemical refinement the imagination derives forms from gross matter, "and draws a kind of
quintessence from things; / Which to her proper nature she
transforms / To bear them light on her celestial wings." At
first one wonders what these two definitions and the stanzas of
Renaissance verse have to do with each other and what both of
them have to do with the promised but unrealized essays on the
supernatural in poetry. What do the words *synthetic*, *magical*,
and *vital* have to do with "the eternal act of creation in the
infinite I AM" and with its finite echo, the I AM existing in the
conscious will?

The answer seems to be that if the very sense that the self
exists is a miracle, it is no wonder that its creativity should be
thought of as miraculous, too. When the self works actively on
the inert world beyond it by analogy with God's forming of
chaos through words, the process might aptly be called magical in that the human echo of the divine I AM, the secondary I
AM, momentarily usurps the divine powers, dissolving previously existing forms and conjuring up new ones. Though
Coleridge's definitions are not entirely satisfying, what they do
is to indicate the mysterious depths of the mind's operations
and to suggest that these depths are so impenetrable that many
sorts of approaches to "facts of mind" might be used to plumb
them. The miraculousness of the mind's various operations in
itself disproves any mechanistic theories of the mind's passive
receptivity to external stimuli. That each person senses himself
to be a miracle, a wonder, with occasional potentiality for
magical acts in moments of joy or ecstasy, provides evidence
for the reality of a spirit yearning for a hidden spiritual world to
which mere visibility cannot testify. This evidence for a spirit
in turn gives evidence of God. The magical operations of the

imagination are not intended as heresy but are viewed as additional evidence of man's supernatural allegiance.

In scattered moments throughout his later lectures on literature and philosophy Coleridge amplifies these arguments by giving further instances of them. He avers that human beings are not natural beings or beasts subject to material sequences of cause and effect; that "man must not be, man cannot be, on a level with the beast. . . . Angel he may be, fiend he may make himself, but beast—that is a privilege which a bad man cannot hope for, it is a punishment which a good man can never suspect."[9] In his *Aids to Reflection* he develops his theme along the lines of *Biographia* 12 by saying that "whatever is representable in the forms of time and space, is Nature. But whatever is comprehended in time and space, is included in the mechanism of cause and effect. And conversely, whatever, by whatever means, has its principle in itself, so far as to originate its actions, can not be contemplated in any of the forms of space and time; it must, therefore, be considered as spirit or spiritual."[10] In emphasizing the disjunction between Nature, "that which is always *becoming*," and Spirit, he finds that "whatever originates its own acts, or in any sense contains in itself the cause of its own state, must be spiritual and consequently supernatural; yet not on that account necessarily miraculous. And such must be the responsible Will."[11] Coleridge indicates that our ability to make new beginnings, to originate acts, proves our supernatural existence. This faith gives Coleridge a personal validation. In "Death and the Grounds of Belief in a Future State," he confesses: "I feel myself not the slave of nature. Not only do my powers extend vastly beyond all those which I could have derived from the instruments and organs, with which nature has furnished me; but I can do what nature per se cannot. Ergo, there is in me, or rather, I am, a praeternatural, that is, a supersensuous thing, but what is not nature, why should it perish with nature? Why lose the faculty of vision, because my spectacles are broken?"[12]

"These views of the Spirit, and of the Will as spiritual, form the groundwork of my scheme," he declares.[13]

Because he can conceive of the vast, it must be there, and he must belong to it. "Every human feeling," he writes in "On Poesy or Art," "is greater and larger than the exciting cause,—a proof, I think, that man is designed for a higher state of existence; and this is deeply implied in music, in which there is always something more and beyond the immediate expression."[14] In his "On the Principles of Genial Criticism, Essay Third," he again argues for free will on the basis of man's desire for it: "We are conscious of faculties far superior to the highest impressions of sense; we have life and free-will."[15]

Coleridge's well-known interest in original sin is also part of his wider interest in proving men free from natural laws. Original sin, an act marking the separation of consciousness from unconscious nature, is a central example of man's power to make true beginnings. Original sin is unmotivated, arising suddenly from no previous cause, and as such it is a mysterious act. Its existence proves that the spirit causing this act is out of nature (at the same time, paradoxically, catapulting that spirit back into nature or death), and therefore the spirit is a supernatural power. Reasoning from the possibility of acting originally that is illustrated in original sin, Coleridge extends unaccountable acts from sin to art. That is, as we can *act* originally, so too can we *create* originally, whether or not nature provides a model. The genius of art, he writes, is "the power of acting creatively under laws of its own origination."[16] Art and evil thus arise from the same freedom of will and separateness from the chains of nature. When, in "The Rime of the Ancient Mariner," "the Mariner hath his will," he is supernaturally empowered to determine change in the passive natural world around him. Original sin is not, then, a sign of bondage but is paradoxically a sign of freedom.

Coleridge's interest in supernatural origination may explain his frequent references to supernatural powers in literature.

When he examines Shakespeare, for instance, he closely attends to ghosts, fairies, witches, and other supernatural phenomena. He lavishes attention on the ghost in *Hamlet*, observing "Shakespeare's tenderness with regard to all innocent superstition: no Tom Paine declamations and pompous philosophy." In *Hamlet* and *Macbeth* supernatural wonders give shape to extreme psychological states: In *Hamlet* the ghost is a "superstition connected with the most [sacred?] truths of revealed religion"; in *Macbeth* the "invocation" of the weird sisters "is made at once to the imagination, and the emotions connected therewith." [17] Coleridge devotes a disproportionate amount of his Shakespeare criticism to justifying those supernatural beings in *Macbeth*, *The Tempest*, and *Hamlet* that the eighteenth century most abhorred. Even when addressing Mrs. Siddons in an early sonnet, he singles out her role in *Macbeth*, elaborating the "fearful dark decrees / Mutter'd to wretch by necromantic spell" and dwelling ghoulishly on "those hags, who at the witching time / Of murky Midnight ride the air sublime, / And mingle foul embrace with fiends of Hell." *The Tempest* gives him an opportunity to call Shakespeare a magician by analogy with Prospero. Echoing Maurice Morgann, he writes: Prospero is "the very Shakespeare, himself, as it were, of *The Tempest*," *The Tempest* as a whole serving as a perfect example of "the imagination . . . which owns no allegiance to time and place." [18]

In dwelling on the supernatural, particularly as it illustrates the imagination's freedom from time and place, Coleridge is clearly different from Hazlitt and other critics in the English empirical tradition, who have little patience with Shakespeare's childish superstitions; and he shows his similarity, if not also his indebtedness, to Schlegel. Schlegel exalts Shakespeare as the "portrayer and philosopher of superstition . . . who distinctly exhibits its origin in apparently irrational and yet natural opinions." He explains that Shakespeare "calls up from their hidden abysses that dread of the unknown, that presage of the dark side of nature, and a world of spirits, which philosophy now imagines it has altogether exploded." Schlegel goes on to say that "in general we find in *A Midsummer Night's Dream*, in *The Tempest*, in the magical parts of *Macbeth*, and wherever Shakespeare avails himself of the popular belief in the invisible presence of spirits, and the possibility of coming into contact with them, a profound view of the inward life of nature and her mysterious springs, which it is true, can never be altogether unknown to the genuine poet."[19]

Coleridge does not appreciate Shakespeare's profound use of supernatural occurrences because they reveal "the inward life of nature and her mysterious springs," as Schlegel did. On the contrary he appreciates them for just the opposite reason. Rather than showing the life of nature, they show the imagination's freedom from nature. Coleridge explores the supernatural aspects of Shakespeare's plays because they show in a pure form the workings of the "imagination . . . which owns no allegiance to time and space," and thus they contribute to his general interest in finding, in original art as in original sin, proof of man's supernatural power.[20]

Coleridge's lectures of 1818 provide further evidence that literature dealing with supernatural occurrences was a guarantee of man's imaginative freedom. On March 3 he discourses "on the Arabian Nights Entertainments, and on the romantic use of the supernatural in poetry, and in works of fiction not poetical. On the conditions and regulations on which such books may be employed advantageously in the earlier periods of education." On March 6 he returns to the subject, lecturing on "tales of witches, apparitions, etc., as distinguished from the magic and magicians of Asiatic origin. The probable sources of the former."[21] Lecturing on Spenser's *Faerie Queene*, he declares that the "land of Faery" is "the realm of mental space." "Imagination," he writes, "is involved with the perception of supernatural life."

Coleridge does not limit his study of the supernatural in literature to works in which supernatural beings actually appear. In his wide aim to assert the priority of supernatural will over nature's inanition, he continues his study of the meaning of language. By the possession of language the supernatural will is most clearly demonstrated. In notebook entry 3810 he speculates: "Words—incompatible with materiality—must they not by their spirituality, as power, have some analogy or ratio to all other spiritual Being?" In his essay on poesy or art he says that speech has always distinguished men from nature, which is mute or dumb. This truism becomes for Coleridge a central proof of his theory. In his opposition to materialism he glorifies the miraculous and inexplicable demonstration of our immaterial nature. "Words, the instruments of communication, are the only signs that a finite being can have of its own thoughts." These "words are things. They are the great and mighty instruments by which thoughts are excited and by which alone they can be [expressed] in rememberable form." Language comes from inside and proves the independence of the mind from the world of matter. The possession of language shows us to be outside of nature, supernatural, and therefore free, whereas nature is a continuous binding chain of cause and effect. "But man," writes Coleridge, "comes from within, and all that is truly human must proceed from within" (*Philosophical Lectures*, pp. 173, 201, 226).

Here, in the importance of language's constituting proof of supernatural will, poetry becomes preeminent in Coleridge's theory. The language of poetry is at its best when it shows the intellect at work; when it merely registers conversations or sensation outside, it is weak. Words are signs of our freedom when they rise from the mere description of observed things. For making this possible, Coleridge praises the medieval schoolmen, the nominalists and realists particularly, who created a language capable of dealing with ideas. Scholastic philosophy "introduced into all the languages of Europe, as far as the languages were susceptible of it, the power and force of Greek and Roman connexion. It forever precluded our falling . . . into the mere aphoristic style of the Oriental nations, in which thought is heaped upon thought by simple aggregation of words" (*Philosophical Lectures*, pp. 290–91). The making of connections expressive of the mind appears most powerfully in poetry. For "poetry also is purely human; for all its materials are from the mind, and all its products are for the mind." He asserts the mind's power over a nature that exists but neither lives nor has form until translated by the signs and symbols "being used to represent *human* thoughts and feelings." Art in general, especially the verbal art of poetry, is "the power of humanizing nature, of infusing thoughts and passions of man into every thing which is the object of his contemplation." [22]

Our ability to speak raises us above beasts, all the more so when this speech is imagined by the poet (whose language is less tied to things than is the language of rational discourse), more yet when the poet voluntarily makes his speech metrical in the excitement of original composition. Meter is a voluntary creation, a sign of will. It is not imitated from nature but is voluntarily forged by the poet responding to his feelings and circumstances, which form part of the meaning of the words. Even the syntax of poetry should be unnatural. Believing that poetry should come from within rather than represent outward voices, Coleridge disapproves of some of Wordsworth's imitations of rustic speech and asks: "Is [poetic language] obtained by wandering about in search of angry or jealous people in uncultivated society, in order to copy their words? Or not far rather by the power of imagination proceeding upon the *all in each* of human nature?" [23] Poetic language is not found; it is imagined.

"The powerful effects which poetry has long been known to produce" derive from this originating assertion of supernatural life. As early as the *Watchman* 3 of March 17, 1796, Coleridge connects these powers with magical operations. Recounting the story of Sigge in a sketch on the manners and religion of the ancient Germans, he writes: "Sigge, the son of Fridulf, commanded the Ases, a Scythian people situated between the Euxine and Caspian seas, when Pompey conducted the Mithridatic war. As the priest of Odin he assumed the name of

Deity. This extraordinary man was the inventor of Runic
characters; and by his persuasive eloquence, his skill in extem-
pore poetry, and his impostures made himself respected as a
deity. The Runic chapter, or the Magic of Odin, is still
preserved as his composition; he enumerates in it the wonders
he could perform with his songs, mingling the operations of
magic with those powerful effects which poetry has long been
known to produce." [24] Coleridge, like Gray and Collins, is
inspired by the legends of Odin, finding in the magical runes a
tradition of magical language similar to the one that he found
in eclectic Platonism. Indeed the gothic mind as a whole,
Coleridge believes, was inclined to invent theories of magical
language because the climate turned men inward to contemplate their own solitary power. The gothic mind, Coleridge observes, "grew in rude forests amid the inclemencies of
outward nature where man saw nothing around him but what
must owe its charms mainly to the imaginary powers with
which it was surveyed" (*Philosophical Lectures*, p. 291).

Coleridge's eagerness to prove man's supernatural life on the
basis of his ability to originate new things through language
helps to explain the mysterious gaps in chapters 13 and 14 of
the *Biographia*. Both his use of the term *primary imagination*
and his proposed essay on the uses of the supernatural in poetry
are aspects of the one proposition that men are supernatural
beings, inasmuch as they are originative. The imagination,
like the will, cannot be subject to nature, for it is an illustration of man's vital innerness in its power to make original
beginnings. This theory of supernatural power modified the
usual suppositions about Coleridge's organic theory: while the
imagination produces organic forms, it does not itself grow
gradually like a plant; instead it works suddenly and freely by a
magical power to call things into being. Organic theory does
not apply to the process of creation but to the interrelatedness
of parts in the thing created; that process itself is antiorganic,
because magical and supernatural.

What Coleridge meant in thinking that the imagination

was magical can be seen more precisely in his late *Philosophical Lectures*. If we read these lectures looking backward through them to his unexplained earlier theories, we can see how they cast light retroactively on the processes which Coleridge had elusively called magical in the poems and in the *Biographia*.

In her introduction to the *Philosophical Lectures* Kathleen Coburn turns to the baffling question of why Coleridge, by 1818 a devout Protestant disdainful even of Catholic idols, should give so much attention to heretics. Coburn explains that Coleridge was anxious to apply their intuitions to science by showing how they anticipated electricity and animal magnetism, thereby leaving religion safe from their touch. This explanation of how Coleridge works to dissociate magic from religion by allying it to science applies similarly to his effort to ally magic to the creative imagination. If he can show that magic, perennially interesting to some of the most profound thinkers in the history of philosophy , can indeed contribute to the history of science and to the psychology of art, even though it has no validity for religion, then the philosophic study of magic will not have been foolish. Coleridge seems to have felt that magic had a truth, though not necessarily the kind it aspired to. Coleridge was searching for a dividing line between religion and these other, often quasi-religious areas where mysteries intermingle; he was happy to find that magic could be made applicable to the workings of the imagination but not to religion where a clear differentiation of powers must be made.

From the lectures we learn that magical philosophies are for the most part imaginative: their makers imagine the universe as functioning in accordance with the way the mind itself works, believing that words answer their own wishes and thereby dissolve time. Discussing the imaginative projections of Pythagoras, Plotinus, Boehme, Agrippa, and Bruno, Coleridge sometimes praises these figures for glorifying the acts of the mind, and sometimes he criticizes them for trying to replace God with imaginary and self-reflexive shadows. The

Philosophical Lectures clarify Coleridge's theories of imagination (and thus indirectly his own practice of poetry) even though in these lectures he was no longer speaking about poetry as such.

In lecturing on Boehme, Agrippa, Bruno, Pythagoras, and on the eclectic philosophers (as he calls Plotinus and his followers such as Porphyry, Iamblichus, Proclus, and Psellus), Coleridge describes their vision of a nature full of magical connections and their glorification of mind. So often does he recur to the animate universe envisioned by the eclectics and others that we should examine his comments before considering their theories of mind.

In the view of these remarkable figures whose opposition to Aristotelian materialism (*Philosophical Lectures*, p. 190) Coleridge shares, nature is alive with spirits. Coleridge divides the early pagan thinkers into practical moralists and imaginative perceivers of a living universe. These last, the inventors of mystery cults, "followed the natural leadings of the imagination or fancy governed by the laws of association." From their own vitality they intuited a life in the universe at large. "They were themselves alive and that they knew, though they did not understand the mode. They moved in consequence of that life and acted. Wherever therefore they saw motion, they supposed that in some way or other there was a vital or motive power; and denying all else but the very law of mind, by which we must necessarily generalize (that is when we look at an immense number of things be impressed by that which is common to them rather than by that which is particular to any one), they conceived that the whole world, everything, must have a motive power. When they contemplated this motive power with regard to particular individuals they called it soul, if with a reference to many souls, they would call it a God. But when they raised their sensuous imagination to the utmost and conceived the indefinite ideal of an All, they carried on the same analogy, and the All was God" (*Philosophical Lectures*, p. 92). In this passage on the widening circles of analogies, Coleridge describes the perception of a vital universe as a clear movement outward from the self, as the imagination comes in contact with the world, projecting on visible nature qualities known to be its own, similar to that "magic power of association" which he describes in the "Lecture on Revealed Religion." This animation is the work of the imagination actively perceiving analogies and likenesses. Such a perception of analogy is, he says in his lecture on dramatic illusion, the "condition of all consciousness"; indeed "the infinite gradations between (likeness and difference) form all the play and all the interest of our intellectual and moral being," gradations that lead us finally to a vision of God.

In the intuitions of the eclectic philosophers the powers in the universe were vastly multiplied, indicating a wonderful wealth of imagination. In the multiplying of the powers and intelligences in the universe, philosophers such as Proclus "connected philosophy with magic, with the power of names and numbers, and the whole secret trade which we know little of, but which they professed under the name of theurgy, was ADDED. What it was it is perhaps of little importance to us to know. I am inclined to think that mere fancy, mere delusion, it was not, but whatever it was, that it was worthless and in its nature of no true value or capable of originating any serviceable laws of mankind seems evident from its impermanence" (*Philosophical Lectures*, p. 250).

This image of a spiritual universe, however misguided, is in Coleridge's opinion an understandable reaction to Aristoteleanism in all its forms. The materialism anticipated by Aristotle and revived by medieval schoolmen and eighteenth-century Lockeans calls forth its opposite. When the existence of the soul apart from the body has been denied, mystics and visionaries naturally rise to affirm it.

They abandoned all ideas, and their principle was that there was an universal life, that this life was distinguished by sympathies and antipathies, that this existed through all nature and that the proper mode of invoking nature was by attaining nature by means of simple substances. Out of this arose the fancy of the transmutation of metals. . . . The same view therefore gave them hope of discovering an universal remedy, a power of keeping life in the highest conceivable state of energy, and on the same principle, carrying on the notion that life is everywhere, and animating the universe, they presented all parts of the world as having symbolical meanings, that there was no shape in nature but had its correspondent in the heaven or under the earth, that it was merely a likeness to something else and therefore capable of acting on some superior being, and in this manner they introduced, indeed, all that was most absurd in fancy or imagination. (*Philosophical Lectures*, p. 282)

The aim of these visionaries was essentially the same as that of poets in general, or of Coleridge himself in his poetic period, whose own philosophy was intended as a refutation of materialism and an affirmation of spirit. The series of correspondences, analogies, and symbols, radiating outward from the imagination for the purpose of keeping life in the highest state conceivable of energy and of animating the universe, may be folly for religion, but is at the root of a poet's genius, for the poet displays his genius in his grasp of metaphor.

Coleridge expatiates on these visions of analogous universes. He shows how the tradition passes to Psellus, and from Psellus to Paracelsus, showing resemblances all the while to the fairy mythology of Persia, Scotland, and northern Germany (*Philosophical Lectures*, pp. 320–21). Time and again he returns to present this world animated by symbols projected from the imagination, returning in reality to theories which dominated his own thoughts twenty years before. Indeed, so warmly does he feel toward these early masters that he cannot resist turning Plotinus, Porphyry, and Iamblichus into potential Christians (*Philosophical Lectures*, p. 295). Because of his own effort to deliver the mind from the shackles of nature, he is impressed by the Cabala, "this most sublime of philosophies . . . [which] possessed certain combinations of sounds, figures, and numbers, by which external nature was to be controlled and governed" (*Philosophical Lectures*, pp. 292–300), and he is impressed by the aims of the eclectics, "especially as the

Eclectic philosophy was connected with the boldest purposes for the extension of the human powers." The powers that Coleridge sees being extended in their thought are the love of knowledge and the love of power.

Now the Platonic philosophy in its degenerate form after Plotinus combined both: here was [no limitation] allowed of, no boundary to the human intellect. It allowed, indeed most fully, that many were the truths which could not be arrived at either by the sense or by the understanding, or even by the reason as far as it was human. But what then? There were mysteries; powers higher than those means, by which they could be united positively with the Deity, and live in him, and in that state partake at once of his omniscience and omnipresence. And these, too, were to be learned; the discipline indeed was severe, the time required in the penances and the watchfulness were perfectly like those of . . . the Brahmins. (*Philosophical Lectures*, p. 295)

Through such disciplines the mind frees itself from the senses and communicates with supernatural beings.

Their eagerness to know the mysteries led to the cultivation of ecstatic experiences toward which Coleridge himself had leaned in his younger days, under the influence not only of eclectics but also of Plato's *Ion* and of bacchic hymns. Coleridge cannot help admiring Plotinus's intimacy with spirits and enjoyment of mystical identification with the divine principle. He becomes even more sympathetic to this experience when he summarizes it in lecture 11 on Bruno, whom he praises as a genius, as the reviver of the Pythagorean system of the universe, and as an early enemy of mechanistic theories of mind. Here he echoes his own theories of symbols and forms as he summarizes Bruno:

Such were the doctrines taught by [Giordano Bruno] but blended with a multitude of the wildest chemical fancies, which, however, as mysticism was not connected with [alchemy], was obliged to apply itself to external objects of nature. . . . It was in a belief that every being, however apparently inanimate, had a life if it could be called forth, and that all along that was called but the law of likeness. In short, the groundwork of their philosophy was the law of likeness, arising from what is called the polar principle (that is that in order to manifest itself every power must appear in two opposites but these two opposites having a ground of identity were constantly striving to reunite, but not being permitted to pass back to their original state, which would amount to annihilation, they pressed forward and the two formed a third something) and in this manner they traced in their [trichotomous] philosophy all the facts in nature and often-times with most wonderful and happy effects. (*Philosophical Lectures*, p. 323)

After this hint as to the source of his own *tertium aliquid*, Coleridge goes on to explain Bruno's animation of the law of likeness:

There is throughout all nature an aptitude implanted that all things may be related to each and to all, for everything that exists in some time strives to be always, everything that perceives anywhere strives to perceive everywhere, and to become that universally whatever it has as an individual; in short each part of nature contains in itself a germ of the omnipresence, inasmuch as it still strives to be the whole, and what it cannot possess at any one moment it attempts to possess by a perpetual succession of development. (*Philosophical Lectures*, p. 326)

Each part longs to abolish time and space and yet to encompass them, to operate on the intricate analogies that course through related things and thus to arrive at a condition of vibratingly alive sympathies. The vision of a universe alive with symbols, each yearning to absorb the whole and to abolish successiveness and fragmentation, was the work of the imagination, which owes no allegiance to time and space. This vision occurs repeatedly from Pythagoras (whose interest in magic rein-forced his belief that the mind itself is an act) onward, reaching a high point of clarity in the thought of Giordano Bruno. In all its revivals—in Alexandria, in Florence, and in gothic Ger-many—it fosters a belief in energy, power, vitality, and life, in opposition to the deadness of inert things. Like the poet the magician wants to keep in motion "the highest conceivable state of energy" and to increase the area of influence of the mind's powers radiating outward.

The dangers of so magnifying the human spirit are the temptation to godhead and the solitude of self-reflexiveness. These are related, for each is a form of megalomania, of "omnipotence of thought." When Plotinus ecstatically enters the godhead he is overstepping his bounds as a human creature; conversely he and his followers try to bring God down to the level of men by various impostures. But it is the self-reflexiveness that seems to concern Coleridge more. Often he refers to the way in which the mind's thoughts call themselves into being. He abhors "the fanatic who abandons himself to the wild workings of the magic cauldron of his own brain, mistaking every form of delirium for reality." He smiles when remembering how his dear Don Quixote "begins with a grave story which he cannot bring himself to deny but goes to a magician to know whether it is true or not," comparing his belief in his own dreams to the work of the imagination. "That which began in imagination . . . has ended in the gratification of it." He detects in Agrippa a "peculiar species of madness, as if the intense desire of power, seizing hold of the mind and becoming a habit in it, had given such an unnatural vividness to certain notions as to impress a belief that they had occurred as events" (*Philosophical Lectures*, pp. 186, 283, 301).

Yet he praises recent artists, including Sir Joshua Reynolds, who "had drunk deeply of Platonism," for realizing that "what is sound must come out of themselves." While he disapproves of "faith watching the effects, imagining the possession of these things to be somewhat in the nature of ceremonies or magical invocations of them, noticing the results," he approves of other forms of imaginative self-summoning. Of prayer he writes in a manner reminiscent of his favorite seventeenth-century poet, George Herbert: "Ask, and in the very energy of asking . . . the energy of the soul to act is by the divine grace made to be the very means of strength, made to be the very wing by which you are to fly and from which alone you can" (*Philosophical Lectures*, pp. 197, 283, 225). Imagination calls the imagined condition into being.

Coleridge opposes the short cuts offered by magic and mysticism. He criticizes the quest for instantaneous experience demanding no moral self-development. But the suddenness and instantaneity which makes such identity inappropriate for religion makes it appropriate for the production of art. Reading Coleridge's praise of the "magic sleeps" in the temples of Aesculapius and Serapis, we are reminded of his own sleep that produced "Kubla Khan," of his ventures into the subconscious, and of his efforts to distinguish sleeping dreams from the submission to literary illusion, where the "suspension of will" is voluntary.[25] Reading his criticism of the eclectic philosophers for populating the universe with living spirits, we are reminded of the spirits in "The Rime of the Ancient Mariner" which Coleridge adapted from Jamblichus and Psellus; reading his ironical praise of alchemy for "transmuting all the dreams of polytheism into reality," we are reminded of the Dejection Ode where he dreams the wind's songs and thereby realizes them.

As much as Coleridge criticizes the many beliefs in magic among his singular choice of philosophers, he admires them also because they enriched his theory of imagination. While he believes in 1818 that "philosophy is mockery unless it is considered the transit from paganism to religion," much as Virgil led Dante only to the gates of paradise, he had been willing in early years to use any theories (no matter how magical, heretical, or pagan) that would help him against Locke's theories of mind. As apologetic as he is here, he insists that these philosophies inherited from the Phoenicians and Egyptians have some glimmers of truth, though these truths have been obscured by the skepticism of "the literati of the last century and a half [who] considered all the ancient oracles to be delusions." He wants to acknowledge "that truths are to be found in those writers, and in my mind, awful truths . . . but

I contend this is not the mode of beginning a truth nor the means of arriving at the very state it pretends to" (*Philosophical Lectures*, pp. 224, 236, 244). He accepts the possibility that analogies and sympathies do run throughout nature, saying that "Natural Magic is the force above human reason which is the active principle in Nature," but these sympathies have been exploited by human greed: "There must be a common law, upon which all can become each and each all; but then the idea was turned to the coining of gold and silver."

The "awful truths" hidden in the magical likenesses of eclectic philosophy seem to reveal the way the mind works when it imagines anything, whether literary or scientific. Coleridge recognizes three qualities of the magical mode of thinking which are particularly appropriate for describing the workings of the imagination, even as they violate Christian principles. These are its instantaneity, its confounding of religion and philosophy, and its materializing of spirit in matter.

Plotinus taught that "men were to arrive at a communion—that is to say at an intellectual, a positive, possession of this Supreme Being which would supersede all knowledge by giving them a higher one. So that what by the efforts of reason we were to acquire painfully, arriving at truth by possession and by all the power (and force) of reasoning, this was to appear in a blessed vision at once—that is the great object." Plotinus assumes "a supernatural something at the beginning, not as in the Christian religion, as a final reward of long exertion." In teaching that there was no boundary to the human intellect, Plotinus and the later eclectics tried to "persuade men that heaven was already practicable on earth." These philosophers tried "not to raise men up to God, but by pernicious practices and contrivances of rites to bring God down to man" (*Philosophical Lectures*, pp. 241–43 passim). In their imaginative invention of a universe reflecting their own symbol-making powers, these philosophers called into being what they asked for *at once.* In inventing a world in line with their imagining of it, the philosophers worked an imaginative magic on what they saw.

When Coleridge defines a man of genius as one who "finds a reflex to himself, were it only in the mystery of being," he implies that there is a similarity between the way these believers in magic imagined a world and the way that poets do the same thing, both experiencing the blessed vision at once, abolishing time and space by seeing everywhere a reflex of themselves. Such instantaneity succeeds in keeping life in the highest conceivable state of energy by cutting out the tedious links of development and arriving suddenly at the vision, regardless of the facts and objects outside. Such an assertion of mind over matter may verge on madness, as it did for Agrippa when "the intense desire for power, seizing hold of the mind and becoming a habit in it, had given such an unnatural vividness to certain notions as to impress a belief that they had occurred as events" (*Philosophical Lectures*, pp. 179, 301). But in poetry it is the way to transcend circumstance, inventing in language the vision imagined.

Coleridge objects to this process in religion, since any substitution of human for divine power leads to imposture; but in dealing with literature he is not so strict, believing as he does that the literary imagination "dissolves, diffuses, dissipates, in order to re-create." Poetic faith is a very different kind of faith from religious faith; our "inward nature" tries to "procure for these shadows of imagination that willing suspension of disbelief for the moment, which constitutes poetic faith."[26]

The achievement of the poem suddenly, out of time, magically called into being and demanding a suspension of disbelief for the moment, results from the synthetic and magical power of the imagination. We should not expect the same magical results in the moral perfection of our souls. When the eclectics tried to persuade men that heaven was practicable on earth, they discouraged men from perfecting their souls for a future life. Teaching that the supreme being could be expected to appear at once, they presented the possibility of magical instantaneous knowledge. But this is not, Coleridge believes, "the mode of beginning a truth nor the means of arriving at the very state it pretends to." Plotinus deludes men into thinking that they have power to see beyond the appearances of fact. And yet realization in the mind is what the imagination does, turning inward upon itself: "With me," Coleridge declares, "the act of contemplation makes the thing contemplated." [27]

The imagination feeds on itself, inventing what it then believes in, as Coleridge explains in a passage already partially cited: "Poetry also is purely human; for all its materials are from the mind, and all its products are for the mind. But it is the apotheosis of the former state, in which by excitement of the associative power passion itself imitates order, and the order resulting produces a pleasureable passion, and thus it elevates the mind by making its feelings the object of its reflexion." [28] This self-fulfilling circular process is typical of the imagination, whose materials are by, from, for, and of the mind. Even though from a Christian viewpoint this self-reflexiveness isolates the soul from God, in Coleridge's early exploration of poetry and imagination this self-reflexiveness seemed accurately to describe the way the mind asserts its freedom from nature.

When Coleridge claims even for scientific (and hence presumably inductive) discovery the preexistence of an idea which then fulfills itself, he gives the example of alchemy: "Magicians and alchemists indulged themselves with these imaginings [so] that certain indulgences became so vivid from hope that they declared they were so, and afterwards many of them, I believe, really believed it. But yet where the whole human faculties were called forth, and with amazing industry, something must come of it; and to the Alchemists we are indebted for chemistry, as it now exists, so that which began in imagination (proceeding and wedding with common sense, and finally with science) has ended in the gratification of it." Alchemy imagined the truths that chemistry later laboriously proved; for "in the imagination of men exist the seeds of all moral and scientific improvement" (*Philosophical Lectures*, p. 283). "In the childhood of those sciences imagination opened a way, and furnished materials on which the ratiocinative powers in a maturer state operated with success." Again, as if by magic, instantaneous vision arose in the sphere of the imagination, working by intuition, immediately beholding the truths of higher reason.

When Coleridge accuses the magicians of confounding religion and philosophy, we remember that such confounding is the touchstone of the synthesizing imagination, which fuses and reconciles "sameness with difference; . . . the general with the concrete; the idea with the image; the individual with the representative; the sense of novelty and freshness, with old and familiar objects; a more than usual state of emotion, with more than usual order." [29] When he accuses magic of materializing philosophy, his terms resemble his own definition of the literary symbol. Magic turns into material forms—such as talismans, charms, or spells—what had previously only been dreams. Such materialization had caused the degeneration of Roman religion and later of Stuart religion ("they were restlessly impelled to materialize the ideas of the Greek philosophers, and to render them practical by superstitious uses") but in art ideas take material form. Coleridge suggests that the source of his own conception of the symbol is present in these occult writers: in "The Principles of Genial Criticism" he says that "the Mystics meant the same, when they define beauty as the subjection of matter to spirit so as to be transformed into a symbol, in and through which the spirit reveals itself." [30] Here spirit is incarnate in matter to give it form, and the embodiment of spirit is the symbol of the spirit. Thought and thing are synthesized in symbol, as "art itself," writes Coleridge in the essay on poesy or art, "might be defined as of a middle quality between a thought and a thing, . . . the union and reconciliation of that which is nature with that which is exclusively human. It is the figured language of thought."[31]

In reading these philosophers, Coleridge encountered what he wanted to encounter: a universe alive with sympathies, a desire to expand the mind's power through conjuration of this living energy and series of likenesses; wishes realized instantaneously as they are spoken by the essentially magical quality of language which brings itself to pass as a spell does; a confounding and materializing, which, like synthesizing and symbolizing, is central to art.

After reading these eclectics at various times throughout his life, Coleridge seems to have applied the magical aspects of their thought to his elusive definition of imagination in something like the following way: the imagination is a supernatural power whose mysterious sources are within and whose workings are instantaneous and miraculous. This power can originate true beginnings and can project living analogies to the self and symbols of inwardness onto the objects beyond it. In perceiving the universe as alive by analogy with the mind, it succeeds in "destroying the old antithesis of *Words* and *Things*, elevating as it were, words into Things, and living Things, too."[32] When it transforms a word into a living thing, accomplishing a true beginning in nature by bringing to pass what it wished for, it proves that "all the organs of spirit are framed for a correspondent world of spirit,"[33] and hence that we are free.

The self-reflexiveness of the magical state of mind, realizing what it imagines, making wishes come true without waiting for a lapse of time, applies to the workings of the imagination when it creates. This similarity of working, carefully explored by Coleridge in dealing with the theological errors of Plotinus, Agrippa, Bruno, and Boehme, informed him of how the imagination functions on a secular level—autonomous because self-generating and self-gratifying. Coleridge's notion of imagination is inspired by and distilled from the instantaneity, self-reflexiveness, and wish-fulfilling omnipotence of thought characteristic of the magical philosophies that he came to refute. "The whole submerged magical system of Romantic aesthetic," to which Frank Kermode alludes in *The Romantic Image*,[34] lies beneath the surface of Coleridge's theories of the imagination.

4 • *Coleridge and the Potent Voice*

In his philosophical theory Coleridge sees the mind operating like a magician by imposing its power on the world, the poet attaining magical possession in order to create ex nihilo, and language itself approximating the "hot magic" of music. Similarly, in his poems, which are often disparaged by critics, Coleridge displays a coherent magical system. From first to last the poems are concerned with the complicated relationship between nature and poetic power, and the sympathetic reader progressively is convinced that the mind transforms nature through language in the same way that the words of the poem transform the blank page. This analogy between the act of writing and the act of animating the universe informs both theory and practice. So much do readings on magic come to bear on his poetry that thirty-three out of eighty-eight original poems written between 1791 and 1804 use the imagery of magic; more often than not magic occupies a central position in the development of the poem, usually where the poet worries whether he can write at all. Therefore it would help us to understand Coleridge's thinking about language if we examine first the development of his feelings about the relative power of nature and mind; second his notion of the shamanistic state that is induced by magical means and that aims ultimately to control the nature around it; and finally the actual moments in the major poems when language imposes its governing powers on the outside world.

The conflict between the respective ascendancy of nature and mind first becomes apparent in early poems about nature when Coleridge tries to assess his own position. Is he apart from nature or one with it? Is his mind omnipotent or is it subject to the impressions of matter? When Coleridge writes "The Eolian Harp," he is expressing a consistent view of a magically organized nature, a view adopted from the writings of Ficino, Pico, Bruno, and Agrippa, and available in the writers of the mid- and late eighteenth century. He comes closer here than in other poems to believing that nature is magically powerful even without man, and later poems reverse this belief. In "The Eolian Harp" nature is vibrant with sympathies that overflow into a "soft floating witchery of sound." The poet is as passive to these magically animate sympathies as a lute, and to passing of the winds across his indolent mind he responds with the poem at hand. "The Eolian Harp" was strummed into existence by the surrounding influences, alive with potential music—"the mute still air / Is music slumbering on her instrument." [1]

Coleridge's early faith in tranquility (or indolence as he otherwise calls it) depends on the belief that nature will cast up songs on its infinite harps if men are passive to it. In "The Eolian Harp" Coleridge is one more sentient thing in a world of sentient things, all responding to one another and bursting into spontaneous song. Such is the ideal state of passivity to nature. The universe is alive, and men yield themselves to this "one life within us and abroad," as he later calls it, refusing as yet to manipulate for their own purposes the sympathies they feel.

Even in "The Eolian Harp" the mind comes to consciousness under Sara's orthodox frowns. The poet has failed to submit himself passively to Christian doctrine, and ironically this poem in praise of the mind's passivity has shown "shapings of the unregenerate mind." The poet has tried to make the Christian Incomprehensible comprehensible in heretically magical terms.

The assertion of consciousness in the very moment of praising passivity suggests in the early poems that the mind is inevitably beyond nature—for good or ill. For example in "Fears in Solitude" the poet in his "green and silent spot" where "sweet influences trembled o'er his frame" is fully conscious, alien from the sun and air, finding significance wherever he looks:

> And he, with many feelings, many thoughts
> Made up a meditative joy, and found
> Religious meanings in the forms of Nature!
>   (p. 257; ll. 22–24)

The green dell leads him not to passiveness in nature, but to "Love, and the thoughts that yearn for human kind." Again, in "The Nightingale: A Conversational Poem," by virtue of the pathetic fallacy the poet suddenly realizes that the nightingale seems "melancholy." A "night-wandering man whose heart was pierced / With the remembrance of a grievous wrong" ascribed to the neutral bird this human quality, thus peopling nature with aspects of himself:

> And so, poor wretch! filled all things with himself,
> And made all gentle sounds tell back the tale
> Of his own sorrow.   (p. 264: ll. 19–21)

Coleridge laments that man must force his consciousness on the world, and wishes that he could relinquish his ambitions and lie back, simply receptive

>   to the influxes
> Of shapes and sounds and shifting elements
> Surrendering his whole spirit, of his song
> And of his fame forgetful! so his fame
> Should share in Nature's immortality,
> A venerable thing! and so his song
> Should make all Nature lovelier, and itself
> Be loved like Nature! But 'twill not be so.
>   (p. 265; ll. 27–34)

As much as Coleridge would like the human song to merge with the sounds of nature, to be as ephemeral and thoughtless as the nightingale's, he knows that this merging cannot be, and he witnesses to its impossibility by writing this poem. Instead of resting in the grass, his mind goes on with its

human and nonnatural tasks because it is irresistibly, unrelent-
ingly outside of nature, above it, and finally supernatural.

More and more, then, the animate universe serves not to
turn man into a thing, but to alert him to his separateness, and
to his power, by acts of will, to fly from the immediate scene.

More and more we find Coleridge using the peaceful vitality
of nature to induce in his own mind a concentration that leads
him beyond nature. Indolence rouses the mind and ends by
blocking out the universe of "little things" and turning the
mind in upon itself. "O! I have listen'd" to the song of the
nightingale,

> till my working soul,
> Waked by those strains to thousand phantasies,
> Absorb'd hath ceas'd to listen!   (p. 93; ll. 12–14)

This "soul-subduing power" does not absorb the soul into the
surrounding world but into the world of its self-born fantasies.
Similarly in "A Stranger Minstrel" the poet lies on a mountain
until his immediate sense of external reality is obliterated, and
he is free to entertain the forms that rise spontaneously within
his mind:

> As late on Skiddaw's mount I lay supine,
> Midway th' ascent, in that repose divine
> When the soul centred in the heart's recess
> Hath quaff'd its fill of Nature's loveliness,
> Yet still beside the fountain's marge will stay
>   And fain would thirst again, again to quaff;
> Then when the tear, slow travelling on its way,
>   Fills up the wrinkles of a silent laugh—
> In that sweet mood of sad and humorous thought
> A form within me rose, within me wrought
> With such strong magic, that I cried aloud.
>
> (pp. 350–51; ll. 1–11)

Forms appear unbidden so insistently that they seem to come
from another world. Certainly they come with a supernatural

luminousness—"with such strong magic, that I cried aloud."
In the "Ode to the Rev. Hort" the poet exclaims, "O skill'd
with magic spell to roll / The thrilling tones, that concentrate
the soul!" (p. 92). Again in the "Ode to the Departing Year"
the poet concentrates his soul and opens it to nonnatural or
supernatural invasion:

> Long had I listen'd, free from mortal fear,
>   With inward stillness, and a bowèd mind;
>   When lo! its folds far waving on the wind,
> I saw the train of the Departing Year!
> Starting from my silent sadness
> Then with no unholy madness,
> Ere yet the enter'd cloud foreclos'd my sight,
> I rais'd the impetuous song, and solemnis'd his flight.
>
> (pp. 160–61; ll. 4–12)

Passivity to nature is only a springboard to an inner mental
involvement. In this state of passivity another power within
the mind goes secretly to work and ends by liberating the mind
from its surroundings. What is this power, asks Coleridge in
"Lines in the Manner of Spenser":

> Was there some magic in the Elfin's dart?
> Or did he strike my couch with wizard lance?
>
> (p. 95; ll. 32–33)

Imaginary forms rise up into the "cloudless Azure of the
Mind" (p. 35; "Ode," l. 9), summoned there invisibly. A
magical power takes over from within the mind at the very
moment when the poet believes himself to be surrendering his
mind.

Despite its freedom from the environment, this power does
not go into operation everywhere. It prefers "enchanted
places" and "enchanted spots." There are "wizard founts,"
strange mountains which hide "the muse's witching charm,"
and "Elfin haunts of the Muses." In his note to "Lewti or The
Circassian Love Chaunt" Coleridge explains that the muses do
not roam freely through the world but dwell in peace in "the

magic haunts of the Muses." When Coleridge urges Cottle to forage for magic herbs on a poetic mount, he hopes that these magic herbs will improve Cottle's verse. These uniquely endowed places are "enchanted ground": they are imbued with more than natural powers, saturated with mana. What makes nature concentrate its strength in one place? Like Wordsworth's "spots of time" these enchanted spots are repositories of layer upon layer of human experiences. They are magical because men have sunk their memories there like buried treasure:

> A savage place! as holy and enchanted,
> As e'er beneath a waning moon was haunted
> By woman wailing for her demon-lover!
>
> (p. 297; ll. 14–16)

The spots come to life owing to the human life "buried" inside, in the same way that Wordsworth's "spots of time" represent the confluence of nature's space (spots) with individual human history (time). We come to discover, in fact, that mere nature will not always arouse the mind to visionary feats, unless it is an enchanted spot; and perhaps it becomes an enchanted spot only because it is the site of a poem. The poet thinks that it was near this beanfield that he dreamed up a poem; and because of that supernatural visitation, the site is alive for him with magical power. He imagines the site as itself a symbol of the chasms and fountains of his own imagination. Thus the more the spot is human, the more it is magical and helps the poet to move into the mind, learning early that "of all we see, hear, feel, and touch the substance is and must be in ourselves." [2]

Paradoxically, therefore, it is through nature that the poet gets into a state eventually to escape nature. When he lies dreaming a "waking dream," watching nature through "half-closed eyelids," and finally not watching it at all, he makes room in his mind for visions. From ecstasy (or stepping outside himself) he moves unconsciously to enthusiasm (or being filled with supernatural powers), reaching the genius within the man of genius, the unconscious stranger below. After being passive to nature, he comes to be filled with a power which is above, or distinct from, nature's. Coleridge's interest in a supernatural life of the mind independent of nature accords with his general belief that any effort of the will is supernatural in that it is original. Acts of the imagination perceive supernatural life, and nature becomes only a medium for the poet's activity as the poet reluctantly realizes his difference from it.

When the poet of the "Ode to the Departing Year" credits the power of his conjurations to holy madness, he is not being altogether rhetorical. He relates that in casting his spells he is thrown into a frenzy:

> The voice had ceas'd, the Vision fled;
> Yet still I gasp'd and reel'd with dread,
> And ever, when the dream of night
> Renews the phantom to my sight,
> Cold sweat-drops gather on my limbs;
>   My ears throb hot; my eye-balls start;
> My brain with horrid tumult swims;
>   Wild is the tempest of my heart;
> And my thick and struggling breath
> Imitates the toils of death!   (p. 166; ll. 103–12)

In this rapture he foreshadows the similar frenzies of the Ancient Mariner and the poet of "Kubla Khan," both of whom must speak before they can be freed of their madness. The mariner explains to the wedding guest why he overpowered him with his spell:

> Forthwith this frame of mine was wrenched
> With a woful agony,
> Which forced me to begin my tale;
> And then it left me free.

> Since then, at an uncertain hour,
> That agony returns:
> And till my ghastly tale is told,
> This heart within me burns.   (p. 208; ll. 578–85)

The physical disabilities of vision are induced artifically for the poet of "Kubla Khan"; after eating his hallucinatory foods, he is taboo, hence dangerous and fascinating:

> And all should cry, Beware! Beware!
> His flashing eyes, his floating hair!
> Weave a circle round him thrice
> And close your eyes with holy dread,
> For he on honey-dew hath fed,
> And drunk the milk of Paradise.

(p. 298; ll. 49–54)

The shamanistic excesses of the poet of part 2 have been carefully examined by Humphry House and Patricia Adair. House, discerning the wildness of the poet and the fear he inspires, declares him to be in a state of "poetic frenzy": "The poet who has been able to realize this fusion of pleasure and sacredness is himself regarded as a holy or sacred person, a seer acquainted with the undivided life."[3] Adair expands this notion by seeing its precedent in dionysian frenzy—the divine madness of bacchic ritual, first shown applicable to Greek drama by Jane Harrison and Francis Cornford. Bacchus, an image for the "energies of nature," says Adair, "was for Coleridge an image of the power of the unconscious, the ideas and impulses which rise unbidden from the depths and can be both a terror and an inspiration."[4] From Thomas Taylor's *Eleusinian and Bacchic Mysteries* (1791) as well as from the *Ion* itself, Coleridge may have adopted the floating hair and the milk and honey which are believed to induce divine madness.

Coleridge's interest in Bacchus thus meshes with his interest in Lapland wizards, Copper Indian curses, and the native bardic frenzies introduced to him in the writing of Gray and Collins. His interest in the Lapland wizard in "The Destiny of Nations" shows his early concern with what we now call shamanism.[5] The Lapland wizard descends into the ocean, envisions otherwise invisible supernatural forms, and fathoms the "penetralium of the mystery" because he first enters a strange trance. The power of his language then releases the danger and majesty of the elements:

> the Greenland Wizard in strange trance
> Pierces the untravelled realms of Ocean's bed
> Over the abysm, even to that uttermost cave
> By mis-shaped prodigies beleaguered, such
> As Earth n'er bred, nor Air, nor the upper Sea:
> Where dwells the Fury Form, whose unheard name
> With eager eye, pale cheek, suspended breath,
> And lips half-opening with the dread of sound,
> Unsleeping Silence guards worn out with fear
> Lest haply 'scaping on some treacherous blast
> The fateful word let slip the Elements
> And frenzy Nature. Yet the wizard her,
> Arm'd with Torngarsuck's power, the Spirit of Good,
> Forces to unchain the foodful progeny
> Of the Ocean stream;—thence thro' the realm of Souls.
>
> (p. 135; ll. 98–112)

Through these mad and rambling phrases the wizard appears as a promethean culture hero and a visionary, giving himself over to ecstasy, risking his bodily life to discover hidden truths. The release is accomplished through the enchantments of "the dread name" that, once voiced, maddens nature. The white magic of the magician overcomes the black magic of the Fury Form, for the primitive wizard-redeemer is the result of a romantic synthesis: the Greek irrational joins with the new study of anthropology.

The poet's enthusiasm arises partly from the distinctly human originative will and derives partly from a frenzied extrahuman surrender of the will. The Lapland wizard and the poetic personae of the great poems share this unnatural quality—abnormal, bizarre, wild. They seem to have been taking herbs, dancing wildly in manic circles, trembling with horror and glee at the visions they alone can perceive. This supernatural state is typical for the magician or shaman when he prepares to cast his spells, and the state presumably continues at least until the spells have been uttered. The poet in Coleridge's view may be thought a magician, not only because of his claim to control things with words but also because of his distinctly shamanistic state. In short, nature first leads the gifted seer to relax in indolence, but paradoxically this indolence releases a supernatural state of mind actively asserting its words on nature.

Personal reasons as well as philosophical ones dictate the use of magical spells as models for his verse. Coleridge reads the magicians to help him with his major task, a task that is painful because it involves, in Coleridge's opinion, the origination of entirely new things rather than the imitation of what already exists. Because of this sense of plunging into the void, of beginning at the very beginning, Coleridge's use of magical forms and references signals his terror before the blank page. He depends on magical references as on laudanum to help him overcome the pain of large adventures or to mesmerize himself into disregarding their magnitude. His own words in asking for words distract him from the tension of launching into a poem. The rhythm of the spell eases the entry into the world where poems are willed—a supernatural world where nature cannot help him. Fearing to begin, Coleridge calls with magical verse for words, and the verse expands as if by magic into the very poem he had dreaded to write. Calling for words breaks the spell surrounding the act of original composition. Spells abound in his poetry; there are spells around writing, and spells caused by writings. There are spells on the poet, and spells that he casts; spells that he needs and spells that he wills. He is caught in the spells of the universe; he in turn commands the universe with spells; he conjures up his own new universes. In poems trivial and profound, Coleridge deliberately uses magical imagery and forms, thereby giving a basis to the "magical" effect so often claimed by his enchanted admirers. Coleridge's interest in magic in his prose is fully borne out in his poetry.

Coleridge seems to be concerned with magic as a way of

getting beyond the deadness of things or at least the thingness of things. In poem after poem he speaks, sometimes with blame, usually with praise, of magic: "wizard spell" (p. 80), "enchanted ground" (p. 76), "magic dews" (p. 46), "Holy Spell" (pp. 36, 152), "Magic smile" (p. 31), "Enchantress pleasure" (p. 25), "necromantic spell" (p. 86), "witching time" (p. 86), "enchanting spot" (p. 94), "soliciting spell" (p. 132), "numbing spell" (p. 482), "a charm to stay the morning-star" (p. 376), "thy mother's name, a potent spell" (p. 176), and "the enchantments of that sudden beam" (p. 113) are only a few scattered occurrences of this concern. Coleridge comes increasingly to focus his magical references on the activity of the poetic imagination and on the language which embodies the forms conjured up by the imagination.

Coleridge seems consistently to think of the imagination as magical, even in the early poems where its powers are bad. In "Religious Musings" Coleridge blames the imagination for leading men to abandon their innocence. He writes, "Imagination conjured up / An host of new desires." The power to conjure up new things is dangerous in a religious context, but this judgment does not apply to imagination as it manifests itself in art. For instance in his early "Effusion at Evening" the imagination is a sorceress:

> Aid, lovely Sorc'ress! aid the Poet's dream,
> With faery wand O bid my Love arise.
>
> (p. 49; ll. 14–15)

This sorceress is a fairy godmother, an allegorical figure who does what the poet does not dare to do himself. A muse with magical power, she evolves from Night in "The Songs of the Pixies" ("Sorceress of Ebon Throne, Mother of wildly working dreams") who summons invisible visions before the poet's inner eye. When Coleridge revises "Effusion" a year later, he dares to summon the spirits with his own spells:

> Spirits of Love! ye heard her name! Obey
> The powerful spell, and to my haunt repair.

> O heed the spell, and hither wing your way,
> Like far-off music voyaging the breeze!
>   (p. 52; ll. 37–38; 43–44)

He longs to have magical power: "O (have I sigh'd) were mine
the wizard's rod, / Or mine the power of Proteus, changeful
God!" The externalized sorceress Imagination eventually becomes part of the poet's mind, its most willful and originative
part; and the "witching spell" that enthralls the poet (p. 156)
turns out to be of his own making. In "The Destiny of
Nations" fancy (not yet distinguished from the imagination) is
linked with the forms which arise in the soul when it is released
from the bondage of appearance. "Fancy is the power"

> That first unsensualizes the dark mind,
> Giving it new delights; and bids it swell
> With wild activity; and peopling air,
> By obscure fears of Beings invisible
> Emancipates it from the grosser thrall
> Of the present impulse.   (p. 134; ll. 80–86)

Once again the poet aims to become blind to outward things,
to free himself from the gross thrall of immediate sensation,
and to prove his freedom by conjuring forms that are new.
Invisible to the outer eye, these forms inhabit a supernatural
world invented by the mind.

Emancipation or, in other words, our ability to wish freely is
possible owing to the power to originate. In "The Silver
Thimble" (a trivial thank-you to Joseph Cottle) Coleridge
recalls heroines whose wishes were magically granted. He
flatters Cottle:

> Such things, I thought, one might not hope to meet
> Save in the dear delicious land of Faery!
> But now (by proof I know it well)
> There's still some peril in free wishing—
> *Politeness* is a licensed *spell*,
> And *you*, dear Sir! the Arch-magician. (p. 104; ll. 11–16)

"Free wishing" separates us from the obligations of gross fixed reality; we wander at will in places that we ourselves have made. Even when he borrows from others, Coleridge borrows strategically to support his hope that the imagination can take us beyond nature. In his rendering of the "Hymn Before Sunrise, in the Vale of Chamouni," the actual mountain is only a means for the persona to rise into a vast and invisible world:

> O dread and silent Mount! I gazed upon thee,
> Til thou, still present to the bodily sense,
> Didst vanish from my thought: entranced in prayer,
> I worshipped the Invisible alone.   (p. 377; ll. 13–16)

The magic haunts of the muses are conjured up by the imagination, which is the archmagician.

Coleridge's use of the metaphor of magic to describe the working of the mind when it creates suggests a new way of understanding his puzzling definitions of the imagination.[6] If he consistently associates poetic creativity with trance, with the state of mind characteristic of the magician or shaman, we can understand that his representation of the imagination as a sorceress and his use of the adjective *magical* for the imagination's power are intentional. Coleridge seems to be moving away from conventional faculty-psychology which locates the imagination as a place in the brain and supposes it to be a continually operating faculty which always does the same things. Instead of seeing the imagination as a faculty, he seems to see it as a power, an unusual condition characterized by more than usual energy. When the imagination attains this heightened state (and only then can it legitimately be called "imagination") it can assert its unifying conceptions on the world outside and give life to this world. At the moment when this new and greater-than-human power fills the mind, the poet is in a state of joy.

The imagination may be considered the emotional and psychological power that enables language to be effective. This definition presupposes that we recognize the powers of imagination only when language has worked well. The poet himself recognizes the imagination when like the Ancient Mariner he feels coming over him the fit that must issue in speech. The energy of the imagination is what creates the excitement of meter, which then sets the wheels of the imagination moving still faster. Here Wordsworth's requirement that a poet be a man with more than ordinarily intense feelings seems to be one of Coleridge's requirements too. Imagination is the mind in a state of unusual creative activity (or imagination is the activity of mind when it is unusually creative). When Coleridge calls the imagination magical he acknowledges that it is unpredictable, sudden, spontaneous, unusual, and mysterious— attributes that suggest it must arise from the exercise of supernatural power. It is a state of mind which becomes divine when it acts, not a faculty of mind that is always divine even when it is inactive.

Accordingly Coleridge's distinction between the activity of the fancy and the activity of the imagination is based on the intensity of energy necessary for each operation, as if for the operations of these powers one could use the analogy of different temperatures required to weld or join different metals. At a certain point such temperature or levels of intensity cease to differ in degree and begin to differ in kind, so that the intensity seems to move outside of a natural order. When E. R. Dodds explains that Homeric gods often represent unaccountable, unnatural, and hence divine aspects of human character or action, he helps us to understand how the human imagination at a certain level of intensity seems no longer to be human but supernatural.[7] Thus the poet who possesses this power—or is possessed by it—is a magician who can call upon supernatural energies and convey this energy to the rest of the world through supernaturally charged language.

This intense activity of the mind is called joy in "Dejection: An Ode," and its connection with the passions is apparent in other poems as well. In "The Monody on the Death of Chatterton" and in "Pantisocracy," "the wizard Passions weave an holy

spell," responding to the moon in their midnight rondelay.
The rapture is bacchic, as the three resident poets dance on the
shores of the Susquehanna. The power to create invades the
poets in the form of strong passions. In that puzzling and
desolate poem "The Pang More Sharp than All," vanished love
leaves its image in the heart, and this image is inscrutably
magical, as is the love itself:

> For still there lives within my secret heart
> The magic image of the magic Child
> Which there he made up-grow by his strong art,
> As in that crystal orb—wise Merlin's feat,—
> The wondrous 'World of Glass,' wherein inisl'd
> All long'd-for things their beings did repeat.

(p. 458; ll. 36–41)

The allegorical love magically enclosed his own image in the
poet's heart, which now exercises a magic of its own. "Life, and
Life's effluence," passion and the image of passion, are both
magical.

This passion becomes a life-force in "Dejection: An Ode,"
for the magical power of the imagination requires not indolence after all but exuberant well-being. Joy makes it possible
for the mind (now decisively separate from nature) to reach out
and to give life to the "inanimate cold world." Although at the
beginning of "Dejection: An Ode" the poet seems to be
begging the winds to inspire him, he loses his passivity as the
poem proceeds until it is he who plays on the wind's stops.
Although in his dejection he thinks himself an aeolian lute, he
ends by breathing his own gusts into the gusts without. And
the poet who in the second stanza saw the universe in layers of
interchanging sympathies learns as early as stanza 4 that his
own voice is "the life and element" of all the throbbing sounds
he hears. The "thin clouds above, in flakes and bars, / That
give away their motion to the stars," seem to do so because
their mutual affinity has been instituted by men: the wedding
garment and the shroud are draped on nature by us—not in
accordance with nature's own love or death, but with ours. The

poet has learned the fallacy of asking for life from nature (for "the objects of nature are essentially fixed and dead"): "I may not hope from outward forms to win / The passion and the life, whose fountains are within." His "genial spirits"—his "shaping power of Imagination"—give life to the universe that already exists but is of itself inert: "In our life alone does Nature *live*" (italics mine).

This imaginative life is manifest most specifically in the "potent voice" which issues from the soul with entire originality, having nothing to do with impressions from without. The sweet and potent voice, in finding the words to write this poem, has at the same time summoned the wind's epic, tragic, and lyric voices; indeed it has caused the wind to rise. The wind is a mighty poet "even to frenzy bold" only because a human poet imagines it to be. Once the poet has found the potent voice that he sought from the beginning and once he has realized how this potent voice animates and then commands nature, he is able to move from the magical imposition of words onto things to bless another human life. He moves here, as in "The Rime of the Ancient Mariner," from spells to blessings, from magic to religion. As in "The Rime of the Ancient Mariner," again, he confers life on outer forms by means of a strange power of speech. And in the same way that the Ancient Mariner's animating words are signs of originative power, this sweet and potent voice is of the soul's "own birth." It rises out of nowhere, it is new. Imagination, the sorceress within, is an expression of the supernaturalism of the will: autonomous and nonmimetic, it decrees what then comes to pass. After the model of Thomas Gray's magical poems, the Dejection Ode (with many others of Coleridge) summons a voice and witnesses its coming. It magically invokes the wind's power ("And Oh! that even now the gust were swelling") and accomplishes itself in the very words of calling for help. The form of the Dejection Ode is thus the paradigm for Shelley's self-fulfilling spell, "The Ode to the West Wind," since both odes celebrate the vital breath of the magician-poet.

This same magical idealism governs "The Rime of the Ancient Mariner." In telling his tale the mariner casts a spell on the wedding guest who thereafter cannot avoid listening; the mariner "hath his *will*," reducing the wedding guest to little more than a passive child. The tale proper concerns the casting and breaking of a spell on the mariner's ship, a spell that is initiated by the mariner's own spiritual state, and that snaps when he moves unaccountably into a loving frame of mind. The sailors who cannot interpret his strange and sudden deeds die. He himself who acts and speaks in bursts of will (even to the point of biting his own arm to let the blood free his parched tongue), is the sole survivor. Speaking his unmotivated and hence supernatural speech, he alone *lives*, whereas the others are as passive as nature itself. "The dream-like inconsequence" of the external happenings is a function of their arising from the internal events of the mariner's mind, so that the ocean's tipping, the silence, and the appearance of slimy things are projections of his mind as dreams are, since "in our life alone does Nature live." Even when interpreted as a magical demon or natal spirit, the albatross does not on its own make the ice split or the winds flag.[8] Instead the hero's attitude toward it—hailing it as a Christian soul or shooting it with a crossbow—determines the progress of the spectral and imaginary journey, a journey that begins to end only when he speaks his blessing.

Having been granted holy madness, the mariner is enthralled by a vision. To escape its thrall he in turn must enthrall another, with his strange power of speech brought on by recurrent agony. The magic, active in a state of shamanistic possession, has its effect through language. The mariner's own act sets the spell in motion, and nature turns dark because his vision does. His own unconscious act of blessing releases the spell and sanctifies nature: "The burden of breathing life into [external nature] falls wholly upon the creative imagination," as Patricia Adair perceives.[9] Coleridge was concerned with acts that are true beginnings in that they are not the consequences of other acts. The power of origination is exclusively human, not an attribute of nature, since nature depends on cause and effect. Here the man with "strange power of speech" acts instantaneously; his acts are not explained by his environment. The instantaneousness of these unmotivated acts inheres in magic. Even Coleridge's refutation of Mrs. Barbauld emphasizes the magical quality of this origination—his own in writing, the mariner's in acting. Condemning the overtness of the moral in his own poem, Coleridge would have preferred his "Rime" to resemble a tale in *The Arabian Nights:* "It ought to have had no more moral than the *Arabian Nights'* tale of the merchant sitting down to eat dates by the side of a well and throwing the shells aside, and lo! a genie starts up and says he *must* kill the aforesaid merchant because one of the date shells had, it seems, put out the eye of the genie's son" (*Table Talk*, May 31, 1830).[10] His description of the Arab tossing his date pits centers on the inexplicable events, unpredictable causality, and sudden visitations of magic. By writing poems that are magical the poet can prove his independence of nature, his freedom of will which is manifest in imaginative creation and free wishing.

The idea that the mind no longer relies on nature to provide it with images is related to the imagination in "Kubla Khan." Both Humphry House and Patricia Adair, opposing the usual critical laments over the "failure" of the poem, interpret it as a joyful assertion of the originative mind.[11] To believe that the poem affirms the magical power of the imagination is to think that parallelism exists between the emperor and the poet, between the emperor's "decree" which commands a city to rise and the poet's song which commands even the emperor. Owing to his imperial power, Kubla himself is not subject to nature. House observes that "it is [Kubla's] decree that matters, for it images the power of man over his environment and the fact that man makes his Paradise for himself. Just as the whole poem is about poetic creation at the imaginative level, so, within the work of the imagination, occurs the creativeness

of man at the ethical and practical levels."¹² In a fashion
similar to Kubla's, the poet is empowered to people the air and
to construct domes with the magic of his poem:

> That with music loud and long,
> I would build that dome in air,
> That sunny dome! those caves of ice!
> And all who heard should see them there.

His longing to revive within himself the symphony and song
of his dream is granted retroactively, as if by magic; and in his
visionary trance he is admitted to a paradise of his own
making. Despite the momentary danger of the unfulfilled
subjunctive ("Could I revive within me / Her symphony and
song"), the existence of the poem proves that the song has been
revived, not only for the private contemplation of the poet, but
for all to see in their mind's eye, even as they listen. The "music
loud and long" bewitches the imagination into believing that
it sees what "all who heard should see." As this poem transforms the impressions of the ear into the visions of the eye,
while both are simultaneously an imaginary projection of the
sacred rivers and chasms of the mind, just so the coming of the
poem to Coleridge was an inexplicable and magical occurrence. Visiting him in a dream, "all the images rose up before
him as *things*." The sudden world of the poem enthralled him
with its charms, so that, rushing to record it, he dreaded the
charm's end and the evaporation of the mind's *phantom*. To
describe this dread he quotes his own earlier poem, "The
Picture; or, The Lover's Resolution":

> Then all the charm
> Is broken—all that phantom-world so fair
> Vanishes, and a thousand circlets spread,
> And each mis-shape['s] the other. Stay awhile,
> Poor youth! who scarcely dar'st lift up thine eyes—
> The stream will soon renew its smoothness, soon
> The visions will return! And lo, he stays,

And soon the fragments dim of lovely forms
Come trembling back, unite, and now once more
The pool becomes a mirror.   (p. 296; ll. 91–100)

Coleridge suggests that he knows the fragments do come trembling back and that the pool does recollect itself as the poet waits over it, reconstituting those fair phantoms that had momentarily fled from the mind. In writing Coleridge was subject to a charm; the emperor conjured up his empire with magical language; the poet of the last stanza conjured the foregoing vision with a song; and Coleridge summoned the whole series of interlocking acts of language into a form, while he stared into the pool at images of his own mind.

In Coleridge's view nature exists, but nature is not (despite the early claims of "The Eolian Harp") inherently alive. It depends for its life on the sensitive magician, in the same way that the crops and hunts in a primitive community are believed to depend on the magician's ritual spells. Nature becomes animate when men think about it and use the concepts in language to deal with it. Nature vanishes when the mind gazes inside on its own smooth and phantom-peopled stream, its sacred river. The imagination commands nature because it comes originally from somewhere outside it or above it.

While the poet lying on the hill learns to be passive, this passivity is a temporary state which leads ultimately to a defiance of the merely natural. When a supernatural power momentarily fills the emptied mind with its originating power, the poet is able to exercise his will on nature, and thereby give it a life it had hitherto not possessed, because it was inert. Charged with supernatural—almost divine—activity, the poet can magically call a poem into being: he can speak, make decrees, sing, invest the inanimate cold world with an ideal animation, and build his palaces in the vacant air.

Assuming the animate pantheistic universe of things in "The Eolian Harp," Coleridge goes on to realize that what he does in writing poems is to command this universe and to raise up forms independent of it. This realization leads him to glorify "the magical power of the imagination" which mediates between the opposing worlds of things and the self as the Holy Ghost mediates between the Incarnation and the mind of God in the Christian Trinity.[13]

How intensely Coleridge pursued the theme of the magician (to postpone for a moment considering his magical form) is apparent in his plans for a long poem on the medieval magician Michael Scott. He reveals these plans at great length in *Table Talk* (February 16, 1833), but claims that he had outlined his work long before reading Goethe's *Faust*. His longstanding jealousy of Goethe is painfully obvious; whether we should believe Coleridge was originating or plagiarizing here is a difficult question. "Before I had ever seen any part of Goethe's Faust, though, of course, when I was familiar enough with Marlowe's, I conceived and drew up the plan of a work, a drama, which was to be, to my mind, what the Faust was to Goethe's. My Faust was old Michael Scott; a much better and more likely original than Faust. He appeared, in the midst of his college of devoted disciples, enthusiastic, ebullient, shedding around him bright surmises of discoveries fully perfected in after-times, and inculcating the study of nature and its secrets as the pathway to the acquisition of power. He did not love knowledge for itself—for its own exceeding great reward—but in order to be powerful. This poison-speck infected his mind from the beginning." Coleridge's Michael Scott is imprisoned and grows gloomy and desperate, until he is tempted: "Accordingly to witchcraft Michael turns with all his soul." Michael raises the devil, and in a torment realizes that it is he who is being commanded, not he who commands. Although the elements of plot are similar (even to an Agatha—Margaret—whom Michael tries to ruin), Coleridge criticizes the motivation of *Faust*, which his own work would have corrected: "The intended theme of Faust is the consequences of a misology, or hatred and depreciation of knowledge, caused by an originally intense thirst for knowledge baffled. But a love of knowledge for itself, and for pure ends, would never produce such a misology; but only a love of it for base and unworthy purposes. There is neither causation nor progression in the Faust; he is a ready-made conjurer from the very beginning; the *incredulus odi* is felt from the first line." One of Coleridge's major projected works was therefore to have been a narrative poem on the life of a great magician. The long poem on magic was to hold the central place in Coleridge's literary career that *Faust* held in Goethe's.

Much earlier, in a letter to Sotheby on August 26, 1802, he had proposed writing a long poem on Medea. Unlike the "mad magical witch poem" that he later plans (notebook 4138), this poem was intended to deal with the aftermath of sorcery, with the way the exercise of magical powers blights and separates the practitioner. Like both "The Rime of the Ancient Mariner" and "Cain" this poem was to deal with healing criminals, with learning to live after willfully originating a break in the natural order. Coleridge believes that he has discovered "a subject of great merit in ancient mythology hitherto untouched"— Medea after the murder of her children. Having described her position in the court of Pelias and her ruse to have his daughters kill their father with magical rites in a magic cauldron, he describes his vision of her: "the character of Medea, wand'ring & fierce, and invested with impunity by the strangeness & excess of her Guilt—& truly an injured woman, on the other hand & possessed of supernatural Powers." Such a poem, with Medea's incantations, her devotion to the goddess Diana, her revenge, and her exile, would have given Coleridge further opportunity to explore the effects of supernatural origination and to experiment with many varieties of the suspension of disbelief, even as it demonstrated the powers of delusion. But the poem did not appear.

Nor did *Medea* and *Faust* exhaust his plans for poems on related topics. Along with the projected hymns to the elements in the manner of Ficino, he projected an analysis of Boehme's system and a biography of Giordano Bruno. He also planned an ode to music with a magician summoning songs from the depths, and this ode might have done what many of his other poems had done—made the possessed magician the center of the universe, organizing it with his magical incantation. Moreover we should not forget his magical play, *Osorio*, contemporary with his best poems, and later reworked as *Remorse*.[14]

Two months after the publication of the "Ode to the Departing Year" on December 31, 1796, Coleridge had begun work on this magical play; and between March and June 1797 he had written two and a half acts of it. Encouraged by the Elizabethan and Jacobean tradition, he relied heavily on magical materials. Alvar is disguised as a magician; magic potions, magic herbs, and a magical picture dominate the metamorphoses of the plot. The hero not only mutters spells, but also disenchants his corrupt brother by his protean disguise. The heroine is sensitive, and therefore susceptible to magic:

> She is a lone enthusiast, sensitive,
> Shivers, and cannot keep the tears in her eye.
> Such ones do love the marvellous too well
> Not to believe it. We will wind her up
> With a strange music.   (p. 536; ll. 32–36)

Alvar, too, is a lone enthusiast; as the wizard in the mountains, he is "he that can bring the dead to life again." Significantly the link between his magical power to bring the dead to life and the magical power of the artist is not overlooked:

> You are a painter—one of many fancies—
> You can call up past deeds, and make them live
> On the blank canvas, and each little herb,
> That grows on mountain bleak, or tangled forest,
> You've learnt to name.   (p. 544; ll. 180–84)

As the enthusiastic poet of the "Ode to the Departing Year" had called up past deeds and made them live by his commands, this magician gives inanimate things life by naming them:

> There's a strange power in weeds
> When a few odd prayers have been muttered o'er them
> Then they work miracles!   (p. 545; ll. 210–12)

Alvar uses magic to rouse himself to action. He conjures his own spirit:

> Hear, sweet spirit! hear the spell
> Lest a blacker charm compel!
> So shall the midnight breezes swell
> With thy deep long-lingering knell.
>
> And at evening evermore
> In a chapel on the shore
> Shall the chanters sad and saintly, . . .
> Doleful masses chant for thee,
> Miserere, Domine!   (p. 552; ll. 44–57)

Mixed with elements of Christian chant, this spell invokes power from the breezes. Magic confers instantaneous strength, whereas Alvar's model, Hamlet, had to wait the length of the play. Magic likewise takes the place of the play within the play; Alvar catches the conscience of his brother by a magic picture. "I will uncover all concealed things," (p. 551; l. 9) he proclaims, as he probes the secret crimes of the moonlit chasm.

> I dare no longer
> Be present at these lawless mysteries,
> This dark provoking of the hidden powers,
>   (p. 850; ll. 116–18)

the loved Maria is made to say in the revised *Remorse*. But Alvar is consistently interested in his own magical role and in his power over nature:

> Ye too split
> The ice-mount, and with fragments many and huge,
> Tempest the new-thaw'd sea, whose sudden gulphs
> Suck in, perchance, some Lapland wizard's skiff.
>   (p. 551; ll. 31–34)

The hero is outcast, artist, and wizard. He brings those who are supposed dead to life, and he reasserts his rightful claims by magical disguise. The play's reliance on magical changes may be the cause of its weakness; for the instantaneous transformation of dramatic situations is unconvincing on stage, where the means of transformations must be visible and credible. But the themes and methods that may not have worked well in the play are central to the great poems that follow it.

We saw that the potent voice, the strange power of speech, the symphony and song, the decree, and the music loud and long in the major poems verify the supreme position of the poet in a world of things that he controls through language. In line with his fascination with the divine Logos, the central theme of his proposed Magnum Opus, Coleridge shows an interest in human echoes of the Word. In the beginning was the Word, and the beginning of each work of poetic creation, too, is a Fateful Word, a Name, a Potent Song. In a poem as silly as "On the Christening of a Child," Coleridge calls the mother's name a "potent spell." The Lapland wizard knows the "dread name," which, when uttered, will "Let slip the Elements." In the "Ode to the Departing Year," too, the single word "Liberty!" is a spell that has power in two directions depending on its use.

Because Coleridge knows the power of the Name to hold in sounds, printed letters and ideas the essence of the thing that is named, he is all the more aware of the force of words in rhythmical combinations. From his interest in curses passed through the eyes (in "The Three Graves" and in "The Rime of the Ancient Mariner") he would naturally turn to explore verbal curses, more permanent and therefore more terrifying. His interest in a heavily incantatory meter, apparent in poem after poem, is integral not only to his interest in the power of words and sounds but also to his belief in the supernatural legacy and mission of the poet, who influences nature and society with his strange power of speech. His gift and his torture involve more than a man speaking to men. He suffers and passes on his new knowledge to make ordinary men sadder and wiser. The mariner alone survives; the poet of "Kubla Khan" revives the dream; the poet of the Dejection Ode gives "the life and element" to the world with his potent voice. "Christabel" carries this faith in the poet's peculiar language even further, since the bard of the poem not only animates nature but must also reform a bewitched society. To do this he must affect men, even against their will, as the mariner keeps the wedding guest from the hearty but thoughtless festivities; and the meter of his verse is designed to penetrate below the rational mind.

While part 1 of "Christabel" dramatizes the triumph of Geraldine's evil magic ("Off wandering mother, peak and pine, / For I have power to bid thee flee") and the silencing and pacifying of Christabel (who loses her power to speak), part 2 hints that a holy magic may prevail when the songs of the bard cleanse the polluted land. A voice is not a negligible commodity for Coleridge, for when Geraldine's spell deprives Christabel of her tongue, she is unable in any other way to assert her virtue. Mute and transfixed, she loses her freedom and her will: like the wedding guest she is reduced by another's magical power to the passivity of a child. Lacking the words actively to enforce her feelings and understanding on the world, she becomes as inert as any natural thing, relinquishing her peculiarly human traits.[15] Only when the orphic singer rouses himself to action can this defeat be revenged, and the deluded king and his enchanted land be returned to nonreptilian order.

Had the poem continued, it is possible that Bard Bracy's role would have widened, following the pattern of Coleridge's other major poems in glorifying the imaginative mind and its medium, the potent voice. The poem, however, unlike "The Rime of the Ancient Mariner" and the Dejection Ode, does not ascribe the evil power to the hero, but suggests for the first time that evil is not necessarily a quality of the human will projected onto the world, but the result of a mysterious rival force, which the hero must combat. White and black magic thus war for the soul of Christabel, suggesting that there may be supernatural forces besides our own at work in the world.

In recognition of this almost Manichaean rivalry, the bard must enhance his verbal supremacy: no longer just a gift, his songs must be powers which can overwhelm the forces of evil. For this purpose language must be strange, arcane, insistent, not ordinary or casual. To achieve such language, the poet provokes madness and frenzy in himself, learns occult lore, and, in the magical shamanistic tradition, gets in touch with the supernatural so that his poems do not imitate the deadness of mere things, but instead re-create a semidivine vitality.

The peculiar importance of language for the well-being of the world explains in part the urgency of the spell-like verse forms that Coleridge cultivates in spite of Wordsworth's scorn. Because words have a mission to inform and organize, they must use every resource available—alliteration, assonance, repetition, pounding meter—to separate them from everyday conversational speech. The poet is a strange person (it is not normal to write poems) with a strange mission, who must use a suitably strange language to dignify and particularly to enforce his will.

With these beliefs in the uniqueness of the poetic voice, as well as his own sense of inadequacy when faced with the supernatural task of original composition, Coleridge is motivated to use the forms of the spell. In "A Stranger Minstrel," for instance, the possessed poet summons the spirits of the mountain:

> "Thou ancient Skiddaw by thy helm of cloud,
> And by thy many-colour'd chasms deep,
> And by their shadows that for ever sleep,
> By yon small flaky mists that love to creep
> Along the edges of those spots of light,

. . . . . .

And by this laugh, and by this tear,
I would, old Skiddaw, she were here!

. . . . . .

Thou ancient Skiddaw, by this tear,
I would, I would that she were here!"

(pp. 351–52; ll. 12–71 passim)

In response the mountain praises Mrs. Robinson's own magic
song, and the vision of her comes to the poet "with such strong
magic, that I cried aloud." In "The Rash Conjurer" again
Coleridge plays with meter:

Strong spirit-bidding sounds!
With deep and hollow voice,
Twixt Hope and Dread,
Seven Times I said
Iohva Mitzoveh
Vohoeen!
And up came an imp in the shape of a
Pea-hen!
I saw, I doubted,
And seven times spouted
Johva Mitzoveh
Yahóevohāen!   (p. 399; ll. 1–12)

In his "Soliloquy on the Full Moon, She being in a Mad
Passion," a casual poem found by George Whalley in Sara
Hutchinson's collection of poems by her "poets,"[16] Coleridge
experiments again with the colloquial humorous rhymes and
dashing meters of "The Rash Conjurer" and "The Silver
Thimble." Like these other poems to friends, this one turns
easily to imagery of magic—of "Conjuring, / Sky-staring, /
Loungering, / And still to the tune of Transmogrification."
The moon regrets that "Ventriloquogusty Poets" bay at her,
that a poet, "one Wordsworth by name," claims the voice of a
"wizzard" is in the wind and in his search for "witch rhymes"
in *Peter Bell* turns her into a canoe.

From this strange Enchantment uncharm'd by degrees
I began to take courage & hoped for some ease

When one Coleridge, a Raff of the self-same banditti
Past by.   (p. 6; ll. 33–36)

This Coleridge transforms the moon into half of a small
cheshire cheese; then, his brain addled by moonlight, he
changes her into an ostrich egg. Before this Coleridge, this
loon, can change her into a bowling ball she cries out,

> And still Heaven be prais'd! in contempt of the Loon,
> I am I myself I, the jolly full moon.   (p. 7; ll. 65–66)

She, the ancient symbol of change, insists on her identity,
despite the efforts of moon-struck lunatic poets to give her
other names and forms in racing lines of incantation.

In "Fire, Famine, Slaughter" more variations of the incantatory forms appear:

> No! No! No!
> Myself, I named him once below,
> And all the souls, that damnèd be,
> Leaped up at once in anarchy,
> Clapped their hands and danced for glee.
> They no longer heeded me;
> But laughed to hear Hell's burning rafters
> Unwillingly re-echo laughters!
>   No! No! No!
> Spirits hear what spirits tell:
> 'Twill make a holiday in Hell!   (p. 237; ll. 6–16)

The poet of the "Ode to the Departing Year" who has been
engulfed by "holy madness" raises his song, a series of summonings that rises to the climax "Rise, God of Nature! rise"
(p. 160; l. 102).

> Hither, in perplexèd dance,
> Ye Woes! ye young-eyed Joys! advance!
>   (p. 161; ll. 21–22)

When Coleridge intones

> About, about, in reel and rout
> The death-fires danced at night;

> The water, like a witch's oils,
> Burnt green, and blue and white,
>
> (p. 191; ll. 127–130)

and

> In the touch of this bosom there worketh a spell,
> Which is lord of thy utterance, Christabel!
>
> (pp. 224–25; ll. 267–68)

and

> And all who heard should see them there,
> And all should cry, Beware! Beware!
> His flashing eyes, his floating hair!
> Weave a circle round him thrice,
> And close your eyes with holy dread . . . ,
>
> (p. 298; ll. 48–52)

he does so after much experimentation in earlier poems, and with a theory of magical language close to his heart.

Certainly reading and hearing *Macbeth* helped him (as it had helped Gray and Collins) to devise an appropriate meter. In his "Sonnet to Mrs. Siddons" Coleridge reveals how her role as Lady Macbeth had enthralled him. As early as 1796, and probably long before, he began perfecting his ability to charge up that fearful sound, as if with his own special electricity. The meter of the hags' incantations—the familiar "Double, Double, toil and trouble"—echoes throughout his work.

Moreover, in the theory of meter scattered through his works, Coleridge suggests that the incantatory sound of these many verses is actually based on principles of deliberate visceral rhythm. His remarks on meter in *Biographia Literaria* (chapter 18) reflect his faith in the balance of the voluntary and the involuntary, of sense and nonsense, so evident in the rhythms of the magical spell.[17] At once lulling and rousing, meter in general (and particularly meter which aims to enchant the listener) combines two countervailing elements: "that spontaneous effort which strives to hold in check the workings of passion" and the effect of meter "to increase the vivacity and susceptibility both of the general feelings and of the attention." Meter balances the compulsion to move with the check to motion. "There must be not only a partnership but a union; and interpenetration of passion and of will, of *spontaneous* impulse and of *voluntary* purpose." [18]

The asseration of will toward which the spell is directed is couched paradoxically in visceral rhythms. The heavily accented trochaic tetrameter of the spell is most nearly akin to those mindless forms—the nonsense rhyme, the nursery rhyme, the counting-out rhyme of popular Germanic tradition. Syntax is frequently pulverized for meter's sake. "The supervening act of the will and judgment" is foiled by the insistence and speed of the sound. And thus in this union of head and heart, the involuntary rhythm (the heart-beat) rules. Sound overwhelms sense, and enthralls it as if by a spell. The most voluntary act of the mind—the bewitchment of another—is enacted through an involuntary and primitive medium.

Drawing on Renaissance texts besides *Macbeth*—*Friar Bacon and Friar Bungay, Dr. Faustus, The Tempest, A Midsummer Night's Dream,* and *Comus*—Coleridge exploits the metrical conventions of the spell. Trochaic tetrameter, end-stopped lines, dense rhymes, alliteration, repetition, and frequent parataxis are essential to the ancient form. The heavily accented meter (often initiated in imperative verbs) moves vigorously, keeping the reader or listener from contemplation. With his disbelief suspended, the reader does not question transformations, and he recognizes invocations as instantaneously granted. Bewitched by the overwhelming strangeness of the meter, the reader thinks himself in a magical situation and succumbs to its enchantments, for the conventions of the spell establish their own atmosphere. The effect on the reader is dual: on the one hand the packed texture of the spell forces him to hear the spell as a powerful, almost stationary unit. The spell asserts itself on the memory as a thing. It has in its very solidity escaped the bounds of mere transitory language. No longer a description of a thing outside of itself, it becomes a memorable talisman, fearful to repeat. Words have become things, and living things, too.

For all Coleridge's emphasis on articulation, he often uses the lack of articulation—as for instance in the spell's parataxis—as a way of pointing out the inadequacy of a civilized logical view of the sources of poetic power. Similarly the heavy accentualism (part of the program in "Christabel") counteracts his interest in the subtleties of meter by recalling the primitive origins of poetic inspiration. He even turns his classical periodic sentences into spells (as in the "By . . . By . . . By . . . ." structures in the "Ode to the Departing Year"), and converts a technique that is normally a guarantee of order into a technique promoting suspense and menace. The reader awaits the resolution of this periodic sentence not so much with delight in its grace as with dread of its power.

There is nothing disguised about the meter. All the resources—the big guns—are concentrated in an effort to force language to one's attention. Natural, easy, eliding speech it is not. One is forced to the conclusion that the intricate dense clump of words is autonomous: it has a life of its own; stepping out from the more relaxed narration surrounding it, it asserts: "I am language; I have power."

The sense of urgency rises in the prevalence of commands. The imperative verb begins the line on a strong accent. Leaving little room for hesitation or introspection, these commands indicate the authority of the spell and suggest that its power is unquestionable. Strong opening accent, coupled with the corrosiveness of diction, creates an aura of compulsion. We are compelled to believe in the powers that are invoked and to believe that what is invoked will come to pass, even though we might normally doubt it. Confronted with this urgent, corrosive, authoritative language—compressed into a unit—the reader must begin to believe there is more to the universe than what the eye can see. With all the aural resources of language aimed at him, he begins to listen with fear to unknown animate powers, to the sound of magical sympathies and antipathies pulsing through nature at the command of words.

Accelerated by alliteration, internal rhyme, and the short line, the spell picks up yet more speed at the refrains. Unlike the refrain of the ballad, the refrain of the spell gains its force in the context of magic: the formula, reiterated, becomes more certain to succeed. The repetition of words that are inherently powerful gives the poet yet more power over his victim. The refrain suggests that a magical operation is indeed being performed, and the more it is repeated, the more inexorable it seems. Thus diction, meter, alliteration, assonance, rhyme, repetition, and refrain join to form a dense spell, a paradigm for the power of poetry generally.

Coleridge's interest in the way music casts a spell over the listener—causing him (as in "Kubla Khan") to confuse sound with sight in a magically induced synaesthesia—is apparent already in some early poems. "To the Reverend Hort" is one example. Hort's music is a spell; Hort is a magician. For Coleridge poetry is not intended to "approach the condition of music" by abjuring content but rather by acting to enchant men, affecting all their senses through the ear (all other senses spreading out from that one) as music does, making them suspend their disbelief and submit to the mesmeric sound. Suspending disbelief is part of the condition of enchantment and thus the aim of the enchanter. Coleridge's interest in music is part of his larger concern with the ways in which music, like rhythm and meter, enforces the magician's unique power over his hearers. Mesmeric and vitalizing, the spell enlists our credulity, and also intensifies the poet's own energy: the very rhythm of the meter causes the excitement that makes the poet write. He oils his own wheels by moving, as lines of verse magically generate new lines of verse and the summoning of poetic power turns into the poem summoned. The meter transports both the poet and the audience into imaginative realms where there is more to the world than meets the eye, where changes occur faster than the eye can see. It is a world

conjured by the rhythms that meet the ear and pass unconsciously into the body. It is a world where any word said
invents instantly the thing or the feeling that it names. What
is said is done; the decree precedes and creates the reality.

Once Coleridge frees the mind from its passivity to nature
by discovering that the mind leads an independent and creative existence, defying by its irresistible activity the indolence
that nature at first induces, he is then free to imagine for his
words a nearly divine power. Thinking "in the beginning was
the Word," he charges up his words with the electricity of the
spell's rhythm, intending to affect through these vibrations the
very substance of things as well as the listener's image of these
things. Thus, when he continually pumps out these auditory
vibrations, he is taking upon himself "the burden of breathing
life into the world," and this central, organizing, and vitalizing role applies to all his heroes—the poets of the "Ode to the
Departing Year," of "Kubla Khan," and the Dejection Ode,
the Reverend Hort, Osorio, Michael Scott, Bard Bracy, and
the Ancient Mariner. It applies most specifically, of course, to
himself, anxious to radiate out from himself the energetic
language which should be the life and element of inert things,
anxious to bear the responsibility, but, alas, too often overcome by fear of taking up the task. The effort required to cast a
spell over another is awesome, from the first trancelike absorption to the final burst of speech. Casting a spell is not casual,
but sublime and exhausting. Always on the peaks, never in the
valleys among ordinary men, the magician must be busy,
frenzied even, to keep the world around him going, believing
it waits for its next breath on the incantation that must be
forthcoming. Coleridge's speaking—the marvel of his university contemporaries and of his later admirers at the Gillman's—kept his listeners rapt. His voice went on and on.
More intensely in poetry, the potent voice, the symphony and
song, must also go on and on to keep the world in the highest
conceivable state of energy, to keep it from relapsing into the
deadness and fixity of things. The strain of this responsibility

may account, then, for some of the difficulties Coleridge met in the fateful act of original composition, in which it was his business not only to achieve a state of trance, not only to choke out the saving words, but also to make these words so mesmerically powerful that they should enforce man's supernatural life on the natural world, thereby proving that man hails from a different and higher sphere, free from the causalities and associations and sensations of nature.

Coleridge's interpretation of poetry as the expression of magical power is thus tributary to his larger philosophical theory asserting the supremacy of spirit over matter, sound over sight, idea over the object of an idea; and this interpretation illuminates the gulf between his own philosophical views and Wordsworth's, so that in the flash of the magical metaphor we can see two grand diverging rivers influencing subsequent poetry—one river flowing toward incantatory verse and visionary fabrications, the other toward imagism and hard-edged objectivity: one impelled by a belief in the originating power of the word; the other impelled at least to begin with by a fidelity to the existing and visible universe of things.

5 • *Wordsworth's Arguments against Magical Words*

Since Earl Leslie Griggs began to reveal the disagreements between the two great founders of English romanticism, Wordsworth and Coleridge, the legendary cooperation between the two friends has seemed less and less harmonious. S. M. Parrish, William Heath, and Stephen Prickett have pointed out that Wordsworth and Coleridge disagreed on their conceptions of the imagination, on their attitudes toward the dramatic protrayal of character, and on their diction.[1] Moreover a close reading of sections of *The Prelude* of 1805 in the light of *Peter Bell* shows that basic disagreements exist about the relation of words to things, about the relation of supernatural to natural, and about the effect of language on moral stability. From such fundamental disagreements personal conflicts naturally arise, for the two poets are working in different directions and hence threaten each other's work.

My focus involves the disagreement between Wordsworth and Coleridge as seen through Wordsworth's eyes; perhaps it would be more accurate to call the disagreement a dialogue, with Coleridge as the imagined interlocutor. Wordsworth himself is not interested in the magical tradition except when he thinks of it as a metaphor for the errors of thinking that he sees in his friend. These errors, impinging on theories of language, books, freedom, reality, and the self, become increasingly apparent to Wordsworth, whose complex feelings toward his friend are difficult to understand if we persist in idealizing their friendship. But if we allow this friendship to have the normal jealousies and tyrannies of a literary friendship, we can understand that many of Wordsworth's poems are intended to correct Coleridge, even sometimes to prove his dependency. Like Geraldine, Wordsworth's star rises as Coleridge's seems to set; symbiosis has often seemed the appropriate botanical analogy, but parasitism applies also to certain areas of the friendship. It is not at all times clear, moreover, which friend is the mistletoe and which the oak.

To justify himself, to define his views against Coleridge's, to affirm his healthy growth against a diseased or stunted one, Wordsworth turns readily in his poems to the subject of Coleridge, often in terms of the magical metaphor, with all that it implies. I will avoid the abyss of Wordsworth's theories about nature and will examine this personal and aesthetic concatenation of thoughts and images.

In the midst of his adulation of Wordsworth, Coleridge recognizes early that there are fundamental differences between them. In writing to William Sotheby, Coleridge says of Wordsworth's preface that "[I must] set you right with regard to my perfect coinc[idence with] his poetic creed" (letter 444; July 13, 1802). Already in 1802 he voices his disapproval of the way Wordsworth imitates the speech of rustic people, a disapproval that he elaborates in the *Biographia* much later; to Sotheby he writes: "In my opinion, Poetry justifies, as *Poetry* independent of any other Passion, some new combinations of Language, & *commands* the omission of many others allowable in other compositions / Now Wordsworth, me saltem judice, has in his system not sufficiently admitted the former, & in his practice has too frequently sinned against the latter. —Indeed, we have had lately some little controversy on this subject—& we begin to suspect, that there is, somewhere or other, a *radical* Difference [in our] opinions." He repeats this discovery in a letter to Robert Southey (449; July 29, 1802), discussing Wordsworth's latest poems: "The greater number of these to my feelings very excellent Compositions / but here & there a daring Humbleness of Language and Versification, and a strict adherence to matter of fact, even to prolixity, that startled me / his alterations likewise in Ruth perplexed me / and I have thought & thought again / & have not had my doubts solved by Wordsworth / On the contrary, I rather suspect that some where or other there is a radical Difference in our theoretical opinions respecting Poetry— / this I shall endeavor to go to the Bottom of." He does explore the radical difference in the *Biographia*, where he explains the promise of genius as "the choice of subjects very remote from the private interests and circumstances of the writer himself." "At least," he continues, "I have found that where the subject is taken immediately from the author's personal sensations and experiences, the excellence of a particular poem is but an equivocal mark, and often a fallacious pledge, of genuine poetic power." He wishes that Wordsworth would write poetry that is, as Coleridge says in the Lecture on Poesy or Art, purely human, and from the mind, not imitated from the world the senses remember.

This radical difference seems to have concerned more than aesthetics, to have involved their moral lives. We can begin to understand this opposition by considering two long remarks by Coleridge, one from the notebooks of October 26, 1803, the other cited in *Inquiring Spirit*. We will see that Coleridge's doubts about Wordsworth were paralleled by Wordsworth's doubts about Coleridge. In notebook entry 1616 Coleridge records "a most unpleasant Dispute with W. and Hazlitt Wednesday Afternoon," and complains: "Dear William, pardon Pedantry in others & avoid it in yourself, instead of scoffing & reviling at Pedantry in good men in a good cause and becoming a Pedant yourself in a bad cause—even by that very act becoming one! —But surely always to look at the superficies of Objects for the purpose of taking Delight in their beauty, & sympathy with their real or imagined Life, is as deleterious to the Health & manhood of intellect, as always to be peering & unravelling Contrivances may be to the simplicity of the affections, the grandeur & unity of the Imagination— O dearest William! Would Ray, or Durham, have spoken of God as you spoke of Nature?"

Coleridge believes that Wordsworth's concentration on the superficies of things denies the existence of a spiritual principle. Always seeking balance, he avers that it is as destructive of imaginative power to depend for the experience of beauty on the external impressions of things as to rely on the meddling intellect alone; while Wordsworth seems never to have tired of criticizing Coleridge for overemphasizing the powers of the intellect.

Coleridge regrets Wordsworth's preoccupation with what the eye sees, believing that his preoccupation keeps him from imposing his own spirited words on fixed objects. In the *Inquiring Spirit* he explains how words generate a fiery vitality greater than that imagined by Wordsworth for things:

> The Focus exercises a power altogether different from that of the rays not converged—and to our sight and feeling acts precisely as if a solid flesh and blood reality were there. Now exactly such focal entities we are all more or less in the habit of creating for ourselves in the world of Thought. For the given point in the Air take any given *word*, fancy-image, or remembered emotion. Thought after Thought, Feeling after Feeling, and at length the Sensations of Touch, and the blind Integer of the numberless number of the Infinitesimals that make up our sense of existing, converge in it—and there ensues a working on our mind so utterly unlike what any one of the confluents, separately considered, would produce, and no less disparate from what any mere Generalization of them all, would present to us, that I do not wonder at the unsatisfactoriness of every attempt to undeceive the person by an analysis, however clear. The focal word has acquired a *feeling of reality*—it heats and burns, makes itself be felt. If we do not grasp it, it seems to grasp us, as with a hand of flesh and blood, and completely counterfeits an immediate presence, an intuitive knowledge. And who can reason against an intuition?[2]

In this complex passage Coleridge describes the convergence of feelings, perceptions, memories, and ideas into the burning focus of a word; and this concoction works upon us in a mysterious and powerful way, much more mysteriously and powerfully than any of the separate elements would work lacking a joining word. This new power, transubstantiated from its parts, seizes us. The spiritual principle incarnates itself in words, to the extent that they have bodies, being midway between thoughts and things. In radical opposition to Wordsworth, Coleridge believes words to be more real than things, even giving off a heat and light which "dead things" do not. Even while Coleridge in the *Biographia* praises Wordsworth's ability to spread the tone, he fears that Wordsworth is unable to rise above things, and occasionally, as abject as he usually is before Wordsworth, Coleridge extends this criticism to apply to Wordsworth's moral life. He writes of Wordsworth to Poole on October 14, 1803: "I trembled lest a film should rise, and thicken his moral eye." Faith in the superficies of things may lead to moral opacity.

At the same time that Coleridge was recognizing that the poet he had counted on to write a long philosophical poem was seeing the superficies of things rather than giving to language its focal role, Wordsworth was working out his opposition to Coleridge's method and to the moral character that he found implicit in it. Wordsworth's opposition to supernatural transformations and to the changes that language works on nature is presented in simple form in *Peter Bell*. Here the evidence of parallel plots leads us to believe that he is directly mocking Coleridge's "Rime of the Ancient Mariner." In the prologue to *Peter Bell* he argues against the Coleridgean mode of receiving inspiration through supernatural possession, and in the tale proper he carefully argues that character developed under the influence of urban rather than natural forms, of books, words, and other artifices, may be unstable.

The premise of the poem in all its parts is stated in the letter dedicating it to Southey, another "lover of the supernatural": "The Poem of Peter Bell, as the Prologue will show, was composed under a belief that the Imagination not only does not require for its exercise the intervention of supernatural agency, but that, though such agency be excluded, the faculty may be called forth as imperiously, and for kindred results

of pleasure, by incidents within the compass of poetic probability, in the humblest departments of daily life."[3]

This purpose is obvious in the prologue where a moon-
shaped boat (supernaturally empowered like the Ancient
Mariner's) carries the poet against his will to pry among the
planets, forgetting "that little earth of ours." But the poet
becomes homesick, voyaging in these mysterious, shadowy,
spectral distances, haunted by the disembodied music that
haunted the Ancient Mariner. In the magical boat the supernaturally possessed poet pines for earth, where he feels he is a
man. He rejects the voyages to a "secret" land where "human
feet did never stray," and rejects "the realm of Faery," "among
the lovely shades of things." The wayward boat longs to show
him how "earth is taught to feel the might of magic lore," but
the poet, lonely for the green earth of reality, pays no attention;
turning his face away from the temptations in the shades of
things and those fantasies invented in the solipsistic, insen-
sible mind, he also turns away from words:

> "Temptation lurks among your words;
> But, while these pleasures you're pursuing
> Without impediment or let,
> No wonder if you quite forget
> What on the earth is doing." (p. 189; ll. 116–20)

The poet is determined to be different from those who "re-
hearsed the wonders of a wild career."

> "Long have I loved what I behold,
> The night that calms, the day that cheers;
> The common growth of mother-earth
> Suffices me—her tears, her mirth,
> Her humblest mirth and tears.
>
> The dragon's wing, the magic ring,
> I shall not covet for my dower.
> (p. 189; ll. 131–37)

After all these imaginative possibilities couched in magical terms have been refused, the poet is deposited in his own garden by the disappointed boat. He asks nothing beyond life's daily prospect to stir, to soothe, or to elevate him; no supernatural wands, spells, or sprites are necessary to enliven the actual feelings that real people experience. The poet sees his friends gathered at a real table in a real garden, and lands there "on his two poor legs." Here, then, is fit audience.

The poet is disconcerted by his supernatural journey and has difficulty in making the transition from a false, extravagant, possessed lunacy to a true simple sanity:

> I spake with faltering voice, like one
> Not wholly rescued from the pale
> Of a wild dream, or worse illusion.
>
> (p. 190; ll. 186–88)

In this frenzied state he rushes into the central act of the tale without explanation, and a listener corrects him, saying: "Against the rules / Of common sense you're surely sinning; / This leap is for us all too bold; / Who Peter was, let that be told, / And start from the beginning" (ll. 196–200). Wordsworth himself makes a similar criticism of the unmotivated acts of "The Rime of the Ancient Mariner," whose "dreamlike inconsequence" he abhorred. Instead of bold leaps and inspired ravings, he believes that the feelings inspired by nature are enough: "A potent Wand doth Sorrow wield; / What spell so strong as guilty Fear!" Even as he rejects magical themes and imagery, he deliberately describes natural events in magical terms to prove that nature works its own magic more powerfully than that of imaginary supernatural worlds. In general the poet decides for things rather than the *shades* of things, for the earth itself rather than for the words which lead away from it into magical realms of transformation and distortion.

Whereas the prologue criticized magical sources of inspiration and magical themes in poetry, the tale applies these same criticisms to ordinary life, arguing that books, supernatural visions, and literary romancing breed weak men.

The poet, dazed by his otherworldly journey, is asked to speak as a man to men, calmly to start from the beginning and explain the environment that built up Peter's mental structure, to show the "growth of the mind" instead of a sudden and unmotivated action. Where does Peter come from? What was the world that formed him? Only after this is clear can the poet tell what Peter did, for the impressions seeded on the mind in youth blossom into the acts of adulthood. Acts have roots; they do not sprout out of nothing. They are not supernaturally original. Because Peter had "never felt / The witchery of the soft blue sky," because he was subject to "whatever vice / The cruel city breeds," because, for lack of natural forms, he was "always playing with some inward bait," he cruelly whips the ass. Then out of fear and guilt he dreams terrible fantastic shapes, lending to the rocks and woods around him the fancies of his mind. He suffers from the "ugly witchcraft" (ll. 264–417 passim) of his own self-inflicted paranoia.

An act (like the Ancient Mariner's) which is not based on associative causation is unrealistic in Wordsworth's early view; for acts can be explained by the accumulation of causes that impress themselves on the innocent mind. Indeed the quality of a mind can be gauged by the surroundings that shaped it, and, conversely, improved surroundings can ultimately produce a healthy mind. Wordsworth believes that young minds impressed by urban forms will shrivel with various kinds of paranoia, violence, and introversion, while young minds impressed by natural forms will grow to self-reliance. Thus Wordsworth's Peter is related to Godwin's Caleb Williams, villain by circumstance; Wordsworth here agrees with Godwin that an act is to some extent the product of an environment, and he therefore disagrees with Coleridge, who sees acts as miraculous, original, and free of circumstance and who criticizes Wordsworth's "*biographical* attention to probability" in the *Biographia* (2.103). In Wordsworth's view Coleridge's insistence on free will fails to respect our original dependency on nature. Like Comus or like Spenser's Archemago, Coleridge seems to pit his manipulative will against the solid reality and, like the alchemist in Chaucer's Canon's Yeoman's Tale, to substitute the falsely willed for the truly given.

Imaginary visions, such as those in which Coleridge specialized, are not only false subjects but symptoms of a diseased mind that cannot rest in the sufficiency of natural things. Like the books they often arise from and subsequently become, these imaginary visions bewitch the mind into the charmed circle of words and lure it away from the solid reality of things. Peter looks like a new Narcissus into a pool, seeing among the inverted trees ghostlike images, imps, fairies, spirits. Thus fancying,

> He looks, he cannot choose but look;
> Like some one reading in a book—
> A book that is enchanted.   (ll. 518–20)

The enchanted pages of the self-reflecting image produce fantastic distortions. In *Peter Bell* Wordsworth criticizes the multiple dangers of books, magical words, imaginary visions, and distant journeys. He implores the dread Spirits of Fancy to spare his susceptible and bookish friends and to work instead on evil men like Peter:

> Dread Spirits! to confound the meek
> Why wander from your course so far,
> Disordering colour, form, and stature!
> —Let good men feel the soul of nature,
> And see things as they are.   (ll. 761–65)

> From men of pensive virtue go,
> Dread Beings! and your empire show
> On hearts like that of Peter Bell.   (ll. 773–75)

Wordsworth conjures the false shadows away from his book-enchanted friends, one of whom is Coleridge. However, if Peter or Coleridge or Hazlitt had received the impressions of nature in their youths, their minds would not now rely on images of their own making or on images from books. Then the spirits of the mind would not cast their spells on the mind, and the mind would not distort nature with its transforming power.

Together with the airy lunar boat of the prologue and the other Coleridgean reminiscences of the tale (the sudden unmotivated crime against a humble Christianized animal), there are many direct hits at attitudes typical of Coleridge— the obsession with books and with the occult significance of words, and the urban upbringing. Lines 736–85 make fun of a gentle soul reading late into the night, whose dazed vision produces a ghostly "Word" standing on the page. The "potent Spirits" of books trouble even good men, making them tremble with remorse. *Peter Bell* demonstrates for Wordsworth that to elaborate nature is to falsify both nature and the soul, and that potent spells, witchery, magic rings, states of visionary possession, imaginary voyages beyond the here and now, words, and enchanting books betray *"things as they are"* (italics mine; l. 765).

When we see the antagonism toward supernatural fantasy displayed in *Peter Bell*, and the insistence on the need "to see things as they are," the importance of real things in Wordsworth's theory seems to increase. The stanza

> And now the Spirits of the Mind
> Are busy with poor Peter Bell;
> Upon the rights of visual sense
> Usurping, with a prevalence
> More terrible than magic spell.   (ll. 916–20)

can be taken as a epigraph for what follows. According to this stanza the mind works by supernatural agency to tempt men away from what is visibly and sensibly right; the mind's effect on character can be compared to the nefarious power of a magical spell, distorting visible reality by inventing forms that drive men mad. Potent spirits of the mind work by magic to separate a man from his bodily sense, the first means for measuring reality. The omnipotent mind usurps the wholeness of the man; words enchant him away from stability. With the fate of Peter Bell in mind, we can see why Wordsworth feels it necessary to make his "verse / Deal boldly with substantial *things*" (*Prelude* 12.233–34). He can be heard throughout the *Prelude* of 1805 fending off the temptation that lurks among words and warning the lonely recipient of that grand poem (who wanders restlessly at the time of its composition on the exotic island of Malta) to do the same.

Wordsworth's attitude toward "things" is complicated and controversial. Following Arthur Beatty's view that Wordsworth was "at once the interpreter and poet of associationism"[4] and Herbert Read's view that Hartley's "psychology dominates the Wordsworth of the great and poetically decisive period,"[5] John Jones sees Wordsworth's persistent concern with "things" as a "search for particularity," an "insistence upon constancy, boundedness, and irreducibility [which] betrays the imaginative impression of a traditional English materialism."[6] In contrast Melvin Rader and Newton Stallknecht have stressed Wordsworth's almost Coleridgean belief in the creativity of the transcendental mind.[7]

Wordsworth's own statements support both views. When he writes that "there is no object standing between the poet and the image of things," he supports Paul de Man's view that Wordsworth's verse "sacrifices in fact, the demands of consciousness to the realities of the object." When he writes that "the poet has a disposition to be affected more than other men by absent things as if they were present; an ability of conjuring up in himself passions, which are indeed far from being the same as those produced by real events," and that he "has acquired a greater readiness and power in expressing . . . those thoughts and feelings which, by his own choice, or from the structure of his own mind, arise in him without immediate external excitement," he seems to give evidence for a transcendental view of imaginative power. While he exults in the *Prelude* that "outward sense / Is but the obedient servant of her will," he also proclaims in apparent contradiction that "there is no need to trick out or to elevate Nature," for he has "faith that no words, which his fancy or imagination can suggest, will be to be compared with those which are the emanations of reality and truth."[8]

A compromise between these two opposing views is achieved in some recent studies that show Wordsworth developing his transcendental imagination from an early sense of particularity, growing to freedom after first seeing and feeling the visible and tactile things among which he grew.[9] He steadies himself by touching substantial things before rising into the vast uncharted regions of the mind, which he comes to believe to be the haunt and main region of his song.[10] It has been argued that in his attempt to make the mind the "lord and master" he fails, halted, unable to break through the present impulse to the fullness of imaginative freedom.[11] If it is true that Wordsworth failed to grow beyond a reliance on things and objects seen, one reason for this failure may have been the persistent example of Coleridge before him, for Coleridge seemed to suffer in many ways from his transcendentalism, and Wordsworth had carefully to weigh these two modes of development. In following the view of Wordsworth as a poet who grows and who watches the processes of growth, I would like to emphasize the circumstances which Wordsworth believed produce the most healthy growth in the early years, rather than stressing the freedom that may eventually arise if these early circumstances are favorable.

Thus, whereas things, particularly the forms of nature, had seemed real, substantial, and steadying for Wordsworth as he grew, words seemed despite all their power to counterfeit these things to move even further away from the truth. Both words and metaphors arise from the mind's arrogance, for the mind presumes to think that by changing the name of a thing it can change the thing's nature. Knowing the name of a thing, as in all magical theory, is to control it; and metaphors, ranging among discrete things with their indiscriminate "likes" and "ases," are interchangeable not only with one another, but also with mental conceptions, fancies, and dreams. Metaphors merge objects with subjects, things with thoughts, realities with unrealities, in a system of imagined correspondences that are made to seem possible because the outside world is all one to the mind. Metaphor works like magic to abolish the boundaries between fact and fancy, as Ortega y Gasset has perceived: "All our other faculties keep us within the realm of the real, of what is already there. The most we can do is to combine things or to break them up. The metaphor alone furnishes an escape; between the real things, it lets emerge imaginary reefs, a crop of floating islands. . . . The metaphor disposes of an object by having it masquerade as something else," he says, explaining his observation that "its efficacy verges on magic."[12]

Seemingly independent of "reality," words lose their identities and claim new ones; merging one thing with another they change the nature of things. As Circe changed men into pigs, words and metaphors release hidden qualities and even go on to conjure up forms that do not exist. The mind imagines a world and equates this shadow with the substance outside; throwing out its fables with complete disregard for fact, the mind, which Coleridge believed to be "the very focus of all the rays of intellect which are scattered throughout the universe,"[13] seems to proceed in spite of reality.

To Wordsworth the mind's promiscuity falsifies "the truth that cherishes our daily life." In the illusory realm of words, metaphors, and dreams, the mind aspires to a false power. Wordsworth's fidelity to sensible nature leads him to believe that the mind cannot derive real power at the expense of outward impressions. For such impressions mean the difference between a mind grounded solidly in verifiable truth, and one wandering among "barren intermeddling subtleties" (*Prelude* 11.204). For him, things are more permanent than the words that describe them.

Indeed, as he begins his praise of books in book 5, it is their impermanence that causes Wordsworth to lament and that gives to this poignant section—with its quixotic dreams, belated regrets, and descriptions of secondariness—its elegaic tone. Coming after his exultant memories of the power of nature's threatening and guiding forms, the description of the effect on him of these "powers only less than Nature's self" provokes an outburst of sorrow. Why, he asks, "Oh! why hath not the Mind / Some element to stamp her image on / In nature somewhat nearer to her own? / Why gifted with such powers to send abroad / Her spirit, must it lodge in shrines so frail?" (5.45–49) Until now Wordsworth's mind has looked "upon the speaking face of earth and heaven / As her prime Teacher." As he turns here to the productions of man's spirit, he grieves: "And yet we feel, we cannot chuse but feel / That these must perish" (5.19–20). As influential as they may often be, books are nevertheless fragile vessels of human spirit, which may easily be swept away by cataclysms, floods, winds, and upheavals—the revenge of nature's huge life. Wordsworth moves toward an affirmation of the creativity of the mind as "a thousand times more beautiful than earth" after first facing its frailty—the sad human song on the silent plain, the slim conch murmuring our history in the desert.

Because of this fragility, one should not rely exclusively on books and words to supply the growing mind with truths. Those who have done so, in the absence of natural forms, have usually suffered. Thus, while Coleridge listens for invisible voices both literary and theological and shuns the objects which "as objects are essentially fixed and dead" in his view, Wordsworth allows himself occasionally to succumb to the "absolute dominion of the eye" (9.176), the eye that made dear to him "the common range of visible things" (2.182) and that bound his feelings "by an unrelenting agency" (3.166). Language for Coleridge has power to conjure up living mental forms, but for Wordsworth it seems to intervene between his experience of things and the things themselves. He seeks for an alliance "both of the object seen and eye that sees" (12.379). "I conversed with things that really are" (2.412–13), and these things should shine through language as through clear glass. He writes: "It is not, then, to be supposed that any one, who holds that sublime notion of Poetry which I have attempted to convey, will break in upon the sanctity and truth of his pictures by transitory and accidental ornaments, and endeavor to excite admiration of himself by arts, the necessity of which must manifestly depend upon the assumed meanness of his subject." [14] Language, he declares in "The Essay on Epitaphs," "if it do not uphold, and feed, and leave in quiet, like the power of gravitation or the air we breathe, is a counter-spirit unremittingly and noiselessly at work, to subvert, to lay waste, to vitiate, and to dissolve." [15]

Although Wordsworth concludes his book 5 with a beautiful tribute to the "mystery of words" embodying within them both the visionary power radiating from the mind and the motion inherent in the winds outside of it, he is often suspicious of words, fearing that the magical language then coming into vogue would compromise the irreducibility and boundedness of things. When the intricate turnings of verse preserve the objects that they embody in recognizable forms, then language is functioning appropriately. Its veil is transparent, circumfusing forms and substances, joining them into an atmosphere, spreading the tone, and illuminating them "in flashes, and with a glory scarce their own" (5.625–29 passim). Within the aura that language casts around things, the "forms and substances" nevertheless "present themselves as objects recognis'd."

Explaining the nonverbal side of Wordsworth's thinking, David Perkins says that "Wordsworth insists again and again that thought—especially what he called insight or vision—can be non-verbal and hence far more subtle, profound, and comprehensive than the words found to represent it." [16] The experience that counts for him is "far hidden from the reach of words." Shelley believes that Wordsworth's passive and speechless wonder before objects stems from a lack of imagination. In his *Peter Bell the Third* he claims that Wordsworth

had as much imagination
As a pint-pot;—he never could
Fancy another situation,
From which to dart his contemplation
Than that wherein he stood.[17]

But this attack would be incomprehensible to Wordsworth, who felt that to dart his contemplation away from the spot where he stands is to falsify that spot at the very moment when he wants to render it whole. To impose the mind on nature ("To bend the Sabbath to [his] use") is heresy for him, whereas for Coleridge to refuse to impose the mind is an abdication of responsibility. Wordsworth's distrust of the mind's manipulation of things limits his experience to "what the eye cannot choose but see." He holds "communion with the invisible" most intensely when the invisible is grounded in "sensible impressions" (13.103–5).

The quarrel between Wordsworth and Coleridge over the relative importance of words and things frequently involves the metaphor of magic. This metaphor in turn determines the shape of their opposed formulations on the nature of reality and the practice of art. Things and words, eye and ear, passive mind and active, visible things and invisible ones diverge into natural and supernatural. By extension this divergence on basic principles seems to have split the possibilities for English poetry down the middle. Wordsworth's side fostered the truth of things and their verification through the eye; Coleridge's side fostered incantatory words that summon supernatural vision through rhythms reaching the ear. For Wordsworth the mighty forms of nature are a major source of our early knowledge, and to require supernatural inspiration is to neglect this reliable source, the visible world men see and "feed" on. For Coleridge a supernatural authority may supply ideas that the impressions of nature do not. The will, in Coleridge's view a supernatural power, is linked not with the matter of things but with the spirit, so that its inventions defy sensuous proof. Against this belief in the supernatural (which by its very

postulation suggests the insufficiency of the natural), Wordsworth asserts that "there is no necessity to trick out or to
elevate nature." Thus the division of the *Lyrical Ballads* into
"natural supernaturalized" and "supernatural naturalized" as
subjects for poetry appears to have had this basis: Wordsworth
was to start with the visible and suffuse it with light; Coleridge
was to start with the invisible and conjure it up. Perhaps
already in 1797 Wordsworth associated Coleridge with the
supernatural, the inventions of the mind, and the distortions
often caused by words and metaphors.

Increasingly Wordsworth realizes that his own intentions
should be subtly opposed to Coleridge's; in reaction to the
magus aspect of Coleridge, he expresses a distrust of the
omnipotence of thought inherent in a magical view of language. As we saw, in the prologue to *Peter Bell* Wordsworth
shows that supernatural fancies and visions debilitate the
artist; in the tale he shows that visions and words undermine
the springs of moral action in ordinary men. In both cases he is
directing his warnings as much to Coleridge as to anyone else,
for Coleridge's preoccupation with proofs of the spirit's supernatural existence and his search for the logos in heterodox
sources seemed to be destroying his art and his moral life.

Wordsworth's intuition in the 1798 *Peter Bell* that a certain
kind of attitude to words is debilitating is intensified in the
following years. One of the many reasons is that between the
trip to Germany taken by the two friends immediately after
the completion of the *Lyrical Ballads* and Coleridge's departure
for Malta in 1804, Coleridge noticeably deteriorates. Before
Coleridge leaves it seems to both William and Dorothy that
the trip is the event that might save him. At the time that
Wordsworth was writing the early books of the *Prelude*, Coleridge was in a low state, his malaise being psychological as well
as physical, as the notebooks reveal. His love for Asra, his
squabbles with his wife, his indolence, his addiction, and
countless other ailments which in his letters are repeated to his
correspondents in ever-increasing notes of woe make the con-

trast with the industrious Wordsworth all the more painful for him, and they make him all the more abject in his sense of failure. When he leaves, the Wordsworths write about him in their letters nearly always as "poor Coleridge."[18] Knowing that his silence is a sign of his misery, they are dismayed that they do not hear from him, and when they do the letters often describe some terrible attack of gastric misery, which Dorothy or William describes to other correspondents in pitying words. In order to arouse Coleridge's energies William begs him to comment on the parts of the *Prelude* that have already been written, and this tactic does not seem to make Coleridge any more communicative.

Coleridge's long awaited return from Malta and then from London, where he lingered because, as Wordsworth explained to Sir George Beaumont, "he dare not go home, he recoils so much from the thought of domesticating with Mrs. Coleridge" (September 8, 1806), brought misery to everyone. The Wordsworth letters are full of the incompatibility of Coleridge and Sara, of Coleridge's general unhappiness, and of his ill health. From August 1806 to February 1807 they often refer sadly to him in their letters. But by the following November their pity shows signs of turning into disapproval, presumably because Coleridge seems to be bringing his misery on himself. Dorothy writes to Catherine Clarkson (November 4, 1807), for example: "Poor soul! he is sadly to be pitied. I fear all resolution and strength of mind have utterly deserted him." She writes to Catherine Clarkson again, on December 6, 1807, that she and her brother "do not think that Coleridge will have the resolution to put this plan [of educating his sons] into practice; nor do we now even think it would be prudent for us to consent to it, C. having been so very unsteady in all things since his return to England. . . . we had long experienced at Coleorton that it was not in our power to make him happy; and his irresolute conduct since, has almost confirmed our fears that it will never be otherwise; therefore we should be more disposed to hesitation; and fear, of having our domestic quiet disturbed if he should now wish to come to us with the Children." Their many worries about Coleridge's state of mind show that Coleridge occupied their thoughts, and thus it is not surprising that his unhappiness and an analysis of the reasons for it should form some part of the theme of the *Prelude*, which Wordsworth was writing during the beginning of Coleridge's troubles.

In the *Prelude* there is already an inkling of the belief that Coleridge was destined to be unhappy by his own character as it had been developed in unfavorable circumstances, and this inkling of feeling becomes important later on, when on May 28, 1809, Wordsworth can write Daniel Stuart that "of the Friend and Coleridge, I hear nothing, and am sorry to say I hope nothing. It is I think too clear that Coleridge is not sufficiently master of his own efforts to execute anything which requires a regular course of application to one object. I fear so—indeed I am assured that it is so—to my great sorrow." He is far more emphatic in his terrible letter to Poole of May 30, 1809, where he writes: "I give it to you as my deliberate opinion, formed upon proofs which have been strengthening for years, that he neither will nor can execute any thing of important benefit either to himself his family or mankind. Neither his talents nor his genius mighty as they are nor his vast information will avail him anything; they are all frustrated by a derangement in his intellectual and moral constitu- tion—In fact he has no voluntary power of mind whatsoever, nor is he capable of acting under any *constraint* of duty or moral obligation" (letter 165). In subsequent letters he and his sister return to the theme of Coleridge's weakness, irresolution, and "utter want of power to govern his mind, either its wishes or its efforts" (June 15, 1809). His conviction, formed after "years" of brooding upon it, that Coleridge suffers from a "derangement in his intellectual and moral construction" comes out into the open in the quarrel with Coleridge in 1810, after Wordsworth has warned Montague not to take Coleridge into his house, but his conviction can already be seen glimmering under the surface of occasional passages in the *Prelude* of 1805.

Given Wordsworth's painful awareness of his friend's disabilities, he could not help wondering why the life of the friend whom he once called the most wonderful man he had known should have been sad and ineffectual, as it then seemed. Wordsworth's complex feelings of pity, affection, admiration, envy, and disappointment are visible in the poem to Coleridge, as he tries to analyze how a poet comes to be strong. Writing during Coleridge's absence, and distressed by his silence, Wordsworth sees Coleridge as a more pitiful figure than he might have had Coleridge been nearby. He also sees him as more of an emblem and tries to draw conclusions from his life and upbringing to discover the conditions necessary for creating someone with basic stability. One of these necessary conditions was, as we shall see, a grounding in the permanent things of nature.

The antagonism to words and fantasy seen in *Peter Bell* reappears in the *Prelude*, again with reference to strength, stability, resoluteness, and moral health; for the themes of the early poem continue to worry Wordsworth, and Wordsworth's fears for Coleridge have increased, as have his efforts to justify his own kind of growth, and his belief that the mind grows best "not with the mean and vulgar works of Man, / But with high objects, with enduring things" (1.435–36).

At the same time that the *Prelude* is a Miltonic epic on the fall from paradise and the return to it, a prelude to vision, possibly an act of therapy that purges the author of the memory of his mother who betrayed him by dying,[19] it is also one side of Wordsworth's dialogue with Coleridge. Coleridge is present in the poem as a sounding board and as an antagonist and adviser. As Dorothy records in her journals, Wordsworth calls the work in progress "The Poem to Coleridge." This fact, together with the many references in the text to Coleridge as the imaginary recipient of the finished poem, shows that the dedication of the poem to Coleridge was more than casual.

Many times in the *Prelude* Wordsworth's narrator remembers his audience, saying, "Thus far, O Friend, did I . . . ," "I spare to speak, my Friend, of what ensued . . . ," "But, O dear Friend!," and "Call back, O Friend, a moment to thy Mind. . . . " He claims that were it not for Coleridge's love and sympathy he would not have spun out this "tedious tale":

> Nor will it seem to thee, my Friend! so prompt
> In sympathy, that I have lengthen'd out,
> With fond and feeble tongue, a tedious tale.
>
> (1.645–47)

He need not be embarrassed if he fails in his aim:

> Yet should these hopes
> Be vain, and thus should neither I be taught
> To understand myself, nor thou to know
> With better knowledge how the heart was fram'd
> Of him thou lovest, need I dread from thee
> Harsh judgments. . . ."   (1.653–58)

Coleridge supports him by being his inspiration:

> and Thou, O honor'd Friend!
> Who in my thoughts are ever at my side,
> Uphold, as heretofore, my fainting steps.
>
> (3.199–201)

Wordsworth never forgets that Coleridge is there:

> Throughout this narrative,
> Else sooner ended, I have known full well
> For whom I thus record the birth and growth
> Of gentleness, simplicity, and truth.   (6.269–72)

If we recall these passages of direct address along with many others, we see that the shadowy listener begins to hover behind the lines, to some extent determining the subject and tone of the narration. With this shadowy figure in mind, we find that many passages previously thought to refer to Wordsworth's internal struggles refer at once or instead to discussions with

Coleridge. The poem can be seen as a vindication of Words-worth's development—a wistful, occasionally self-righteous explanation of how Coleridge's life would have prospered had he grown up in more favorable circumstances and an analysis of the causes for Wordsworth's success and Coleridge's failure.

Indeed the very subtitle of the poem assigned later on—"Growth of a Poet's Mind"—expresses the argumentative bent of the poem. The obvious but controversial statement within this subtitle is that the mind grows. The poem studies the way it grows, assuming that it is not whole from the start, that it is like a plant in absorbing elements from the surround-ing atmosphere and turning these elements, along with ele-ments from its own depths, into itself. At the heart of this statement is a claim that Coleridge would dispute: that the mind is not at first free of its environment, entering this alien world of things from a supernatural realm. Instead it grows to freedom if it has been strengthened by the permanent forms of nature at its earliest stages. If the influence of nature's perma-nence has molded the mind, the mind will then be strong enough in maturity to stand alone, needing occasional returns to nature only in moments of crisis, when nature restores the strength that it originally gave. Along these lines it is clear that anyone who claims to be free of nature usually falters emotionally, psychologically, and professionally. It may seem heartless, but it was his friend Coleridge who gave Words-worth an example for this theory. Coleridge sought in occult studies and metaphysics a philosophy to verify the freedom of the soul from its surroundings. But look at him now: he is sick, sad, broken, uncreative, and pitifully addicted to laudanum, and unable to find a woman to love him.

Coleridge's presence in the background of the *Prelude* brings to focus criticism that otherwise seems unfocused. When Wordsworth criticizes romances, words, fantasies, transforma-tions, distortions, and shifting urban forms, he associates these changing specters with magic, and occasionally with Coleridge himself, whom in turn he connects with insecurity and change. Wordsworth establishes a chain of circumstances that help to explain Coleridge's failures: as we shall see, the isolation of the city where men live side by side as "strangers" in their "labyrinths" (7.120), the poverty of real images and thence the excessive solace of books lead to an insubstantiality of language and from there to the instability of character. The life of words is an illusion, and environment has in part engendered the need for such a life. In Wordsworth's view Coleridge's life as well as his poetry betrays the spell that binds him.

Narrating his own Alpine wanderings in the *Prelude*, book 6, Wordsworth is reminded of Coleridge's Maltese exile; but Wordsworth wants to show that Coleridge's wandering arises from causes very different from his own. Coleridge had taken ship almost a year before the writing of this section to escape his failures—marriage, health, will, and *The Watchman*. His long absence and comparative silence in that dreary but exotic outpost worried his friends:

> Far art thou wander'd now in search of health,
> And milder breezes, melancholy lot!   (6.249–50)

Wordsworth tries to understand why Coleridge as a grown man should still be aimlessly wandering, while his own wanderings had ended with his youth. What explains this difference in their fates?

> I, too, have been a Wanderer; but alas!
> How different is the fate of different men
> Though Twins almost in genius and in mind,
> Unknown unto each other, yea, and breathing
> As if in different elements, we were framed
> To bend at last to the same discipline,
> Predestin'd, if two Beings ever were,
> To seek the same delights, and have one health,
> One happiness.   (6.261–69)

Although their "capacities" were "twin," they had breathed in different elements, and for that reason Coleridge has since failed "to bend to the same discipline" and failed also to be healthy and happy. Coleridge's unhealthy "element" since age nine was the city. Thus Wordsworth aims in the first five books to "record" for Coleridge's benefit how he himself grew in a favorable element, thereby illustrating the contrast between their two lives:

> Throughout this narrative,
> Else sooner ended, I have known full well
> For whom I thus record the birth and growth
> Of gentleness, simplicity, and truth,
> And joyous loves that hallow innocent days
> Of peace and self-command.   (6.269–74)

Wordsworth's element, nature, favored the development of inner peace and self-command—qualities that Coleridge notably lacked. Had Coleridge developed them, he would have been able to bend to the discipline that now drives Wordsworth on to write his ambitious poem.

Wordsworth thus establishes a fundamental difference between himself and Coleridge:

> Of Rivers, Fields,
> And Groves, I speak to Thee, my Friend; to Thee
> Who, yet a liveried School-Boy, in the depths
> Of the huge City, on the leaded Roof
> Of that wide Edifice, thy Home and School,
> Wast used to lie and gaze upon the clouds
> Moving in Heaven; or haply, tired of this,
> To shut thine eyes, and by internal light
> See trees, and meadows, and thy native Stream
> Far distant, thus beheld from year to year
> Of thy long exile.   (6.274–84)

Cut off from nature in the metropolis, imprisoned in school and in a constricting uniform, and too weak to take sustenance from the distant clouds, the liveried school boy escapes into his own mind. Shutting his eyes, he looks within where he hides his worn-out memories of nature, hoping that they will sustain him in his separation. In the absence of natural forms, Coleridge is forced within himself, and the inwardness of his vision later distinguishes him:

> I have thought
> Of Thee, thy learning, gorgeous eloquence,
> And all the strength and plumage of thy youth,
> Thy subtle speculations, toils abstruse
> Among the Schoolmen, and platonic forms
> Of wild ideal pageantry, shap'd out
> From things well-match'd, or ill, and words for things,
> The self-created sustenance of a mind
> Debarr'd from Nature's living images,
> Compell'd to be a life unto itself.   (6.305–14)

The profusion of Wordsworth's praise in the first four and a half lines suggests an undertone of regret, as if Coleridge's learning had come to nothing. Even before we discover that Coleridge's early splendor was only pageantry (a showy exhibition of ideas without substance), "youth" sets the note of elegy, and "plumage" suggests that his learning (and learning itself is suspect) is seasonal and external. "Gorgeous" adds an impression of something overdone and gaudy, particularly in proximity to "plumage," and when connected with "eloquence" (since Wordsworth thinks words vitiate and dissolve), the impression of display is hard to avoid. The learning and eloquence of the young Coleridge is a show, disconnected from essential truths. To these insinuations the adjectives "subtle" and "abstruse" add a sense of sinuous convolutions. When Coleridge then lumps "platonic forms" together out of unrelated things and confuses these things with words, he commits a central Wordsworthian sin. He tries to set up the mind as a power independent of nature. An exile from "the huge and mighty forms of nature" since the age of nine, Coleridge presumes to think that he can devise his own images in place of

natural ones. Wordsworth, however, knows that this cannot
be done: "debarr'd from Nature's living images," one has no
other vital sources of images. Separated from nature's living
images (other images being dead) the urban mind tries to be its
own source of life, and yet even for a great spirit, such
self-sustenance is difficult at best.

Wordsworth elaborates this contrast between strong outer
forms and sickly inner forms in book 8. Writing of the
adolescent who perversely distorts the truth, Wordsworth
shows how he himself had succeeded in escaping the lure of
this "wild ideal pageantry," because he was supported by "a
real solid world of images" rather than abandoned, like Coleridge, to sickly inward dreams:

> Yet in the midst
> Of these vagaries, with an eye so rich
> As mine was, through the chance, on me not wasted
> Of having been brought up in such a grand
> And lovely region, I had forms distinct
> To steady me; these thoughts did oft revolve
> About some centre palpable, which at once
> Incited them to motion, and control'd,
> And whatsoever shape the fit might take,
> And whencesoever it might come, I still
> At all times had a real solid world
> Of images about me; did not pine
> As one in cities bred might do; as Thou,
> Beloved Friend! hast told me that thou didst,
> Great Spirit as thou art, in endless dreams
> Of sickliness, disjoining, joining things
> Without the light of knowledge.   (8.594–610)

Wordsworth was lucky in his upbringing, and he made the
most of his luck: the forms that steadied him were "distinct,"
"palpable," "real," and "solid." They ordered and at the same
time energized his mind. Coleridge, however, was not so
lucky: bred in the city, without distinct and solid images to
steady him, he pines hopelessly for some center. In the half-

light he mistakes the counters of things for the things themselves.

Coleridge's interest in imaginary and insubstantial words and dreams was leading him far afield into his magical studies. Since his urban environment was an illusion, Coleridge was doomed to be separated from the ground of truth—the nature that "fed" Wordsworth's lofty speculation. No wonder Coleridge did not respect the solidity of real things, for in his formative years he had been surrounded by falsity.

But the illusory Babylon of London had no such debilitating effect on Wordsworth, because he visited there when he was old enough to withstand the mirage. The impressions of nature stayed with him and "diffused,"

> Through meagre lines and colours, and the press
> Of self-destroying, transitory things
> Composure and ennobling Harmony.   (7.738–40)

He was immune to London's triviality, because in his childhood he had spoken

> Not with the mean and vulgar works of Man,
> But with high objects, with enduring things,
> With life and nature.   (1.435–37)

An urban environment makes bad men, claims Wordsworth: "the increasing accumulation of men in cities" is one of several causes "now acting with a combined force to blunt the discriminating powers of the mind, and unfitting it for all voluntary exertion to reduce it to a state of almost savage torpor."[21] Indeed Coleridge's dreams of sickliness are examples of this urban torpor which affects even the highest minds. Only men bred in nature can keep the metropolis in perspective:

> Living amid the same perpetual flow
> Of trivial objects . . .
>
> .   .   .   .
>
> Oppression under which even highest minds
> Must labour, whence the strongest are not free;

> But though the picture weary out the eye,
> By nature an unmanageable sight,
> It is not wholly so to him who looks
> In steadiness, who hath among least things
> An under-sense of greatest; sees the parts
> As parts, but with a feeling of the whole.
>
> (7.701–2, 705–12)

The city is an accumulation of manmade, trivial, and basically sickly shapes, vanishing over the enduring foundations of the land. Only for the man steadied by the great things of nature is the city safe. As the sad example of Coleridge shows, a city upbringing has inescapable consequences, for the city conditions the mind to weakness and inwardness. Coleridge's misery is the inevitable result of having been bred among manmade forms, as Wordsworth's pleasure is the inevitable result of his childhood among the living images of nature.

Forcing the mind inward, the city leaves the child with substitute truths: reading, talking, and dreaming are the poor bones the urban mind gnaws on, disjoining, joining things without the light of knowledge. Though he exaggerates in his "The Tables Turned" and "Expostulation and Reply" when he exclaims, "Books / 'tis a dull and endless strife!" and remarks puckishly that books convey "the spirit breathed / From dead men to their kind,"[22] he nevertheless continues to have reservations: the works of Homer, Shakespeare, and Milton may be "Powers . . . only less . . . than Nature's self," (5.219–22), but the "speaking face of earth and heaven" is still the "prime Teacher" (5.12–13).

Wordsworth's reservations about the primacy of literature focus on books from "the hemisphere of magic fiction." For instance to read *The Arabian Nights* on the river Derwent defrauds one of the natural beauties that the fisherman should feel:

> For a whole day together, I have lain
> Down by thy side, O Derwent! murmuring Stream,
> On the hot stones and in the glaring sun,

> And there have read, devouring as I read,
> Defrauding the day's glory, desperate!
> Till, with a sudden bound of smart reproach,
> Such as an Idler deals with in his shame,
> I to the sport betook myself again.   (5.508–15)

Even more fraudulent are Ossian's fancies, which are spurious
because they show no vision of things, only an incantation of
barren words: "From my very childhood I have felt the falsehood that pervades the volumes imposed upon the World
under the name of Ossian. From what I saw with my own eyes,
I know that the imagery was spurious. In nature every thing is
distinct, yet nothing defined into absolute independent sin-
gleness. In Macpherson's work it is exactly the reverse; everything (that is not stolen) is in the manner defined, insulated,
dislocated, deadened—yet nothing distinct. It will always be
so when words are substituted for things." [23]

Because it distorts the observation of things, romance also
distorts the feelings of those who read it. When it teaches men
to ignore the real suffering of other men, it gives a false sense of
escape. At the sight of a dead man the adolescent Wordsworth,
dallying with *The Arabian Nights*, is unable to respond:

> for my inner eye had seen
> Such sights before, among the shining streams
> Of Fairy Land, the Forests of Romance.   (5.475–77)

When they are "uneasy" and "unsettled," men have "cravings
for the marvellous"; they read romances instead of strengthening their souls amid natural forms. Full of praise for
"dreamers, Forgers of lawless Tales," they fall into vicarious
satisfactions and instantaneous gratifications:

> We bless you then,
> Impostors, drivellers, dotards, as the ape
> Philosophy will call you: then we feel
> With what, and how great might ye are in league,
> Who make our wish our power, our thought a deed,
> An empire, a possession; Ye whom Time

And Seasons serve; all Faculties; to whom
Earth crouches, th' elements are potter's clay.

$$(5.548-55)$$

Books of romance substitute magical words for real things. In them wishes are accomplished; thoughts are automatically enacted; great countries are within grasp; time, change, and all the mighty elements are subservient to the merest mental whimsy. They give us a sense of our might, which is far better than the moralisms received from utilitarian tales; but in the long run they lead to illusion.

Literature trusts that the earth crouches before it, waiting to be transformed, that like clay the earth is passive until men give it form. Such a presumption is in Wordsworth's opinion a fearful distortion of reality. Instead of being inert, the earth is permanently true and living, while human structures move fleetingly across it. To reverse this evaluation is a sign of madness, since men impose their psychoses on immutable reality. When Wordsworth at thirteen believed momentarily in "words for their own sakes, a passion and a power" (5.590), he quickly changed his mind, and came to affirm the greater power of "things forever speaking." "Lifted above the ground by airy fancies," he touches base again to rediscover, like the poet of *Peter Bell*, "what on earth is doing."

The transformations that words work on things not only distort things and feelings, but are entirely unnecessary, for nature works her own magic, which human artifice cannot rival:

> A single Tree
> There was, no doubt yet standing there, an Ash
> With sinuous trunk, boughs exquisitely wreath'd;
> Up from the ground and almost to the top
> The trunk and master branches everywhere
> Were green with ivy; and the lightsome twigs
> And outer spray profusely tipp'd with seeds
> That hung in yellow tassels and festoons,
> Moving or still, a Favorite trimm'd out

By Winter for himself, as if in pride,
And with outlandish grace. Oft have I stood
Foot-bound, uplooking at this lovely Tree
Beneath a frosty moon. The hemisphere
Of magic fiction, verse of mine perhaps
May never tread; but scarcely Spenser's self
Could have more tranquil visions in his youth,
More bright appearances could scarcely see
Of human Forms with Superhuman Powers,
Than I beheld, standing on winter nights
Alone, beneath this fairy work of earth.   (6.90–109)

With only one metaphor of the ash as winter's mistress,
Wordsworth glories in the thingness of the tree: extravagant
fancies blind men to the loveliness of stark reality; fiction's
magical power disguises the truth with words, setting up
human imaginings and supernatural transformations in its
place.

A single real image outshines all imaginary paradises because the magical changes that words induce are superfluous:

Beauteous the domain
Where to the sense of beauty first my heart
Was open'd, tract more exquisitely fair
Than is that Paradise of ten thousand Trees,
Or Gehol's famous Gardens, in a Clime
Chosen from widest Empire, for delight
Of the Tartarian Dynasty composed;

.   .   .   .

Scene link'd to scene, an evergrowing change,
Soft, grand, or gay! with Palaces and Domes
Of Pleasure spangled over, shady Dells
For Eastern Monasteries, sunny Mounds
With Temples crested, Bridges, Gondolas,
Rocks, Dens, and Groves of foliage taught to melt
Into each other their obsequious hues
Going and gone again, in subtile chace
Too fine to be pursued; or standing forth
In no discordant opposition, strong

And gorgeous as the colours side by side
Bedded among rich plumes of Tropic Birds;
And mountains over all embracing all;
And all the landscape endlessly enrich'd
With waters running, falling, or asleep.

But lovelier far than this the Paradise
Where I was rear'd; in Nature's primitive gifts
Favor'd no less.   (7.119–25, 129–46)

These unearthly paradises, the pleasure domes and shady dells,
reminiscent of "Kubla Khan," are the products of dream, not
"things oracular." The quest for the strange and artificial is
once more seen as an escape from the abiding paradise here.
Like the Coleridgean eloquence of book 5 the gorgeousness of
Coleridgean paradises is suspicious: it is subtle, obsequious,
and replete with plumage. The images melt into one another,
"going and gone again" like the fabrications of magic, showing a dreamlike inconsequence.

Exotic stimuli lead us to seek ever more fanciful extremes.
The adolescent mind enraptured by romance is exhausted by
it, rather than renewed:

Yea, doubtless, at an age when but a glimpse
Of these resplendent Gardens, with their frame
Imperial, and elaborate ornaments,
Would to a child be transport over-great,
When but a half-hour's roam through such a place
Would leave behind a dance of images
That shall break in upon his sleep for weeks;
Even then the common haunts of the green earth,
With the ordinary human interests
Which they embosom, all without regard
As both may seem, are fastening on the heart
Insensibly.   (8.159–70)

Unlike manmade metaphor and fable, the common haunts of
the earth give us strength. Metaphor in general inflames the
adolescent mind, drawing it away from nature's own miracles.
Books are a Circean lure:

> There came among those shapes of human life
> A willfulness of fancy and conceit
> Which gave them new importance to the mind;
> And Nature and her objects beautified
> These fictions, as in some sort in their turn
> They burnish'd her. From touch of this new power
> Nothing was safe: the Elder-tree that grew
> Beside the well-known Charnel-house had then
> A dismal look; the Yew-tree had its Ghost,
> That took its station there for ornament:
> Then common death was none, common mishap,
> But matter for this humour everywhere,
> The tragic super-tragic, else left short.   (8.520–32)

The "touch of this new power," magical, metamorphic, distorting, may be compared to Coleridge's "Midas touch of life and joy," for imaginative language transforms the things when it renders them, willfully forcing natural things into the mind's categories by ornamenting and exaggerating what already suffices.

When Wordsworth attacks the extravagant adolescent style he is once again referring his corrections to Coleridge, here suggesting that Coleridge has failed to move out of the adolescent interest in "the touch of this new power." Wordsworth has outgrown this style, but Coleridge still affects it:

> Beside our Cottage hearth,
> Sitting with open door, a hundred times
> Upon this lustre have I gaz'd, that seemed
> To have some meaning which I could not find;
> And now it was a burnished shield, I fancied,
> Suspended over a Knight's Tomb, who lay
> Inglorious, buried in the dusky wood;
> An entrance now into some magic cave
> Or Palace for a Fairy of the rock.   (8.569–77)

Alluding in this passage to Coleridge's romance "Love," Wordsworth seems to be suggesting that any adult poet who still transforms a rock into a shield or magic cave must be an extravagant adolescent at heart, still enchanted with "words for their own sakes," still victimizing nature. If comparisons must be made, they should be to ordinary things, not to fantastic ones. In the 1815 preface Wordsworth comes to deal with this problem of the "conferring, the abstracting, and the modifying powers of the Imagination," in an analysis of his own "Resolution and Independence." In that poem, where the old leech-gatherer is compared to a stone and then to a sea-beast, "the stone," explains Wordsworth in retrospect, "is endowed with something of the power of life to approximate it to the Sea-beast; and the Sea-beast stripped of some of its vital qualities to assimilate it to the stone; which intermediate image is thus treated for the purpose of bringing the original image, that of the stone, to a nearer resemblance to the figure and condition of the aged Man; who is divested of so much of the indications of life and motion as to bring him to the point where the two objects unite and coalesce in just comparison."[24] He justifies his own comparisons here by showing that all three of these natural beings exist on the margins of animation and can be shown to shift back and forth imperceptibly between life and nonlife. Such subdued "operations of the mind upon those objects" remain faithful to the essential beings of the things themselves.[25]

Shakespeare and Spenser, whose imaginary visions and magical themes had enthralled other eighteenth-century writers, had in Wordsworth's view helped to defraud nature, great though they were. Their pastoral shepherds, for instance, were artificial, whereas Wordsworth's shepherds in *The Lyrical Ballads* and in *The Recluse* are true to life. Wordsworth asserts this faith in his own humble characters in spite of the mockery heaped upon them by Hazlitt and Coleridge, who claimed that no peasant ever spoke as Wordsworth's peasants did.[26] Because both Hazlitt and Coleridge criticize the unreality of his shepherds, Wordsworth argues that his shepherds are far more true than visions of resplendent imperial gardens or than the pastoral fancies of Theocritus, Shakespeare, or Spenser

(8.185–91). He seems to speak sharply to the critics who have charged him with giving to the shepherds an unrealistic nobility:

> Call ye these appearances
> Which I beheld of Shepherds in my youth,
> This sanctity of Nature given to Man
> A shadow, a delusion, ye who are fed
> By the dead letter, miss the spirit of things,
> Whose truth is not a motion or a shape
> Instinct with vital functions, but a Block
> Or waxen Image which yourselves have made,
> And ye adore.   (8.428–36)

His rage against critics of his "realism" is the rage of a righteous Moses, castigating the worshippers of the golden calf; to him they are idolators prostrate before a counterfeit reality. In their blindness they call the truly sanctified spirit of things a "shadow, a delusion."

Judging the solid things of nature to be shadows, they locate reality in language—in the dead letter. Ignoring the spirit of things, they concoct a derivative reality of words, and then bow down before it, worshipping a surrogate of their own making. But how could Hazlitt or Coleridge be expected to do otherwise, when both of them had been nurtured on surrogates, bred in a manmade city, and thrown back on fancies, romances, dreams, and the self-made delusions of words?

When he criticizes the "hemisphere of magic fiction," imaginary paradises, artificial pastorals, and the literary tradition, the dead letter, the waxen image which men have made and then solipsistically adore, Wordsworth continues his long argument with Coleridge about the relative powers of things and words. He is arguing with Coleridge about nature's truths and the mind's falsities, which turn in ever-narrowing circles of self-reference and ultimately lead to personal instability.

Some of the interests which Wordsworth worries will sap men's strength he satirizes in the portrait of the prodigy in book 5. Stunted in adolescent verbosity, incapable of moving to "a time of greater dignity," the prodigy is swamped with knowledge:

> His discourse moves slow,
> Massy and ponderous as a prison door,
> Tremendously emboss'd with terms of art;
> Rank growth of propositions overruns
> The Stripling's brain; the path in which he treads
> Is chok'd with grammars; cushion of Divine
> Was never such a type of thought profound
> As is the pillow where he rests his head.
> The Ensigns of the Empire which he holds,
> The globe and sceptre of his royalties
> Are telescopes, and crucibles, and maps.
> Ships he can guide across the pathless sea,
> And tell you all their cunning; he can read
> The inside of the earth, and spell the stars;
> He knows the policies of foreign Lands;
> Can string you names of districts, cities, towns,
> The whole world over, tight as beads of dew
> Upon a gossamer thread; he sifts, he weighs;
> Takes nothing upon trust. His Teachers stare,
> The Country People pray for God's good grace,
> And tremble at his deep experiments.
> All things are put to question; he must live
> Knowing that he grows wiser every day,
> Or else not live at all; and seeing, too,
> Each little drop of wisdom as it falls
> Into the dimpling cistern of his heart.   (5.320–45)

Eloquence, variety of learning (divinity, grammar, politics, astronomy, travel), the endless accumulation of knowledge, the admiring teachers, the display of traditionally inviolable secrets—these are all the attributes of the prematurely learned man, bred "among the deformities of crowded life" (8.464), nurtured on books, and cut off from a vision of the whole.

Wordsworth ends his portrait of the prodigy with a call back to earth reminiscent of the end of *Peter Bell:*

> Meanwhile old Grandame Earth is grieved to find
> The playthings, which her love designed for him,
> Unthought of; in their woodland beds the flowers
> Weep, and the river sides are all forlorn.   (5.346–49)

Here is the warning (with echoes of "Lycidas"), perhaps addressed to Coleridge, who has soared off in his magic boat in search of unearthly visions among the shades of things, and who can be seen far off skirting the rocks and reefs that shipwreck wandering mariners. Wordsworth warns him not to listen to the magic songs but to come down to earth, letting nature's images fasten insensibly on his heart.

Wordsworth stops his own thought from straying into magical excesses, thinking as he does so of Coleridge's errors in this direction. Wordsworth compares his own adolescent obsession with metaphor and words and magical romances with Coleridge's mature interests. In book 11 he comes to compare his own years in France with Coleridge's years as "a rigorous student." He is struck by his own momentary resemblance to Coleridge. Wordsworth as Man of Reason is very much like Coleridge in his subtle speculations: both are caught up in "toils abstruse," unsteadied by the permanence of nature. Both are "debarr'd from nature's living images."

When Wordsworth himself returned from France after two years of "Man's perverseness," he found himself "dead / To deeper hope" (11.23–25). His long sojourn in the realm of rationalism was like Odysseus's enforced sail. Odysseus smelled "the fragrance which did ever / Give notice of the Shore," and Wordsworth returns to rediscover "the breezes and soft airs that breathe / The breath of Paradise and find a way / To the recesses of the soul." The power that kept Odysseus out on the barren sea, unable to go to the harbours of "blessed sentiment and fearless love" was a magical power: "What avail'd, / When Spells forbade the Voyager to land" (11.48–49). As a magic power, it was an evil one, keeping the voyager (at once the legendary Odysseus and the real Wordsworth) apart from his true feelings and making these true feelings appear to be "perfidious." This magical power was reason. It "promised to abstract the hopes of man / Out of his feelings" (10.809–11).

Wordsworth begins his long description of the effects of the exclusively mental life on the totality of life. Again reason is a power that cuts men off from Paradise:

> Thus strangely did I war against myself;
> A Bigot to a new Idolatry
> Did like a Monk who hath forsworn the world
> Zealously labour to cut off my heart
> From all the sources of her former strength;
> And, as by simple waving of a wand
> The wizard instantaneously dissolves
> Palace or grove, even so did I unsoul
> As readily by syllogistic words
> Some charm of Logic, ever within reach,
> Those mysteries of passion which have made,
>
> .   .   .   .
>
> One brotherhood of all the human race.
>
> (11.74–84, 88)

Reason, divided from the whole self, creates unnatural strife. In its devotion to an otherworldly life of ideas, it is ascetic and life-denying. Sickly, in being cut off from the natural sources of strength, it is idolatrous, worshipping the waxen image it has made. Above all, this self-sufficient life of the mind is like a wizard, for whom the only realities are words. The wizard's words seem to have power to change reality by the very redefinitions of their own self-reflexive terms. Whatever the wizard does he does instantaneously, not gradually and steadily. He can never sustain his act because words can change though things are permanent; and the wizard's effect is always to unsoul, as the prodigy was without feelings, and as the elaborations of metaphor kept the common earth from fastening on the heart of the child who read romances. The "plumage" of Coleridge's youth (the "gorgeous eloquence" and "subtle speculation") was a wizard's "charm of Logic." His eloquence was a pageantry of ideas shaped out "from things well-match'd, or ill, and words for things." Those who believe in the self-created sustenance of the mind are in an eclipse where even the books with which they live lose their meanings. In this eclipse they forget that things defy words. They forget "the laws of *things* which lie / Beyond the reach of human *will* or *power*" (11.97–98). The willful fancy, the adulterate power (as he calls the activities of the mind elsewhere) are transient pretensions to the truth of nature. The wizard does not know that his words only *seem* to have insights into reality.

Wordsworth began his portrait of Coleridge with the idea of wandering. Here, with the figure of the Wanderer Odysseus escaping the magic falsity of Circe's island, he sees his own life turn away from all wandering. He abandons manmade dilemmas and returns to nature. Like Penelope nature has been faithfully waiting, and because he had been first molded by nature, Wordsworth is able to resume his fructifying life with her. But Coleridge is not so fortunate. He had been forced to leave for the city before the huge and mighty forms of nature had enacted their "severer ministrations" on him, giving him the stability to stand alone. Under the circumstances it is no wonder that Coleridge should be sick, indolent, and sad, his "ten thousand hopes / For ever wither'd." The forms that impressed his young mind were mean and vulgar; he was doomed from the start.

For Wordsworth words like ghosts and spirits are spectacles or pageants that the wizard makes appear by trickery and illusion. They do not correspond to a substance. When Wordsworth wants to speak of superficial change (as when he dressed himself to look like a Cambridge scholar), he says,

> Strange transformation for a mountain Youth,
> A northern villager. As if by word
> Of magic or some Fairy's power, at once
> Behold me rich in monies, and attir'd

> In splendid clothes, with hose of silk, and hair
> Glittering like rimy trees when frost is keen.
> (3.33–37)

Here a metamorphosis (like the literary metamorphoses of his fitful youth) is imposed by rules of human civilization which are extraneous to his own organic growth. Forced to partake of frivolous academic society and to defraud the time, he finds the interruption a sleight of magic, like the gorgeous plumage of his friend. Money and dress are glittering surfaces over the true Wordsworth (steadied by the early impressions of nature) who preserves himself below.

When Wordsworth writes in the same book of the "vague and loose indifference" of his days at Cambridge, he again attributes his changes to magic. He sees his separation from truth as the work of an outside power, not a choice he would have made from his own heart:

> Rotted as by a charm, my life became
> A floating island, an amphibious thing,
> Unsound, of spongy texture, yet withal,
> Not wanting a fair face of water-weeds
> And pleasant flowers.   (3.339–43)

Once more he is adrift, divided, sickly, superficial—merely a face, and that, weedy. Some insidious charm has bewitched him, loosed him from even an island's hidden connection to earth.

London, too, is just such a superficial interruption. In describing the spectacle or pageant—here again are the words with which Wordsworth describes the play of ideas—he says:

> As when a Traveller hath from open day
> With torches pass'd into some Vault of Earth,
> The Grotto of Antiparos, or the Den
> Of Yordas among Craven's mountain tracts;
> He looks and sees the cavern spread and grow;
> Widening itself on all sides, sees, or thinks

He sees, erelong, the roof above his head,
Which instantly unsettles and recedes
Substance and shadow, light and darkness, all
Commingled, making up a Canopy
Of Shapes and Forms and Tendencies to Shape
That shift and vanish, change and interchange
Like Spectres, ferment quiet and sublime. . . .
. . . .
              The senseless mass,
In its projections, wrinkles, cavities,
Through all its surface, with all colours streaming,
Like a magician's airy pageant, parts,
Unites, embodying everywhere some pressure,
Or image, recognis'd or new, some type
Or picture of the world.   (8.711–23, 731–37)

Here, then, in London is a magician's airy pageant, with its
elaborately shifting forms, shadows, and mists, and disembodied figures. They are merely pictures of the world, not
substantial realities.

Thus, for Wordsworth, evanescent spectacles, fancies,
elaborate metaphors, inventions, fables, dreams, trivial forms
that pass and dissolve, and words that flow out volubly from a
mind supercharged with thoughts can all be ascribed to a false
magic like Prospero's when he called up the colors and clouds
of his final pageant. Wordsworth rejects this; for magic trades
in appearances and artifice. It tries to change the facts by
devious sleights-of-hand; it tries to trick the eye with illusions
of the brain. Above all it tries to impose verbal categories on
the flux of the outer world.

Coleridge figures almost invariably in the context of
Wordsworth's criticisms of illusion, particularly if this illusion
is magical. In failing to distinguish between true and false,
Coleridge grafted the shapes of fancy upon the feelings of the
imagination. He is left joining and disjoining dreams, while
Wordsworth "speaks no dreams, but things oracular," that
circumfuse the inward and the outward in a flash. The image of

the wizard comes for Wordsworth as an important metaphor of man setting himself against wholeness, adrift in a mental world not ballasted by the perception of natural forms. The wizard is a wanderer; he employs the mind to fragment the fundamental totality; he separates words from the things to which they ultimately refer. The products of the wizard mind (words, dreams, books, and the city) are false. Wordsworth's farflung but carefully related attacks become a rebuke to Coleridge's whole system of thinking, and to Coleridge's life as a liveried London schoolboy, Cambridge scholar, endless conversationalist, and opium dreamer. Although Coleridge began with a great spirit, he had no forms on which to exercise it. He has been forced into a mental world of dreams, cut off from experience, to juggle the ideas of things without reference to the things themselves. Wordsworth acknowledges the great spirit thwarted by circumstance, but his disapproval extends to Coleridge's moral as well as his poetic sickliness.

When Wordsworth in the preface to *The Lyrical Ballads* avers that purifying language will purify the heart, he sets up a principle according to which he later connects Coleridge's lack of center in language to his lack of center in life. The disdain for Coleridge evident in the letter to Poole of May 30, 1809, quoted earlier in the chapter, culminates in the great quarrel of 1810, when Wordsworth advised Montague not to allow such an unstable man as Coleridge to stay at his London home.[27] Already in the first version of the *Prelude* these criticisms of his friend emerge. When marriage, health, and poetic power were collapsing for his friend, Wordsworth was anxious to discover why his own sorrows were not similarly destroying him.

Coleridge was the shadow figure against which Wordsworth could define himself, a kind of Conradian double, about whom Wordsworth could say: "There, but for the grace of God, go I." Twin spirits, their minds had been nurtured differently and their fates diverged accordingly. Because Coleridge's mind was molded by manmade forms and manmade fantasies, he was conditioned to think that men could impose their metamorphic powers at will. Thus deluded, Coleridge could not help his creative and moral decline.

When Wordsworth sees Coleridge enchanted by a book, endlessly pouring forth "voluble phrase" to substitute for one single vibrant natural thing, and fabricating metaphors and fanciful paradises, he is consistently elaborating a theory of reality which Coleridge does not share. Coleridge—the magus—offends against this reality by trying to transform it and by valuing the projections of the mind above it. He offends reason by turning his observations inward, then presuming to impose these inner structures on the outer reality—the reality of "living images," of "things forever speaking." Coleridge's stress on the power of the mind and its symbols to manipulate and weld into a living whole the disparate aspects of a previously fragmented universe—a "universe of little things"—is anathema to Wordsworth. Wordsworth believes the universe is a coherent whole.

It is not simply a matter of Wordsworth believing that Coleridge is wrong. But Coleridge's sorrow and weakness— his neglect of dull Sara Fricker, his laudanum, his debts, his inability to appear at his scheduled lectures, his wandering abroad, his long-winded monologues, his early "loss" of poetic genius—could be explained first by his childhood and urban shadows, then by his literary bewitchments in the "hemisphere of magic fiction."

Perhaps the opposition between Coleridge and Wordsworth on the subject of words, fables, and transformations can be summarized by looking closely at Wordsworth's vision of druids on Salisbury Plain (12.312–79) in the 1805 version. In recounting this vision, summoned abruptly on the flat and empty plain, Wordsworth speaks directly to Coleridge, contrasting his own ideas of the imagination with Coleridge's. The passage from lines 320 to 352 is one of the rare instances when Wordsworth not only lets the light of sense go out but also invents in the resulting darkness a scenario with no precedent in things remembered. Unlike the spots of time (the gibbet or the drowned man) this scene is not a memory unearthed from a trove of Wordsworth's personal past; it is outside of real time and space, drawn only from myths suggested by the ominous ruins of Stonehenge. The druidic rites practiced amid these inscrutable hulks can only be imagined; certainly Wordsworth has not seen them and thus must invent them. He does so here as he does almost nowhere else; for the Arab-Quixote of book 5 (often seen to parallel the druid) is after all a figure in someone else's dream, though Wordsworth claims it as his own in the 1850 version.

The plain is a "wide waste," no track breaking its vacancies, except the "bare white roads / Lengthening in solitude their dreary line" (ll. 315–17). Unguided by other specific visual images, the poet is "overcome" "by the solitude," falling inside himself in a reverie. He fills the blank plain with visions of the past:

> I had a reverie and saw the past,
> Saw multitudes of men, and here and there,
> A single Briton in his wolf-skin vest
> With shield and stone-axe, stride across the Wold;
> The voice of spears was heard, the rattling spear
> Shaken by arms of mighty bone, in strength
> Long moulder'd of barbaric majesty.   (12.320–26)

The next line is particularly striking in its deviation from Wordsworth's usual method: "I called upon the darkness; and it took," with the word *took* naturalized in the next line as taking shape. What does this cryptic line mean? It means, I think, that the calling took effect and produced the vision as summoned. His words of calling invented what he saw, contrary to his usual method whereby his words try faithfully to reproduce what he sees, however distant from the original event. When this line is taken together with the unusual word "lo!" (329), we are struck by the effect of conjuring. "Lo!," an exclamation denoting a sudden, miraculous appearance, often magically invoked, is a word much more to be expected in the poetry of Coleridge than of Wordsworth, for Wordsworth customarily disdains these "strange transformation[s]." Nevertheless, here, in response to the conjuration, a new scene materializes: "again, the desart visible by dismal flames! / It is a sacrificial Altar, fed / With living men" (12.329–32). As Prospero summoned with his charms the swiftly alternating scenes of mimes and banquets in his final flurried displays, so Wordsworth brings before us one imagined scene after another. The sacrificial victims scream in their wicker baskets, the bearded druids gesticulate to the stars; music filters in from everywhere. But like Prospero's final magic, this, too, is Wordsworth's farewell.

Immediately after these remarkable, powerfully drawn scenes, there is a pause. This pause, indicated by a paragraph break, is followed by a decisive dismissal of the entire vision preceding it. "This for the past, and things that may be view'd / Or fancied, in the obscurities of time" (12.354–55). So much for visions. The pause, then, is not one of satisfaction with the fierce descriptions, or a dramatic pause giving the narration air, but a skeptical pause that says in effect: You see, I can do it, but it should not be done, because it falsifies the permanent forms of nature. So much for the kind of imagination which claims to be above nature.

He goes on to elaborate his position, turning his argument directly to Coleridge. Saying "Nor is it, Friend, unknown to thee, at least / Thyself delighted, who for my delight / Has said, perusing some imperfect verse / Which in that lonesome journey was composed, / That also then I must have exercised / Upon the vulgar forms of present things / And actual world of our familiar days, / A higher power" (12.356–63), he recognizes that Coleridge had admired the visions from the lonesome Salisbury journey. But in praising Wordsworth for imposing on these vulgar things and familiar days—"vulgar" as in "dead," "inert," or "little" things—Coleridge had misinterpreted Wordsworth's general intention. As he did when he asked Wordsworth to write a long philosophical poem about the mind's power, Coleridge ascribed to Wordsworth his own view that poetry should transform nature, a view which Wordsworth eventually accepted in the preface of 1815. In the discussion following the druid scene, Wordsworth tries to convince his friend that he is deliberately doing something different from what Coleridge expects.

His friend may have praised these verses, but he did so for the wrong reasons. The vulgar forms of present things which Coleridge praises him for transforming are in reality the substantial things with which the true poet must deal by illuminating them with a glow, a gleam, or a flash. At the very time that Coleridge was praising his power to transform the waste, Wordsworth himself was realizing that poems should not ignore the things that are, but should intensify their thingness "by an ennobling interchange / Of action from within and from without" (12.376–77). He says tolerantly that Coleridge's misplaced appreciation must have come from his loyalty: "Call we this / But a persuasion taken up by Thee / In friendship."

Coleridge's praise of Wordsworth's druid visions is rebuked even more distinctly in the 1850 version. Coleridge apparently had claimed that in inventing the Druids Wordsworth was finally using his imagination. "Thou . . . hast said," writes Wordsworth,

> That then and there my mind had exercised
> Upon the vulgar forms of present things
>
> .   .   .   .
>
> [A] higher power.   (13.355–56, 358)

But Coleridge's praise was only half-knowledge:

> Call we this
> A partial judgment—and yet why? For *then*
> We were as strangers; and I may not speak
> Thus wrongfully of verse, however rude,

> Which on thy young imagination, trained
> In the great City, broke like light from far.
>   (13.360–65)

In awkward and obscure syntax Wordsworth seems to be
saying that when Coleridge praised this work he did not know
better, because he was starved by long residence away from the
"base . . . whence our dignity originates" (1805: 12.373–
74). If his druid visions helped Coleridge, then he would not
want to criticize them, as partial as they are, even though at
that very time he was discovering

> That in life's every-day appearances
> I seemed about this time to gain clear sight
> Of a new world.   (1850: 13.369–71)

These everyday appearances were the new world that did not
need to be tricked out or defrauded by being transformed into
something else. They did not need Coleridge's "magical power
of the imagination" to give them supernatural glamor.

  Wordsworth and Coleridge did not agree, then, about the
definition of the imagination. Wordsworth first sets up a
situation that satisfies Coleridge's notion of the word, where it
signifies a free invention of absent scenes on a blank canvas; but
then no sooner has Wordsworth given us this Coleridgean
situation than he rejects it. In following Coleridge's demands
for a sea change, a transformation of the bare, meager, and even
vulgar facts of existence into something rich and strange, he
has, in his own view, falsified the truth of nature. This
onesided dialogue at the end of book 12 sets their disagreement into dramatic form. It shows how immediately and
consistently the two friends carried on their arguments—one
for the poetry of absent things, the other for the poetry of
present things, one seeing the imagination as a "higher
power," a power apart from and supernaturally above nature,
the other seeing it as "a power like one of Nature's," "proceeding from the depth of untaught things," a power which is the
"best power / Both of the object seen, and eye that sees"

(1805: 12.378–79). For Coleridge that blank dreary space is a vacancy that needs to be filled; for Wordsworth the "visible forms" "of Nature have a passion in themselves" where he "is enabled to perceive / Something unseen before."

Coleridge's own criticisms of Wordsworth follow the same alignments, opposing words to things. In Wordsworth's work Coleridge sees a certain monotony, a refusal to go beyond observed phenomena to a larger significance. His eagerness for Wordsworth to go ahead with a long philosophical poem reflects his distress that Wordsworth clung to a mass of little things instead of creating a poem from the mind. Coleridge worries that Wordsworth is bound to particulars, whereas Wordsworth worries that Coleridge is wandering aimlessly among the shadowy words which veil particulars. Shelley's criticisms of Wordsworth will later follow the lines that Coleridge set down.

Both Coleridge and Shelley, favoring a visionary rhyme, see Wordsworth ringed around with objects. The peripheries of the thing demarcate the limits of his poems; they set a boundary on what Wordsworth dares to say. As if drawing from life, Wordsworth's eye is constantly on the object, constricted within the limits of the immediately visible as it is recollected in tranquillity. Wordsworth does enter the vanishing point, but only after he has stared long and hard at a thing and has seen it blur into the middle distance. Left alone with a mind unpunctuated by sights, he frequently panics. Wordsworth's ability occasionally to pass into the invisible world "where the light of sense goes out" depends on his having first been grounded solidly in sensuous nature, which originally gave him strength to abandon sense. His early awareness of natural things made him endure but always distrust the invasions of invisible powers.

However loyal to eighteenth-century associationism and to an outside measure for reality Wordsworth may seem to be, it is essential to remember that he believes he is in revolt against eighteenth-century artifice. He believes that he is returning poetry to a contemplation of stark truth, and this belief has for him aesthetic and also moral aspects, with the moral ones shading into religious questions at one end and at the other into a self-righteousness that allows him to watch his friend's misfortunes, as if to say sadly: "I told you so." But at its best Wordsworth's belief gives foundation for his own masterful lyrics and also for the clarity of early twentieth-century verse, and it provides a careful statement of an enduring position: the mind's transformations not only diffuse the intensity of the single sacred thing but they distort it, and aim ultimately to render it, rather than themselves, superfluous. Devious and illusory, magical words are the work of Circe, substituting the transformations of the mind for a proper humility to the truth of nature.

Wordsworth's opposition to Coleridgean magic modifies a tradition beginning with Chaucer and culminating with Milton. He modifies Milton's view in a way that is significant for modern poetry. Wordsworth's view is as negative as Milton's but for different reasons. Milton sees Comus's magic as fleshly, sensual, and spirit-subverting. Wordsworth, however, sees magic as antiphysical, as an intellectual distortion through metaphor and fable of the true nature of things. Both see magic ultimately destroying virtue. Milton believes that magic lures men to revel in things as they are, forgetful of the virtue that comes from the contemplation of ideal platonic chastity. Wordsworth believes that the magic in words divorces men from the stability originally given to them by visible sensible things, a stability which is the source of virtue because it is the source of strength. Both believe magic undermines virtue, but Milton sees magic leading men away from ideas into things, while Wordsworth sees magic leading men away from things into ideas. Both use magic as an emblem of all that is impermanent, transitory, and unreal, but differ in their views of where permanent forms exist, Milton locating them in God and in the mind, Wordsworth locating them in nature and then in those minds nourished by nature's mighty forms.

Milton's magic is physical; Wordsworth's is mental; Milton's lies in nature; and Wordsworth's exists out of nature.

Wordsworth's view of magic is akin to Thomson's, in that both see magic as a dream loosening the dreamer's hold on reality, leaving him wan and impotent, distracted by fantasies. Wordsworth's view reveals yet other similarities with the views of Spenser and Pope, whose Archemago and Magus respectively deceive ordinary men with glittering jargon, becoming in both cases images of false literature.

6 • *Shelley's Political Enchantments*

Despite Wordsworth's carefully modified warnings, poets of
the second generation of English romantics were bewitched by
Coleridge's poems, lectures, and *Biographia*. They read his
work avidly and saw him as a hooded eagle among owls, as
Shelley would later describe him. Thomas Carlyle's description
of the influence on young men of the aged Coleridge bears out
Wordsworth's fears. To Carlyle Coleridge appeared "as a kind
of *Magus*, girt in mystery and enigma; his Dodona oak-grove
[Mr. Gillman's house at Highgate] whispering strange things,
uncertain whether oracles or jargon." Carlyle was deeply suspicious of this poet swathed in language, and he believed that
"the moaning singsong of that theosophical-metaphysical
monotony had a charm much more than literary, a charm
almost religious and prophetic" and that Coleridge "had,
especially among young inquiring men, a higher than literary,
a kind of prophetic or magician quality." [1] Like the young Pico
della Mirandola to whom Lamb had compared Coleridge in his
essay "Christ's Hospital Five and Thirty Years Ago," the old
Coleridge of Carlyle's portrait mesmerizes his audience by
pouring forth words that have a mysterious power regardless of
whether or not they correspond to sensible realities.

Inspired by Coleridge's influence and guided by his own
early proclivities, Shelley worked from his earliest juvenile
poems to his late "Witch of Atlas" to devise a theory of
language, a language that would help to precipitate the golden
age. Throughout his poems—most pervasively in *The Revolt of
Islam* and *Prometheus Unbound*—and in *A Defence of Poetry*
Shelley calls attention to what he hopes will be the magical
power of his language by repeating the words *charm*, *incantation*, *spell*, *enchantment*, *words*, and *songs* and by showing that
political and cosmic change occurs through their agency. If the

poet is to be the legislator of the world, it must be through the rhythms, the syntax, and the drive of his words that his laws of love are enacted. But how in fact could the corrupt world be revolutionized by poetry?

Shelley's early speculations on this matter were naively sensational. He began reading magicians, occultists, and Neoplatonists as a child raiding his grandfather's library; he read Agrippa, Albertus Magnus, and Paracelsus; and he practiced conjuring "Cornelius" from a hole in the garden. He intoned "incantations for raising ghosts and devils" before going to Eton; at Eton he was discovered drinking from skulls and conjuring over fires with a spell that began, "Demons of the air and of the fire. . . . " His tutor, Dr. Lind, helped him in occult as well as scholarly studies and taught him ritual curses.[2] When Shelley fell under the rival influence of William Godwin in 1812, he wrote to Godwin that he thought he was cured of his "passion for the wildest, most extravagant romances" and that he had lost interest in the "ancient books of Chemistry and Magic [which he had] perused with an enthusiasm of wonder, almost amounting to belief."[3] In thus announcing himself cured to Godwin, he seems to have felt that his early extravagances were incompatible with politics, though this feeling may not have lasted long. Ross Woodman argues that Shelley returned to his magical studies as early as 1813 when he joined an occult group headed by John Frank Newton.[4] Perhaps in that year he discovered that politics and occultism were related.

Shelley's juvenile poems reflect this sensational approach to supernatural appearances, though the references are scattered and unsystematic. Borrowing from gothic novels and from the poems of Gray, Collins, and Coleridge, he fills his poems with spells that are intended to penetrate the fertile womb of nature with their maddening rhymes, fatal words, and secret powers. In order to utter his incantations, the youthful poet of "The Wandering Jew" (1810) must surround himself with "reliques of magicians dead." He hears the earth answer his spell with

her "soul-appalling verse," and he trusts that he can compel
the giant witches in the earth's center because he knows "the
magic spell / To summon e'en the Prince of Hell."⁵ Shelley's
hero Ginotti in *St. Irvyne; or The Rosicrucian* dies by the
influence of a murderous natural magic. Similarly inexplicable
causes govern the action of *Queen Mab* and *The Daemon of the
World*, which are both filled with the trappings of magic: the
major figures fly in "magic cars," wave their wands in mul-
tiples of three, and intone their spells in a "Hall of Spells,"
calling on the elements to awake, and urging the souls of the
virtuous to rise up.

But as early as *Alastor* (1815) Shelley seems to have begun to
use this sensational imagery to speak about the mind and its
possible effect on the outside world. In *Alastor* the solipsistic
hero seeks knowledge in charnel houses and in voyages to the
near east; calling himself "an inspired and desperate al-
chymist," he tries to make "such magic as compels the
charmèd night / To render up thy charge." Nearly crazed by
his quest for strange truths, he prays for Medea's alchemy to
renew him; he prays

> O, that the dream
> Of dark magician in his visioned cave,
> Raking the cinders of a crucible
> For life and power, even when his feeble hand
> Shakes in its last decay, were the true law
> Of this so lovely world!   (ll. 681–86)

If the magician can continue to dream a perfect world in the
cave of his mind despite his physical mutability, perhaps the
poet can do the same. Such a hope becomes the "true law" of
The Revolt of Islam and *Prometheus Unbound*, and this early dark
magician foreshadows the later brighter Witch of Atlas dreaming a new world in the cave of the mind. The morbidity and
self-absorption which destroy him are denounced at the end of
a later poem, "The Hymn to Intellectual Beauty," where the
poet allows himself to be filled from without by the spirit of
beauty. Her "spells did bind" him to love all human kind. The

poet who had previously "called on poisonous names" submits himself to these benevolent spells and escapes the prison of his solipsism.

At the end of the preface to *Alastor* Shelley criticizes the hero of his poem by saying: "Those who love not their fellow-beings live unfruitful lives, and prepare for their old age a miserable grave"; almost two years later he concludes his preface to *The Revolt of Islam* with the pronouncement that "love is celebrated everywhere as the sole law which should govern the moral world."[7] How is this new law to be communicated to a world roiling in despair and injustice as Shelley sees it? Introducing this ambitious poem, Shelley sets himself the highest aims and says: "I have sought to enlist the harmony of metrical language, the ethereal combinations of the fancy, the rapid and subtle transitions of human passion, all those elements which essentially compose a Poem, in the cause of a liberal and comprehensive morality." He wishes to kindle "within the bosoms of my readers a virtuous enthusiasm for those doctrines of liberty and justice"; he would "awaken the feelings" to the "love of mankind." He hopes to show in this poem that he possesses "that most essential attribute of Poetry, the power of awakening in others sensations like those which animate my own bosom." His poem, then, will arouse feelings of love and benevolence, kindling them directly through language and rhythms rather than arguing them as ideas; his poem will work; and significantly the hero of the poem, the hero who inspires the revolt, is himself a poet whose songs kindle and arouse the entire population.

How can the language of poetry work quickly to cause this change? In the years leading up to the writing of *The Revolt of Islam* Shelley had enriched his adolescent enthusiasm for "maddening rhymes" with extensive reading in the tradition that Coleridge had cultivated in his poetry and lectures, and this reading, beginning with Plato's *Symposium*, was corroborated in Shelley's studies of science.

In the *Symposium*, which Shelley studied with Dr. Lind,

Diotima speaks beautifully of the power of Love: "Through Love subsist all divination and the science of sacred things as it relates to sacrifices and expiations, and disenchantments and prophesy, and magic." Neville Rogers argues that Diotima's speech as a whole encouraged Shelley's belief in demons as beings halfway between natural and supernatural;[8] in addition it may have encouraged his hope that songs, properly empassioned, can work on the universal vibrations of the spirits. The notion that love is the radiating energy in the universe is also described by Plotinus. Plotinus speaks of the universe as "one universally comprehensive living being, encircling all the living beings within it and having a soul, one soul, which extends to all its members in the degree of participant membership held by each." At the center of this pulsing universe sits Plotinus's magician, the man who is most sensitive to these vital interactions and knows how to shift the patterns of energy. "The wise magician is the one who assimilates himself to the universe and practices his work in accordance with his capacity, for he makes use of love in one place and makes use of mastery in another." Plotinus's magician senses the sympathies and works them to his will, either by singing songs that transform the sympathies or by sending out passionate feelings of love. Love, a principle of accord, is in Plotinus's words, "the first wizard and enchanter."[9] The Florentine Neoplatonist Marsilio Ficino adapts Diotima's speech to his own Plotinian belief that love is throbbing through the universe and is directed by the magician singing his incantations. In Ficino's translation Diotima asks: "Why is Love called a Magus? Because all the force of Magic consists in Love. The work of Magic is a certain drawing of one thing to another similitude. . . . From this community of a relationship is born the common drawing-together; and this is the true Magic." Magic consists of all the binding passions in the living universe. Giordano Bruno also believed that love was magical, as Frances Yates explains: "In marrying higher things with lower, the magus enters into an erotic relation to nature which is fundamental for sympathetic magic. [He] enters with loving sympathy into the sympathies which bind earth to heaven, and the emotional relationship is one of the chief sources of his powers." [10] Pico della Mirandola describes in more erotic terms how the magus discovers the secret harmonies in nature and works on them; his magic "draws forth into public notice the miracles which lie hidden in the recesses of the world, in the womb of nature, in the storehouses and secret vaults of God, as though she herself were their artificer. As the farmer weds his elms to the vines, so the 'magus' unites earth to heaven." [11]

From such a notion of a magnetic power drawing together the impulses in the universe and radiating outward along them into the individual minds, political states, and cosmic forces comes a subtle concept of revolution. The platonic and neoplatonic theories of love do not contradict Shelley's hope for political change but in fact reinforce it. Critics of Shelley who struggle between a view of Shelley as an eighteenth-century empiricist politician and a view of Shelley as a Platonist might reconcile their views by seeing that actual political change is the phenomenal form of the platonic or neoplatonic change occuring in the noumenal world. The outer world and the inner world respond simultaneously to the radiating energies of the magus or singer. Indeed it is not alien to the tradition to envision political reform as its end; Giordano Bruno himself, as Yates has shown, hoped that his magical signs and images could introduce into the chaotic situation of sixteenth-century Europe a hermetic peaceful Egyptian system; for this purpose he sang orphic songs and actively supported the candidacy of Navarre. [12] Shelley's political involvement is similarly extended over the whole area of the universe and the spirit; because of the hidden sympathy of thing to thing and of word to the thing it names Shelley is encouraged to hope that internal impulses of thought will immediately cause external changes.

Such a congruence of practical politics and neoplatonic philosophy has been observed. In the wake of Yeats's pioneering "The Philosophy of Shelley's Poetry," where Yeats noticed that Shelley's "early romances and much throughout his poetry show how strong a fascination the traditions of magic and of the magical philosophy had cast over his mind," Carl Grabo described the syncretism of Shelley's thought, suggesting that Shelley combined scientific and neoplatonic theory, and blended his radicalism with "Platonism, occultism, and science." In a similar vein James Rieger suggested that "Shelley derived many of his major symbols from the magic, hagiology, and obscene creation myths of the Gnostic and dualist Christian heresies." Ross Woodman, too, intended his *Apocalyptic Vision in the Poetry of Shelley* to examine "the growth of Shelley's mind as it wrestled with the somewhat conflicting approaches to truth offered by the rationalist and occult traditions, both of which absorbed his life-long attention."[13]

Not only politics and Neoplatonism reinforce each other in Shelley's thought. Both find further corroboration in contemporary science. Here again Shelley's neoplatonic studies are not refuted by reference to concrete realities but instead are shown to have material and even practical applications. The contemporary study of electricity, gravitation, animal magnetism, and other invisible forces lent credence to the platonic, neoplatonic, and magical assumption that the world is pulsing with secret sympathies and correspondences that could be acted upon by human energies compressed into words and songs. As the occult sciences had been in the Renaissance the imaginative precursors of real sciences, so too the intuitions of a magical energy acting within and without were reinforced by the inductive proofs of Newton, Franklin, and Mesmer. If the universe was full of mysterious life in the eyes of scientists as well as of occult philosophers, a transformation of the political world might be forthcoming. On this possibility as intimated by real and occult sciences, Shelley based his hopes for the effectiveness of his revolutionary poems.

Whether or not Shelley was influenced by Coleridge in his recognition of spiritual analogies to chemical change we cannot prove. But Coleridge's interest in analogical readings of science—in attraction and repulsion, in magnetism, and electricity as images of love—was similar to Shelley's in holding out hope for a discovery of underlying powers susceptible to voice. In *Inquiring Spirit*, for example, Coleridge speculates on the continuity of magic, magnetism, electricity, chemistry, and love, as the boundaries between these otherwise discrete phenomena are seen to roll apart. Coleridge also connects his lifelong study of chemistry with the transformations of music, fragrance, air, and water,[14] seeming in these connections to recall the songs of *Comus* or the airy voices of *A Midsummer Night's Dream*. Sounds affect spirit because both are made of moving air, as D. P. Walker suggests of neoplatonic solarian music,[15] and Coleridge and Shelley both seemed to hope that science would find the underlying principles of these as yet still imaginary connections.

For Shelley it is in the rhythmical words of the poets that the internal and external energies converge, energies that are by turns psychological, political, scientific, and spiritual. Love as an outward moving force is embodied in meters and metaphors; for without a powerful language these impulses of benevolence and unity would have no medium. It is on waves of sound that the new law travels. When read through the eyes of science, these impulses of radiant love could be conceived as a spiritual form of electricity or of light; there is thus both emotional and rational validity to a poetry based on these assumptions.

When Shelley expressed a hope in an 1811 letter for "the eventual omnipotence of mind over matter," he used the term that Freud would later adapt to describe the distortions of the magical outlook. But Shelley thinks of this omnipotence of mind as the achievement all at once on several levels of the golden age, "when present potence will become omnipotence."[16] Such a golden age, when latent energies are activated and oppressive laws are suspended, Shelley described in his 1812–1814 "Essay on Life." Here Shelley repudiates the superficial materialism of his youth, the "shocking absurdities of the popular philosophy of mind and matter, its fatal consequence in morals, and their violent dogmatism concerning the sources of all things"; and he turns to what he calls an "intellectual philosophy." He hopes, as did Coleridge, that at the miraculous center of each man "there is a spirit within him at enmity with nothingness and dissolution," and he subscribes provisionally to Berkeley's view that "nothing exists but as it is perceived." Shelley finds support for his belief in the identity of thoughts and objects from the example of the child's vision. As children, he writes, "we less habitually distinguished all that we saw and felt, from ourselves. They seemed as it were to constitute one mass. There are some persons who, in this respect, are always children. Those who are subject to the state called reverie, feel as if their nature were dissolved into the surrounding universe, or as if the surrounding universe were absorbed into their being. They are conscious of no distinction. And these are states which precede, or accompany, or follow an unusually intense and vivid apprehension of life." Such an intense perception of oneness within and without decays after childhood but survives in the intellectual philosophy. In this philosophy "the difference is merely nominal between those two classes of thought, which are vulgarly distinguished by the names of ideas or of external objects. Pursuing the same thread of reasoning, the existence of distinct individual minds, similar to that which is employed in questioning its own nature, is likewise found to be a delusion. The words *I*, *you*, *they*, are not signs of any actual difference subsisting between the assemblage of thoughts thus indicated but are merely marks employed to denote the different modifications of the one mind."[17] This omnipotence of mind, envisioning the oneness of things and thoughts, becomes increasingly important in Shelley's major poems. The end of the *Revolt* and the end of *Prometheus* are both gathered up into this original unfallen child's view of the universe as one, of the interpenetration of things and thoughts, of the intermingling of mind and the objects it perceives, without the hindrance of separate bodies. In these poems Shelley reproduces the life of words, of objects, thoughts, and feelings, dissolving and absorbing one into the other, as if there were no slips between the representing utterance and the idea beyond it. The phrase "everything is flux" merges with "all is one." Thus child psychology, physical science, platonic philosophy, occult and magical lore, and poetic intuition together provide images for this living, changing and interchangeable universe.

With such congruence in mind sudden change is made possible by changing the words and thus the categories in which men think, and words can be changed by those most skilled in their use—those poets who can weave words together in irresistibly arousing sounds, songs, and rhythms that will alter the listener even when he thinks he is not conscious of changes within him.

The outlines of Shelley's great theory of music and language to be presented in *Prometheus Unbound* are contained in the much-neglected and narratively tedious *Revolt of Islam*, written in 1817, a year before the composition of *Prometheus*. Although the *Revolt* is often clumsy, its stanzas and syntax are sometimes dazzling, and it serves for Shelley as a parade ground for his later strategies. Here, for instance, are the motifs of the poet-hero summoning the masses with his songs, joining his feminine double for the enrichment of spirit and body, travelling to the center of wisdom, hiding in the cave of the mind, and there achieving illumination. Here is the theory of magical words and vibrations already apparent in *Queen Mab*. In the first five cantos of the *Revolt* Shelley assumes that songs can enchant a people and transform the political system, that political, material, and cosmic reality is instantaneously susceptible to language. The hero, Laon, Shelley's ideal combination of poet and politician, learns magical lore from an old hermit, reads "scrolls of mortal mystery," and plans through the power of his exhortations to "waken the multitude." He hopes to find words that will make his thoughts illumine the darkened world. Vibrations of sound, pulses of light, and charges of feeling, work their intricate way through the hearts of individuals, through the classes of men, and finally to society at large. Laon speaks of the radiant powers of his arcane songs, which he hopes will smite the tranced crowd:

> These hopes found words through which my spirits sought
>   To weave a bondage of such sympathy
> As might create some response to the thought
>   Which ruled me now—and as the vapours lie
>   Bright in the outspread morning's radiancy,
> So were these thoughts invested with the light
>   Of language: and all bosoms made reply
> On which its lustre streamed, whene'er it might
> Through darkness wide and deep those trancèd spirits smite.
>
>   (ll. 802–10)

As in the language of theology, the word is light, flashing its intelligence on the mind; the word is radiant, enlightening substance; it weaves together its syllables and rhythms into a fabric. The woven fabric binds, as do the woven words.

The radiant visionary leader must embody his hopes in words in order to move others to follow him. Thoughts are invested in the light of language. Laon studies the literature of the past to learn the most radiant words:

> With deathless minds which leave where they have passed
>   A path of light, my soul communion knew;
> Till from that glorious intercourse, at last,
>   As from a mine of magic store, I drew
>   Words which were weapons;—round my heart there grew
> The adamantine armour of their power.   (ll. 838–43)

The word-hoard is a mine of magic store, heaped with potent weapons. When Laon's knowledge of words is allied with Cythna's singing of the songs he has composed, together they begin to sway the people. The listeners' senses swim; they feel love for one another; the words evoke communal "gaspings." Cythna, like a secret bird, fills the sky with a wild melody:

Hymns which my soul had woven to Freedom, strong
   The source of passion, whence they rose, to be;
Triumphant strains, which, like a spirit's tongue,
To the enchanted waves that child of glory sung.

                                                    (ll. 915–18)

She is enraptured "on the wing / Of visions that were mine"
(ll. 926–27), says Laon:

For, before Cythna loved it, had my song
   Peopled with thoughts the boundless universe,
A mighty congregation.   (ll. 928–30)

Their visionary thoughts are endowed "with music and with
light," flowing like fountains, so that all "Hearts beat as mine
now beats, with such intent / As renovate the world, a will
omnipotent." Cythna has faith in the power of their combined
magic:

There with the music of thine own sweet spells
Will disenchant the captives, and will pour
   For the despairing, from the crystal wells
Of thy deep spirit, reason's mighty lore,
And power shall then abound, and hope arise once more.

                                                    (ll. 1040–44)

The disenchanting music is again liquid, as it was previously
luminous. It is also shining metal armor, as for Cythna

                     truth its radiant stamp
Has fixed, as an invulnerable charm
Upon her children's brow, dark Falsehood to disarm.

                                                    (ll. 1060–62)

"As the charmèd bird that haunts the serpent's den" (l. 1080),
they believe that Laon's "command / Shall then dissolve the
world's unquiet trance" (ll. 1067–68).

   Even when they are captured and tortured, they are rescued
by the old hermit who shares with them his "enchantments"
and his knowledge of secret lore. He says,

Out of the hopes of thine aspirings bold,
Have I collected language to unfold

> Truth to my countrymen; from shore to shore
>   Doctrines of human power my words have told,
>   They have been heard, and men aspire to more
> Than they have ever gained or ever lost of yore.
>
>   (ll. 1516–21)

The world, through these potent words, is under "the sway / Of thy strong genius, Laon . . . , [which] compels all spirits to obey" (ll. 1545–47). Cythna, too, commands a train of wild-eyed women "who, even like a thunder-gust / Caught by some forest, bend beneath the spell / Of that young maiden's speech, and to their chiefs rebel" (ll. 1591–93). "Great is the strength of words" (ll. 1569–70), Laon believes; and Cythna's voice, "whose awful sweetness doth repress / All evil" (ll. 1609–10), turns her foes around by words. "Words of human love" (l. 1646) cast a trance on men. "Uplift thy charmèd Voice!" (l. 1659), cries Laon to her. In the ensuing battle words and shouts magnetize armies; the flood of eloquence is as vital as the flood of blood (ll. 1795–96). Words take such effect that this first hopeful phase is climaxed by a joyful rite to celebrate the equality of all men.

Reality breaks in at the beginning of canto 6. Against the ruthlessness of unenlightened power there is no recourse, except in occasional escapes into solitude. These moments are described as enchanted, too, for in them the hero and heroine are magically healed of their misery. They hide in a spot near "the murmur of the motion / Of waters," "haunted / By the choicest winds of Heaven, which are enchanted / To music, by the wand of Solitude, / That wizard wild" (ll. 2535–39). In their lonely silence they hear the song of the wind, "a wondrous light, the sound as of a Spirit's tongue." Aside from these enchanted retreats attuned to universal vibrations, reality in these central cantos is chaotic and horrible.

How, Shelley asks, does the visionary poet maintain his power in the face of the world's real cruelty? Inevitably he or she is forced to turn inward accumulating lore and ever subtler, more powerful, language. Thus in canto 7 Cythna, now Laone or Laon's female aspect, enters the cave of the mind. There she recounts:

> "My mind became the book through which I grew
>   Wise in all human wisdom, and its cave,
> Which like a mine I rifled through and through,
>   To me the keeping of its secrets gave—
>   One mind, the type of all, the moveless wave
> Whose calm reflects all moving things that are,
>   Necessity, and love, and life, the grave,
> And sympathy, fountains of hope and fear;
> Justice, and truth, and time, and the world's natural sphere.
>
> "And on the sand would I make signs to range
>   These woofs, as they were woven, of my thought;
> Clear, elemental shapes, whose smallest change
>   A subtler language within language wrought:
>   The key of truths which once were dimly taught
> In old Crotona."   (ll. 3100–14)

Having seen the signatures of all things drawn in the sand, she flees on the winds of Laon's songs. Lecturing the mariners on the falseness of what they had been taught, she claims that "with strong speech I tore the veil that hid / Nature, and Truth, and Liberty, and Love" (ll. 3523–24). Nevertheless "Madness, and Fear, and Plague, and Famine still / Heaped corpse on corpse" (ll. 4181–82). With the possible exception of the wilderness of America, no freedom now remains but in death. The two visionaries inscrutably die and are carried to the Temple of the Spirit, where thoughts, words, songs, and actions finally become congruent; sound, knowledge, light, and water flow as one in the omnipotent world of the mind.

In the first half of *The Revolt* there is hope that the combined powers of Laon and Cythna, the powers of invention and the powers of execution in the making of enchanting words, can transform the hearts of the multitude, particularly when these two powers, joined into one with male and female aspects, are further inspired with the occult lore of the old hermit. But the actual slavishness of the mass of mankind is too real to allow this hope. The whole history of the West, fiendishly directed by the Christian faith to subvert human energy and love, is a nightmare from which Laone and Laon are trying to awake. It is a void heaped with corpses, victims of Madness, Fear, Famine, and Plague. Tyrants and their oppressed and oppressive minions try to sustain their false power by sacrificing scapegoats, by subduing any brave and true visionaries who urge the mass to liberty, and finally Laon and Laone must give up their proselytizing and sacrifice themselves willingly in order to flow swiftly in the spirit's boat to the spirit's temple. In such an oppressed state the only possible liberty is inward and imaginative.

The combined politician poets, male and female, escape the round of cruelty and enter an eternal life of bliss, so heavenly in its radiance that their deaths are barely perceptible. They undergo psychic cures in grottoes undersea, as will the lovers in the fourth act of *Prometheus;* they are transformed by love and enter the temple on a swift current of liquid sound. In such a heightened mood, love becomes tangible as liquid and audible as music. All flows together, as if in Plotinus's universal fountain.

Hoping that in an ideal harmonious world language has power to work on the harmonies that it describes, Shelley develops a particular kind of rhythm to enforce this hope. Shelley's particular sound arises from his desire to approximate an incantation that is a mingling of liquidity and luminescence. His incantations reproduce in shape and sound the long motions of winding, weaving, flowing, and glimmering, or shining. Such motions for making fabrics or webs, or for water and light in play, are supposed to resemble the continuous texture of the spell, binding visual, aural, kinetic, and tactile senses in the web of words. This technique arises from the faith, described above, that the charmed voice can enchant the senses and thereby liberate them and ultimately the world. As early as "The Daemon of the World," but more expertly in the final canto of *The Revolt*, Shelley works on this seamless flow of words that are intended to induce, as if by hypnotic power, the harmony that they depict. In this final canto the long lines float as if effortlessly imitating the motions of water or light. When we hear through the imagery of gliding, swaying, winding, weaving, glistening, and shining about the nature of the perfect world, we experience its growth as if it were growing before our eyes and in our ears. The sentences become longer and longer, more and more mellifluous, as if any abrupt stop would break the spell. When Shelley imagines a utopia summoned by a visionary poet's spell, he describes it in the language that originally summoned it. The utopia exists in its summoning syntax, and depends on the perpetual motion of the sound that renders it.[18]

In lines 4731 to 4746 of *The Revolt*, canto 12, this seamless technique is particularly evident, as it will be again in *Prometheus* 4:188–318.

> Then at the helm we took our seat, the while
>   Above her head those plumes of dazzling hue
>   Into the winds' invisible stream she threw,
> Sitting beside the prow: like gossamer
>   On the swift breath of morn, the vessel flew
> O'er the bright whirlpools of that fountain fair,
> Whose shores receded fast, whilst we seemed lingering there;
>
>   XXXIII
> Till down that mighty stream, dark, calm, and fleet,
>   Between a chasm of cedarn mountains riven,
>   Chased by the thronging winds whose viewless feet
> As swift as twinkling beams, had, under Heaven,
>   From woods and waves wild sounds and odours driven,
> The boat fled visibly—three nights and days,
>   Borne like a cloud through morn, and noon, and even,
>   We sailed along the winding watery ways
> Of the vast stream, a long and labyrinthine maze.
>   (ll. 4731–46)

In these lines a polished surface gleams; unbroken it mirrors the imagined utopia of the mind. Lines enjamb; clauses grow out of clauses and return to their source; participles imply the continuous flux of motion and thought and suggest the generation of one from the other. This suspending for longer and longer periods of the life of the sentence, kept from falling by the magic carpet of the words, is not merely an exercise in virtuosity but is an illustration of the powers of magical language in action.

Believing that as an unacknowledged legislator of the world he can bring to pass the ideal conditions that he as a philosopher and politician has imagined, that "all things will become slaves" to his "holy and heroic verse" (2.933–34), Shelley joins Ficino in viewing the sympathy of thing to word as the spirit of love. This sympathy is relayed through the energetic words of the songs, as the love that enchants the universe to harmony presides as "the prime Enchanter." Without the magician's incantatory words of love that sustain the things of the world on their flowing stream, the parts of the universe become fragmented, solitary, and malevolent. Shelley shares with Ficino this hope that his magical songs will keep the love that binds one thing to another in circulation, and keep it in the highest conceivable point of energy, radiating oneness through the light of moving words. Like the poets of the sixteenth-century Pléiade, who were also influenced by Ficino, Shelley wrote songs to charm every element of the world into a loving and liberating peace. The magical words reestablish the animate sympathy of thing to thing and hold them together in a tenuous web of continuously moving words, with waves of words corresponding to the waves of feeling, and gaining effectiveness from the underlying vibrations.

That the perfect world of spirit must be held up on the gliding wings of a ceaseless song will explain why Shelley's *Prometheus Unbound* is so fluid that no dramatic breaks occur and that individual voices flow into one another. In performing their verbal magic in the listening mind, lines are fearful of silence, caught in their own spells, and bound to celebrate the words that they are made of. It is no wonder therefore that the words *word*, *language*, *writing*, *spell*, *uttered charm*, *incantation*, *enchantment*, *sound*, and *songs* recur in Shelley's poems and, in the case of *Prometheus Unbound*, as we shall see, that they magically cause the transformation from evil to good, quickening a new birth. Only in his prose does Shelley occasionally doubt the ability of words to penetrate the mystery of our experience, but these doubts are allayed in the medium of verse as it moves along in the compulsion of its rhythm, suspending such disbelief.

In examining how spells, charms, enchantments, and songs magically cause the transformations in the visionary poem *Prometheus*, we should see that Shelley consolidates in it two major themes of *The Revolt:* the belief that the temple of the spirit is eternal; and the hope that if everything is mind, magically empowered words can change things. *Prometheus Unbound* has been called "the biography of an hour" to excuse its lack of dramatic sequence; but it is not so much a drama as a ritual, or a magical conjuring act, revealing the single instant in time when the nightmare of history is transformed to an eternity of bliss. As in *The Revolt* here rival powers course from mind to mind, and in and out of past, present, and future times, approximating a permanent condition of synchronicity; in this moment out of time, the poet, as Shelley later explains in his *Defence*, "participates in the eternal, the infinite, and the one; as far as relates to his conceptions, time and place and number are not." In abolishing for a magical instant such sequences, Shelley confirms his early faith in "the eventual omnipotence of mind over matter," and anticipates his statement in the *Defence* that "poetry defeats the curse that binds us to be subjected to the accidents of surrounding impressions."[19]

In a play celebrating the poet's power to enchant the universe out of time by means of his songs, it is significant that the hero is himself the inventor and bringer of language. The action of the play, made up of a sequence of invocations, revocations, incantations, summonings, celebrations, psalms, hymns, and spells, consists of recalling the dread spell, reiterating it, and celebrating the end of the tyranny of hate brought about by the finding of a new spell. Characters are differentiated from one another, if at all, by the varying meters of their songs. The play assumes that sudden miraculous change is as possible as the changing currents of electrical energy, and as inevitable as gravitational force, now that "the cloud of mind," as Shelley ringingly declares in his preface, "is discharging its collected lightning." Indeed so dependent is the play on a belief in the power of words in themselves that these words do not require bodies to speak them. Swirling with incantatory songs in place of the substantial characters found in *The Cenci*, the play is a many-voiced poem on the triumph of benevolent songs over repressive decrees. The disembodied voices—clashing, booming, singing alone and singing in duets or in choruses—give the play a resemblance to oratorio. *Prometheus*, which Shelley believed was his best work, does what Shelley says in the *Defence* that Calderón did—that is, return the drama to its original relation to religion and to music and dance.

Prometheus himself is a disembodied voice, the voice of a magician who casts off destructive magic in favor of constructive magic and who organizes with a spell a renovated universe of magical correspondences. His revocation of the curse and his subsequent blessing assumes that there is an electric current of good and evil corresponding to and therefore obeying the pulsations of words, themselves carrying an electrical charge that can switch these currents from negative to positive. Prometheus, summarizing the cruel tortures that he endures at the hands of his shadow Jupiter, has ceased to hate Jupiter, in a miraculous about-face, and he wishes to revoke his curse that brought death on the world. It is a curse uttered thrice three thousand years ago but remembered as sacred to heroic suffering by all the elements and spirits of the earth. The exact words

are treasured and are so fearful that they can be uttered only by
a specter of the already-dead. The words keep power even after
the spirit that first pronounced them has changed his mind.
Prometheus is in the awkward position of seeing his curse
continue to operate when he no longer wishes it to; and
therefore he must, in a formal ritual, recall it in the presence of
witnesses:

> If then my words had power,
> Though I am changed so that aught evil wish
> Is dead within; although no memory be
> Of what is hate, let them not lose it now!
> What was that curse? for ye all heard me speak.
>
> (1.69–73)

"The thunder of that spell," once set free, has a life of its own;
the words are indeed too dangerous for anyone to utter. From
such "dread words" all the voices of nature shrink back, and for
189 lines the voices of the elements tremble to think of their
repetition. The mountains, springs, airs, and whirlwinds do
not dare repeat them but only describe their effect:

> But never blowed our snowy crest
> As at the voice of thine unrest   (1.91–92)

cry the mountains, and the air confesses

> By such dread words from Earth to Heaven
> My still realm was never riven.   (1.100–101)

The springs sing:

> Never such a sound before
> To the Indian waves we bore.
> A pilot asleep on the howling sea
> Leaped up from the deck in agony,
> And heard, and cried, "Ah, woe is me!"
> And died as mad as the wild waves be.
>
> (1.93–98)

The earth and all her streams "preserve" the curse as "a
treasured spell" (1.184). She says: "We meditate / In secret

joy and hope those dreadful words, / But dare not speak them" (1.184–86). The Earth has hoarded these words in their exact, most potent, order, muttering over them like a savage so that the powerful utterance will not be altered and its power snapped.

Only the Phantasm of Jupiter, the shadow of a shadow, is dead and is vicious enough to serve as the unwilling mouthpiece; and he is shattered by the alien independent sounds rising within him, having no relation to his own thoughts or voice. The spell, which is itself alive, uses him to rise up through. He cries: "What unaccustomed sounds / Are hovering on my lips, unlike the voice / With which our pallid race hold ghastly talk / In darkness?" (1.242–45) He is torn open by the words: "A spirit seizes me and speaks within. / It tears me as fire tears a thunder-cloud" (1.254–55). The phantasm is powerless to keep the curse from issuing forth, and the curse booms out over the universe (ll. 262–301).

Shelley is hard pressed to write a spell to justify the terror which all the elements feel before it, but he makes up for its actual weakness by spending most of act 1 elaborating the fact of its power. Prometheus himself is ashamed of his rage and tells his mother Earth that he repents these terrible words now that his mind has become benevolent:

> It doth repent me: words are quick and vain;
> Grief for awhile is blind, and so was mine.
> I wish no living thing to suffer pain.   (1.303–5)

Words may burst forth quickly out of a sense of injured vanity, but do not pass quickly and are not said "in vain." They take on an actual "shape, a throng of sounds" (1.226), and form whirlwinds underground. They have a life apart from the speaker's.

Recanting his dread spell is not enough. Prometheus must replace it by another spell. Until he finds one, he is still tortured by furies who summon before him visions of earthly horrors that he has caused. Having once silenced nature by words of rage, Prometheus must find words to bring nature to life again, by "clothing" his secret new benevolence in words (1.375–76). By the end of act 1, words, voices, and songs are already carrying news of love, and these songs prepare us for the finding of the second spell and the releasing of the world from the old spell in act 2.

This new spell is hidden with Demogorgon, and Asia, variously interpreted as love, compassion, or charity, will retrieve it for Prometheus. Asia and Panthea, their minds flowing in and out of each other, mingle in an osmosis of love, and speak of words, names, songs, and enchantments. "Hark!," says Asia, "Spirits speak. The liquid responses / Of their aëreal tongues yet sound" (2.1.171–72). From all around spirits call "Follow, follow." The women pursue the sound and seek a voice:

Echoes

In the world unknown
Sleeps a voice unspoken;
By thy step alone
Can its rest be broken;
Child of Ocean!   (2.1.190–94)

Through an enchanted forest, by enchanted eddies, they seek this as yet unspoken voice that will release the universe. When this voice is discovered and then spoken, the deep will no longer be imageless. In Demogorgon's realm words, colors, shapes, and music merge; elements, hours, and darkness find voice, for they become sounds that move bodily about the stage: words are the actors and the props, more real than things. These flurrying words circle around a core of yet more potent words that will soon enact immediate reform.

The cave of Demogorgon is the center of sound, where "the oracular vapour is hurled up." Here winds and words unite; wind-enchanted shapes and the enchantments of the moon magnetize Asia and Panthea, until they hear what seems to be the central salvational lyric, the spell that is coiled like a snake

under the seat of power. This spell is the center of the play
(2.3):

Song of Spirits

To the deep, to the deep,	55
Down, down!	
Through the shade of sleep,	
Through the cloudy strife	
Of Death and of Life;	
Through the veil and the bar	
Of things which seem and are	60
Even to the steps of the remotest throne,	
Down, down!	

While the sound whirls around,	
Down, down!	
As the fawn draws the hound,	65
As the lightning the vapour,	
As the weak moth the taper,	
Death, despair; love, sorrow;	
Time, both; to-day, to-morrow;	
As steel obeys the spirit of the stone,	70
Down, down!	

Through the gray, void abysm,	
Down, down!	
Where the air is no prism,	
And the moon and stars are not,	75
And the cavern-crags wear not	
The radiance of Heaven,	
Nor the gloom to Earth given,	
Where there is One pervading, One alone,	
Down, down!	80

In the depth of the deep,	
Down, down!	
Like veiled lightning asleep,	
Like the spark nursed in embers,	
The last look Love remembers,	85
Like a diamond, which shines	

On the dark wealth of mines,
A spell is treasured but for thee alone.
                    Down, down!

We have bound thee, we guide thee;   90
                    Down, down!
With the bright form beside thee,
Resist not the weakness,
Such strength is in meekness
That the Eternal, the Immortal,   95
Must unloose through Life's portal
The snake-like Doom coiled underneath his throne
                    By that alone.

In this artful lyric, stanza one is a series of prepositional
phrases, showing its incompleteness by ending with a comma;
stanza two, also ending with a comma, is a series of similes
describing irresistible movements of one kind or another;
stanza three is a series of adverbial clauses of progression and
direction ("Through" and "Where") pointing toward the
destination in stanza four—the depth of the deep to which the
refrain "Down, down!" has been leading. No declarative
statement has yet appeared. Stanza four begins with a prepositional phrase, moves to four more similes, this time modifying
not the descent but the treasure which rewards that descent.
The stanza arrives finally at the treasure in the first declarative
sentence of the lyric: "A spell is treasured but for thee alone."
This sentence ends with a period. The stanzas of direction,
magnetic movement, and place, have penetrated the depth of
the deep and found there the spell which is like lightning, like
"the last look Love remembers," like a diamond; veiled in
similes, cushioned in likenesses, it is like "a spark nursed in
embers." This spark nursed in embers points to the fading
embers of language in the *Defence;* the spell treasured but for
thee alone recalls Earth's confession that her seas and caves
preserve Prometheus's original curse as "a treasured spell."
Stanza five explains the function of this spell which hides at the

center of the world. The spirits have led Asia and Panthea to
the source of Demogorgon's power. And yet strangely they talk
of weakness and meekness as the source of power:

> Resist not the weakness,
> Such strength is in meekness
> That the Eternal, the Immortal
> Must unloose through Life's portal
> The snake-like Doom coiled underneath his throne
> By that alone.   (ll. 93–97)

By what alone? By the spell discovered in the last stanza
perhaps. Language, not Jovian violence, will direct the snake-
like doom to its positive rather than negative potential. This
language is meek because the spell to which the spirits refer is
in fact the spell that Demogorgon reveals at the end of the play:

> Gentleness, Virtue, Wisdom, and Endurance
>   .   .   .   .
> These are the spells by which to reassume
> An empire o'er the disentangled doom.
>   (4: 562, 568–69)

The meek spells of Gentleness and Virtue, Wisdom and
Endurance will free the serpent now coiled and tangled but
soon, by the force of the spell alone, loosed and turned to good.
The spell treasured like a diamond in "the dark wealth of
mines," has power to redirect the nature of life. Once it is
found, the spell accomplishes instant revolution on its own, as
had the curse. Prometheus's success thus depends not on
himself, but on the existence of the spell, and more generally
on the power of language to work instantaneously and to
create, suddenly and independently of the ordinary delays of
evolutionary process, a new society. Prometheus succeeds because magical language is believed to convert the spiritual
vibrations coursing throughout the universe.

Unless we grant some such conclusion that a new language
with immediate power is the goal of *Prometheus Unbound*, we
may find that the play is static. If we agree with Milton Wilson

that "the dramatic center of the plot is [Prometheus's] conversion, his discovery that 'virtue' is preferable to 'vengeance,'" we see the climax at the beginning of the play and the play itself as an anticlimax. But if we see the importance to the play of the finding of magical words to enact Prometheus's change of mind in act 1, the center moves to the second half of act 2, the physical center of the play, where the spell is found in the depth of the deep. According to this interpretation, act 1 reveals the conversion within Prometheus's mind, externalized through the answering responses of the earth and elements. Act 2 records the quest for the potent speech which will make the conversion effective by embodying it in words; then, after the climax of act 2, scene 3, line 97, when the veil is fallen, acts 3 and 4 describe the rapturous harmony of the universe resulting from the new spell. In a play where "time is all but rendered subordinate to instantaneity," this instantaneity is made possible by the way that magical spells are thought to take effect immediately. Prometheus's decision to revise his words is simultaneous with Asia's descent to the cave of Demogorgon, and both events occasion simultaneously the fall of Jupiter and the liberation of the planets. The play is the biography of an hour and a study in the end of time, but it is a crucial hour when a new magic is sprung into operation.[20] Without the explanation of a magic in operation, the improbable number of unmotivated events that occur in this hour would be unbelievable; with the explanation of magic we accept the improbable, knowing that magic bypasses ordinary processes and enacts otherwise unbelievable transformations.

Prometheus bewitches nature, summons spirits, finds (through his loving aspect, Asia) the magical words that underlie all energy; as a culture hero, "he gave man speech, and speech created thought, / Which is the measure of the universe." He also "told the hidden power of herbs and springs, / . . . and by what secret spell the pale moon is transformed" (2.4.85, 89–90). By changing his own mind and by finding words to express this universal change, he asserts himself over nature; instead of propitiating higher powers, he exerts his own. He is a Prospero orchestrating a magically attuned universe by means of his magic. With his discovery of the spell, tyranny collapses spontaneously and the world is free:

> Hearest thou not sounds i' the air which speak the love
> Of all articulate beings?   (2.5.35–36)

Asia feels the liberating joy of the new magic; she sings: "My soul is an enchanted boat," and becomes suddenly more beautiful. In the new society the senses are renovated, allowing Ocean and Apollo to hear the music of the spheres, and in the cave of the mind where they embrace, to perceive universal harmonies:

> My vision then grew clear, and I could see
> Into the mysteries of the universe.   (3.4.104–5)

"All things had put their evil nature off." Prometheus, like the Ancient Mariner who influences many of his postures, blesses "the water-snakes" "unawares" (see 3.4.73–77). Simultaneity, magnetism, oneness, and universal sympathy prevail, while the spirits dance and sing their incantatory songs:

> Weave the dance on the floor of the breeze
>   Pierce with song heaven's silent light,
> Enchant the day that too swiftly flees. . . .
>
>   (4.69–71)

> But now, oh weave the mystic measure
>   Of music, and dance, and shapes of light
>
>   (4.77–78)

> Our spoil is won,
> Our task is done,
> We are free to dive, or soar, or run   (4.135–37)

> Break the dance, and scatter the song;
>   Let some depart, and some remain.
> We, beyond heaven, are driven along
> Us the enchantments of earth retain.   (4.159–62)

The word *enchantment* appears over and over; wishes are immediately granted, for things have been absorbed as thoughts in the universally correspondent mind. The spell that the magician has discovered frees men into a new heaven and a new earth; through magical language the bringer of speech has become an unacknowledged legislator of the world. Lifting the veil of appearance and penetrating the center of power, his potent voice enforces political change.

With the introduction of magical theory to bridge the gap between the ideal and material realms, Shelley is able to accomplish the transformations he desires, if only in words. The curse revoked, the new spell having been found at the base of energy, all songs now become parts of the music of the spheres, all words, now loving, go instantly into effect. In the harmoniously attuned universal mind, words are lights are clothes are dances are feelings are sounds. Magical words bring about this condition of merging identities, and magical words keep it going: a fountain is an awakening sound; a spirit is a lute, a charmed wind, a low voice of love. Air and sunlight are transformed like all things in these "happy changes" (3.4.84); hours "melt away, / Like dissolving spray" (4.24–25); flying fish and birds forget their distinctions (4.85); spirits, having been spirited out of their bodies, "are free / To dive, or soar, or run" (4.137), regardless of their original species. "Visions of strange radiance float upon / The ocean-like enchantment of strong sound" (4.202–3). The earth beneath her "pyramid of night," sleeps an "enchanted" sleep; Panthea rises from the stream of sound with her own words shaken like drops from her hair.

So entirely have words and things become mental events that evil beings can be dismissed at will: "Be not! And like my words they were no more" (4.318). The deep truth which had been imageless has found an image in the speaking of the hitherto unspoken voice. Amid the "bright visions, / Wherein the singing spirits rode and shone" (4.514–15), come words from all directions:

Ione. There is a sense of words upon mine ear.
Panthea. An universal sound like words: Oh, list!
(4.517–18)

The world has become articulate. Demogorgon speaks and his words are liquid to the drop of dew of earth and wind to the leaf of the moon; to the spirits "thy voice to us is wind among still woods." This voice, finally found, shapes the universe into eternal harmony:

Speak: thy strong words may never pass away.   (4.553)

Demogorgon perorates with a triumphant statement on the nature of the new spell, the strong, palpable, radiant streaming words, which Prometheus, Panthea, and Asia have released. He says of Gentleness, Virtue, Wisdom, and Endurance (l. 562),

if, with infirm hand, Eternity,
Mother of many acts and hours, should free
The serpent that would clasp her with his length;
These are the spells by which to reassume
An empire o'er the disentangled doom.   (4.565–69)

Such is, he says, "the Earth-born's spell." The meek spell will free the serpent, which may again become coiled and tangled but may be loosed and turned to good, by the force of the spell alone.

In *Prometheus Unbound*, then, the use of magical imagery and the theory that it implies has allowed Prometheus's original curse to silence the elements; Prometheus's change of will to reverse the significance of these words; his female aspect to go in search of new words at the center of the earth; and at their finding to release the elements of the world into a musical articulation. The revolution has been accomplished on many levels through sounds, songs, and the reverberations they set in motion; things and events have passed into spirits and become susceptible to the incantations that embody thoughts of change. Because of this miraculous transformation of bodies into spirits, of curses into blessings, and of all things into songs, love can radiate through the universe and be its prime enchanter, setting everything free.

Shelley pursues these hopes for the power of songs in the translations of the following year. He translates charms from Goethe's *Faust* and from Calderón's *Magico Prodigoso*, experimenting with their meters. In his translation of Homer's "Hymn to Mercury" he translates the question demanded of the divine poet:

> What Muse, what skill, what unimagined use,
> What exercise of subtlest art, has given
> Thy songs such power?   (p. 695; ll. 595–97)

and shows the infant Mercury willing his rod to Apollo, "a perfect three-leaved rod of gold unbroken, / Whose magic will thy footsteps ever bless" (p. 698; ll. 709–10).

Shelley's rough draft of "A Midsummer Night's Dream Poem," copied into a notebook in 1822, continues these preoccupations, influenced by the meters that he was learning from Calderón and Goethe. In introducing this poem, previously published only privately by H. Buxton Forman, Neville Rogers explains that "through Goethe, Calderón, and Plato the poet is looking back through the wrong end of a telescope and perceiving his daemons in the form in which he first knew them: the goblins and fairies of his childhood's imaginings at Field Place."[21] The poem begins as a spell of racing anapests followed by quick two- or three-syllable whirling lines:

> Ye goblins black & great ghosts white
> Fairies all green & spirits blue
> Through the white mist on Midsummer's night
> Hither come hither over the dew
>   Not a snake
>   In the brake
>   Shall awake
>   With you
>   But a snail
>   With his trail

> Shall you
> Pursue
> To the cave
> And the grave
> And the wave
> Bid adieu.

The poem darts and turns with mysterious ingredients and voices, echoing Goethe's *Walpurgisnacht* and the sisters of *Macbeth*, and recalling the excited songs of *Prometheus Unbound* 4.

A year after the final composition of *Prometheus Unbound* and contemporaneous with the translations, Shelley synthesizes his scattered theories about the magical origins and powers of poetry in *The Witch of Atlas*. *The Witch of Atlas* expands these elements into an intricate theory of imagination. It does so first by appealing to the Wordsworth-Coleridge quarrel which Shelley had carefully investigated while writing *Peter Bell the Third* a month previous. Against Wordsworthian truth to visible things, which is Mary's preference, he opts for a Coleridgean magical invention, a visionary rhyme. He is all the more intent on writing a visionary rhyme now that he has finished *Prometheus Unbound* and sees himself, as he explains in his *Letter to Maria Gisborne*, as a magician, the magician whose wish became his own at the end of *Alastor*. To Maria Gisborne he writes:

> Whoever should behold me now, I wist,
> Would think I were a mighty mechanist,
> Bent with sublime Archimedean art
> To breathe a soul into the iron heart
> Of some machine portentous, or strange gin,
> Which by the force of figured spells might win
> Its way over the sea.   (ll. 15−21)

He sees himself as inventing in his multitudinous verses "strange and dread / Magical forms" (ll. 43−44). He believes that "Proteus transformed to metal did not make / More figures, or more strange" (ll. 45−46); and more elaborately he describes himself:

And here like some weird Archimage sit I,
Plotting dark spells, and devilish enginery,
The self-propelling steam-wheels of the mind.
                                                        (ll. 106–8)

Memory becomes a witch (l. 132), himself again "an old diviner," hope, "a sad enchantress." Having seen that he himself was an "Archimage, plotting dark spells," he comes to investigate what power it is within him that propels his magical words. Thus in *The Witch of Atlas* he analyzes in magical terms the workings of the imagination.

The poem tries to discover what is magical about the poetic imagination that has empowered the poet of *Alastor*, Queen Mab, Apollo with his magic wand, and Prometheus himself. Shelley tries in *The Witch of Atlas* to allegorize the psychology of creation, and he applies his remarks in the preface to *Prometheus Unbound* that his imagery is "drawn from the operations of the human mind" to an analysis of how the mind generates new forms and through them reaches other minds.

Within the cave of the mind is born a witch with strange powers to transform the world that she watches. Born of the sun and a Titan, the witch develops by protean changes, animating the rocks around her and magnetizing even the gods with her beauty:

The magic circle of her voice and eyes
All savage creatures did imparadise.   (ll. 103–4)

To keep from blinding men she must hide in a veil, woven to mediate her glory. In the deep recesses of her cave are "magic treasures—sounds of air, / Which had the power all spirits of compelling," and also scrolls of arcane learning with formulae for redeeming the earth. These are "the spells of Wisdom's wizard skill" (l. 195). She alternately reads ancient lore and practices her craft, "broidering the pictured poesy" (l. 252). She weaves form, as cloth develops out of the insignificance of thread, almost out of nothing. Line by line as in verse the shuttle crosses to make a complex fabric with the in-and-out of rhymes, the up-and-down of meter, and the intricate pattern of sounds through the texture of a stanza. Like a spider web the woven poetry catches its victims, as Shelley explains in *The Letter to Maria Gisborne:*

> The spider spreads her webs, whether she be
> In poet's tower, cellar, or barn, or tree;
> .   .   .   .
> So I, a thing whom moralists call worm,
> Sit spinning still round this decaying form,
> From the fine threads of rare and subtle thought—
> No net of words in garish colours wrought
> To catch the idle buzzers of the day—
> But a soft cell. . . .   (ll. 1–2, 5–10)

Snaring the images of things in verse, the poet also extrudes his own self like a silk worm, while his spider's web snares his listeners, compelling them to do his bidding. The image of the web is another one for binding. Similarly, from her father, the sun, "the wizard lady" of *The Witch* inherits yet another variety of magical power—the power to change things with heat and light. "The enchantment of her father's power" (l. 202) makes her verse fiery: "She held a woof that dimmed the burning brand" (l. 264). She lies half-asleep, entranced in "an inextinguishable well / Of crimson fire" (ll. 278–79), creating in a waking dream.

The imagination, the witch, flies freely on a magic boat inherited from Vulcan, Venus, and Apollo (a fusion of craft, love, and inspiration) that is "oared by . . . enchanted wings" (l. 407). Voyaging far beyond what the eye can see, she escapes the merely natural sphere, for "the lady-witch in visions could not chain / Her spirit" (l. 419). Time, space, myth, and history present no boundaries such as those erected by the cruel twins, Truth and Error. Freely she rides "like Arion on the dolphin's back, . . . singing through shoreless air" (ll. 484–85). So in the prefatory letter to *Peter Bell the Third* Shelley described his imagination: "The orb of [my] moonlike genius has made the fourth part of its revolution round the dull earth which you inhabit, driving you mad." Learned in magical lore, enchanted by the senses, free to voyage beyond all bounds on her magic boat, the Witch Imagination shows her magical power most evidently when she visits men and bewitches them to a new virtue. The imagination, opening their minds to a larger understanding of other men, has a spiritual and political function. Passing "through the peopled haunts of humankind" (l. 523) she scatters "sweet visions from her presence sweet" (l. 524); under the veil of appearance she discerns the "naked beauty of the soul," "the inner form" (ll. 571–73). Penetrating to the *natura naturans* underneath the superficial *natura naturata*, the imagination is able to conjure the inner form into the permanence of poetry. With her "charm of strange device" (l. 574) she can draw erring men up into a life of the spirit. Kings and soldiers drop their violent and corrupt ways when their imaginations are enlivened, and

> Friends who, by practice of some envious skill,
>   Were torn apart—a wide wound, mind from mind!—
> She did unite again with visions clear
> Of deep affection and of truth sincere.   (ll. 661–64)

"These were the pranks she played among the cities of mortal men" (l. 665), pranks that bewitch men into being just even against their will. Like the Witch Poesy in "Mont Blanc" she touches men with her invisible power and improves them. The Witch Imagination, like Prometheus as magician or the enchanter poet of the "Ode to the West Wind," does more than invent the new forms of poetry: she reforms the corrupt universe with her enchantments and realigns the cosmic harmonies, sitting as she does in the cave of the mind and casting her vibrations around her.

The golden age will come into being when the witch's magical power gives the omnipotent mind a verbal medium through which to operate. The magic of songs is so powerful that it turns injustice to justice in the instant of utterance, and the magician who intones the swaying, gliding, and glowing synaesthetic incantation commands phenomena as easily as he says "Arise!" The poet, "the hierophant of the unapprehended inspiration," as Shelley calls him in the *Defence*, sends forth "as from a magnet the invisible effluence . . . which at once connects, animates, and sustains the life of all." Having studied in his youth not only Plato's *Symposium* but also neoplatonic, occult, and magical commentaries, Shelley arrived at his idealized view of the potency of poetic language that is able to "defeat the curse which binds us to be subjected to the accident of surrounding impressions." He sees all poetry as one poem, a "perpetual Orphic song" that charms away the bestial aspects of man.

Shelley's contribution to the theory of magical poetry inherited from Coleridge is his view of poetry's political effectiveness: the spell bewitches, enchants, charms, and magically coerces men and nations. It works more forcefully than action, because it works immediately by enlarging the imagination, forming "new intervals and interstices whose void forever craves fresh food." Poetry "transmutes all that it touches, and every form moving within the radiance of its presence is changed by wondrous sympathy to an incarnation of the spirit which it breathes; its secret alchemy turns to potable gold the poisonous waters which flow from death through life; it strips the veil of familiarity from the world, and lays bare the naked and sleeping beauty, which is the spirit of its forms." [22] So in the *Defence* Shelley summarizes the intuitions in his poems about the wondrous powers of poetry to transmute, transform, and change all that it touches with its enchanted words. Once individuals have been bewitched by this secret and irresistible power, groups and nations inevitably succumb to the same enchantments. When Shelley commands the wind

> Be thou, Spirit fierce,
> My spirit! Be thou me, impetuous one!

Drive my dead thoughts over the universe
Like withered leaves to quicken to new birth!
And, by the incantation of this verse,

Scatter, as from an unextinguished hearth
Ashes and sparks, my words among mankind!
Be through my lips to unawakened earth

The trumpet of a prophecy!   (ll. 61–69)

he rejoices that the thoughts of his own mind quicken the universe to a new birth, that by the incantation of his verse, he has caused the spring. With words that can light up the world, he sees himself as a Prometheus, suspecting that in the cave of his mind he harbors a witch and that with his knowledge of lore and his skill in weaving spells, he will be able to send his witch out to awaken the earth. Therefore Shelley is more concerned than Coleridge with poetry's effect on the outside world; while Coleridge marvels at the power of words to generate fabulous independent life inside the poem, Shelley thinks of what that power can do beyond the sphere of the poem itself. Shelley's hope for an articulate universe susceptible to music represents a high point of optimism about a theory that had at first opened to late-eighteenth-century poets new sources of creative power within and that had affirmed for Coleridge the miraculousness of being. Byron and Keats will turn the theory in a fatal direction.

As can be seen from the example of Shelley, Coleridge's promise of a freedom attainable through magically intensified language had an enormous influence on the second generation of romantic writers. It led to a search for supernaturally induced change of an instantaneous kind and hence to an impatience with the slow workings of normal narrative time. It led, by the same token, to a search for sudden apocalyptic escapes from normal history and biography either through evanescence or through dying, and to a fantastic merging with the infinite, as in *Prometheus* 4, or, as we shall see, in the final act of *Manfred*. It led, later in the century, to a faith in the efficacy of mere sound, in mellifluous forms to the exclusion of sense. For it began to be supposed that if words had power in themselves, in their very sounds and letters, it would be possible to empty them of intentionally included meanings and the words would nevertheless continue to exercise their powers. By this route magical theories of language led to a disparaging use of the term *incantatory* for the loose rhythms of Poe and Swinburne. The magical theory developed by Coleridge with such care in this way was rarefied in the course of the nineteenth century and increasingly was separated from a sense of the actual existence of observed things. Shelley's intricate theory of magical language stands as a transition from Coleridge's theory to the less clearly defined magic of the later century, particularly because, though derived in part from Coleridge, it expands the area of magical operation outward beyond the perimeters of the poem itself to society at large.

7 • Self-destroying Enthrallments: Byron and Keats

It is not customary to pair Byron and Keats, for they knew well that in their most basic attitudes toward language they were opposed. Keats articulates his understanding of this opposition in letters to his brother and sister-in-law, George and Georgiana Keats: "Byron," he writes on February 19, 1819, "cuts a figure—but he is not figurative." Seven months later he clarifies the contrast between Byron's outward theatrical presence and his own search into the core of words for their essences: "Byron describes what he sees—I describe what I imagine—mine is the hardest task." [1] Byron presents himself to the outer world; he also looks at the outer world in order to render it. Keats, discovering truth through figuration, allows this truth to emerge from within through symbols. Byron's criticism of Keats is more ad hominem than Keats's of him, though he claims to admire the language of the gods in *Hyperion*. Byron's antipathy to Keats's "piss-a-bed poetry" and cockney origins is only laughingly repented in *Don Juan:*

> Poor fellow! His was an untoward fate;
> 'Tis strange the mind, that very fiery particle,
> Should let itself be snuffed out by an article.
>
> (11.60.6–8)[2]

Probably neither poet would appreciate being leagued with the other.

Nevertheless, despite their differences and despite the appeal to different audiences of Keats's palpably concentrated images and of Byron's externally referential statements, both poets react similarly to the tradition of magical language inherited from Coleridge and his predecessors. They are both first charmed by the external trappings of the tradition and the easy mention of adjectives like "magical" and "enchanting" as synonyms for "pleasing." From this casual interest both become absorbed by the transformations which promise to free them from their personalities and their bodies. In the improbable suspensions of time and space both discover the lure of self-oblivion. However, as if responding to Wordsworth's warnings, both finally realize the danger of such self-obliteration. They shake themselves free of the magical changes and near the ends of their brief lives they turn to action in the world as a form of disengagement from language.

The dangers inherent in the magical tradition, dangers foreseen by Spenser, Milton, Thomson, and Wordsworth and fulfilled in the magical theories of late-nineteenth-century symbolists, are implicit in Byron's speculative dramas, in Keats's *Endymion* and "Ode to a Nightingale." They are explicit in such a play as Thomas Lovell Beddoes's *Death's Jest Book*, where Wordsworth's forecasts about the abandoning of life through magic come true. In this discussion of divergent responses to the magical tradition I will not deal with the attitudes of these poets to each other or even with their attitudes toward Coleridge and Wordsworth, which would require a much larger study; instead I will consider their uses and revisions of this tradition, as they hope to be momentarily carried into another realm, enchanted by dreams, impossibilities, suspensions, and forgetfulness.

It is not only in the speculative dramas, of course, that Byron confronts varieties of the supernatural. The supernatural incidents in the final books of *Don Juan*, for instance, stir questions about Byron's religious beliefs, as do legends about Byron's superstitions. But these questions cannot be answered unless we can solve the riddle of Byron's sincerity. How much did he mean? Whom was he mocking? We hardly know what Byron believed about the ghost's appearance in Adelaide's country house any more than we can know the meaning of his horror at the black ribbon on his wife's wedding ring.[3] Since we cannot resolve the tangled ironies of *Don Juan* or of Byron's real-life performances, we cannot decipher what Byron believes from what he pretends to believe in his work. He may use magical transformations as parodies of the gothic narrative, as ridicule of his credulous contemporaries, as fodder for his readers, or even as dramatizations of his own folly.

Moreover, even though the speculative dramas may seem to be seriously dealing with problems of magical changes, they must still be treated with reservation. The very existence of the narrative voice in *Don Juan* casts a mocking shadow over these plays and makes them questionable. They, too, may be part of the game. We can deal with the speculative dramas as if they mean what they say only if we acknowledge at the outset that the narrative voice of *Don Juan* is in the background snickering at us. By this awareness we may partially escape being Byron's dunces as we examine these remarkable and neglected dramas.

The four speculative dramas, as George Ridenour has named the quartet of *Manfred, Cain, Heaven and Earth*, and *The Deformed Transformed*, were written in the aura of Coleridge, Goethe, and Scott. They differ from the historical plays in featuring supernatural events in vast cosmic settings and in questioning the nature of man's life, particularly the limitations set on his spirit. It might be said that they form a tetralogy, however unfinished, on the problems of human limitations and the will to escape from them. *Manfred* deals with the problem in an abstract way, with Manfred symbolizing man, the spirit trapped in time. *Cain* deals with it as a moment in the development of biblical mythology, when man's supernatural life is thwarted and Cain is blamed for God's unjust command. *Heaven and Earth* focuses on this division of man from his supernatural life at a later moment, showing that God forbids the continuing intercourse between men and spirits because He is jealous of man's supernatural powers. *The Deformed Transformed* applies this general problem of limitations to an individual psychological case, where a Byronic cripple tries to escape from his hated body by supernatural means. The tetralogy moves from the general to the particular, from allegory to miracle play to fairy tale; it uses the incantations imagined to have been available to the human being in his free state, before the transcendent God repressed the old religions of a living and communicative world and trapped men in dying forms. It contrasts man's limitations with lost possibilities in worlds without limitations, imagined to have existed before the fall (*Cain*), before the flood (*Heaven and Earth*), in an occult universe (*Manfred*), or in a fairy-tale world like that inhabited by Grimm's frog prince (*The Deformed Transformed*).

Much of Byron's magical theory derives from aspects of Coleridge's theory as it applies to the mind, to language, and to nature; but it is greatly changed. In *Manfred* the magic which permitted all men to think themselves more spiritual than nature is transformed into a magic which elevates the superman over his inferiors. Byron uses magic to lift the extraordinary individual into a supernatural realm, where, by the energy of his will, he tries to make his body vanish. Coleridge's belief that we are supernatural rather than natural beings is exaggerated in this play, where Manfred, the lonely superman, refuses to conform. He will not accept the life of nature in which the chamois hunter, like Wordsworth's leech-gatherer, is at home. Manfred cries:

> My spirit walk'd not with the souls of men,
> Nor look'd upon the earth with human eyes;
> The thirst of their ambition was not mine,
> The aim of their existence was not mine;
> My joys, my griefs, my passions, and my powers,
> Made me a stranger; though I wore the form,
> I had no sympathy with breathing flesh. (2.2.51–57)

So omnipotent does he hope to be that he wants to unmake himself, willfully to conjure away his life, because as a magician he not only discovers knowledge but also originates his own states of being. Seeing life as a scene of death—horror, havoc, misery, and guilt—he believes that it is more vital to be a spirit than a living body enmired in life. Life is really Death-in-Life; the only way to triumph is to have Life-in-Death by becoming a spirit free of clay. Manfred comes closer than Byron's other Manichaean heroes to defying the ineluctable laws of old age and decay. For Manfred almost succeeds in preempting the rival magic of nature; he almost succeeds in making his body evaporate and become, in Keats's phrase, free of space. Manfred rejects the consolations of leech-gatherers and the village kirk, shudders at the approach of mortals, and imagines that he alone is conscious of being a spirit trapped in a mortal cage, beating his wings.

Coleridge's probing thoughts about the self-reflexiveness of language, by, for, and from the mind, are exaggerated in Byron into the posture of incest. The mind gazes on its own products and reflections; there is no Other. Hence Manfred, like other Byronic heroes, has eyes only for Astarte, his sister, who resembles him. Like other postures in *Manfred* (particularly Manfred's remark that he himself is his proper hell, 1.1.251) this incestuous mirroring is borrowed from Milton's Satan, whose self-love makes him desire his daughter, Sin, the product of his own brain, because he sees himself in her. Magical omnipotence of mind becomes narcissism.

Magic has many forms in *Manfred*. The natural life has its own magic, ensnaring the human spirit. Time casts a spell. The spirits of place and of natural forces sing their spells, each with a distinctive rhythm. The spirit of the sea sings:

> In the blue depth of the waters,
>   Where the wave hath no strife,
> Where the wind is a stranger,
>   And the sea-snake hath life,
> Where the Mermaid is decking
>   Her green hair with shells,
> Like the storm on the surface
>   Came the sound of thy spells.   (1.1.76–83)

The spirit of darkness, among others, responds:

> My dwelling is the shadow of the night,
> Why doth thy magic torture me with light?
>
> (1.1.108–9)

The magic in nature is countered by the magic existing out of nature in the energy of will. Living is a bewitchment. Other incantations come from many directions. The hero calls upon the spirits of the unbounded universe to deliver him from his bindings, his weight of sorrowful knowledge:

> I call upon ye by the written charm
> Which gives me power upon you—Rise! Appear!
>
> (1.1.35–36)

He succeeds in summoning the spirits of earth and air with "a tyrant spell, / which had its birthplace in a star condemn'd, / The burning wreck of a demolished world" (1.1.43–44). He begs the spirits for self-oblivion (1.1.144) but is instead stunned by the beautiful apparition of Astarte and by her incantation, which is heard through the air, cursing him to an agony of remembrance:

> By a power to thee unknown,
> Thou canst never be alone;
> Thou art wrapt as with a shroud,
> Thou art gather'd in a cloud;
> And for ever shalt thou dwell
> In the spirit of this spell.   (1.1.206–11)

Astarte enchants him with herself, as a haunting presence always near but not near enough; in words that W. H. Auden will adapt for his elegy on William Butler Yeats, Astarte entrammels Manfred:

> And a magic voice and verse
> Hath baptized thee with a curse;
> And a spirit of the air
> Hath begirt thee with a snare;
> In the wind there is a voice
> Shall forbid thee to rejoice.   (1.1.222–27)

In her incantation Astarte makes a litany of the contents of her magic potion, sucked from Manfred's own corrupted soul:

> From thy own heart I then did wring
> The black blood in its blackest spring;
> From thy own smile I snatch'd the snake,
> For there it coil'd as in a brake;
> From thy own lip I drew the charm
> Which gave all these their chiefest harm;
> In proving every poison known,
> I found the strongest was thine own. (1.1.234–41)

His own treachery serves in the magic potion to be used against him. At the close of the incantation, after more and more ghoulish invocations, Astarte intones,

> Lo! the spell now works around thee,
> And the clankless chain hath bound thee;
> O'er thy heart and brain together
> Hath the word been pass'd—now wither!
>   (1.1.258–61)

Manfred is caught in the compulsions of remorse, in the hell of his own consciousness, and he will try to counter this magic by willing life away, by calling on Earth to "take these atoms" (1.2.109). Like Keats in the "Ode to a Nightingale," he wishes,

>   O, that I were
> The viewless spirit of a lovely sound,
> A living voice, a breathing harmony,
> A bodiless enjoyment—born and dying,
> With the blest tone which made me!
>   (1.2.52–56)

and like Keats he aspires momentarily to the condition of music.

Manfred's own "long-pursued and superhuman art" (2.2. 148) derives, as he tell us, from familiarity with the caves of death. The caves of death, he explains, are the deep caves of arcane knowledge, including specifically the texts of Jamblichus and the Persian Magi. The knowledge gleaned there is fatal because it allows the practitioner to be "familiar with Eternity" (2.2.90). From this knowledge Manfred discovers that being supernatural is not being alive. Being supernatural is wishing oneself away from, outside of, ordinary natural life. The caves of death make Manfred's eyes familiar with eternity but alien to the time in which we exist as living beings. They give him the exit from the ennui of time, from the dreary guilts of this stale promontory. Far more than Shelley's magic Byron's magic abolishes time, development, and process; for Byron the tedium of consciousness should be conquered by willed nonexistence.

Byron gives Manfred magical powers to support theories similar to Coleridge's about the supernatural life of man and about the self-reflexiveness of thought, but he makes them extreme. In Byron's version we can see the late symbolist superman and invert being born, with Coleridge's innocent theories of imagination and language in the background. Art, magic, power, and sex begin to converge for the first time in *Manfred* and later influence Nietzsche, Huysmans, Villiers de l'Isle-Adam, Rimbaud, and even Ibsen in *When We Dead Awaken*, where a hunter on a wind-swept peak, arguing against the hero's suicide, is drawn as much from Byron's play as both are drawn from *King Lear*'s subplot.

Byron in *Manfred* sees magic in much the same way that Wordsworth does, as a nonnatural, fatal, spectral power, deny-ing, by transforming, things that are "real." But Byron, unlike Wordsworth, yearns for this spectral power. He accedes to Coleridge's belief that we are supernatural, and he therefore is glad to deny corporeal things their finality, leaving them victim to the shifting meanings of words in incantation. Byron's yearning in *Manfred* is a yearning for death, for self-annihilation in the face of the ennui of things and of the past. For Coleridge, however, the denial of vitality to things is only to liberate the living, life-fostering transformations of the imagination from the fixity of what is considered real in the common-sense view.

Manfred's yearning for death prefigures that of Hans Castorp in Thomas Mann's *Magic Mountain*. In that sanatorium in the Alps, Eros and Thanatos conjoin in a hermetically sealed, timeless kingdom ruled by Rhadamanthus. The enchanted dreamers in Mann's antiromantic novel imagine diseases and are bewitched by these imaginings into being diseased; they forget that only tombs are hermetically sealed. The necrophilia of this mountain breeds a final creative fever; the imagination races before the swoon, for the magical dream-kingdom is a dead end. Mann's analysis of the conjunction of death, magic, desire, and imagination in the same mountains where Shelley came under the sway of the "spells" of intellectual beauty and Manfred conjured the spirits of the winds is a climax of the romantic tradition: Coleridge points the way to the magic mountain; Byron climbs it, and Mann scrutinizes its decadent morbidity.

Manfred is, then, an allegory of man: the disappointed magus asserts his freedom by summoning elemental forces, rejects the conventional consolations of religion, tries to stand at the edge and lose himself. In escaping by magic from restrictions of time and space and corporeality, he ceases to exist and vanishes, nobly murmuring "'Tis not so difficult to die'" (3.4.151) as he dies.

This desire to be free is a furious compulsion in *Cain*, for Cain shakes his fist at Jehovah for depriving him of an immortal world. Fastened to a dying animal, Cain loathes his life and that of his son Enoch, whose tiny corpse he would dash against a rock. In writing *Cain*, Byron creates a hero who does not want to evaporate as Manfred had but who wants as a man to be free of the paternalistic spiritual order governing men's lives. While the conformists in Cain's family honor the validity of supernatural commands, Cain himself wishes to affirm his humanity, to direct his violence not against himself as Manfred had but against the whole order of divine rewards and punishments, demands for obedience and passivity, and oppression of the fiery spirit of man. Byron chooses in *Cain* to dramatize the pivotal moment in biblical history when "the fruit of our forbidden fruit begins to fall" (1.1.30).

At this moment in the Judeo-Christian mythology, according to Byron's play, men suddenly discover what it means to cease being part of a divine eternity and to learn how alien from God are men, how strangely designated "mortals." Cain alone realizes what this division means, how final it is, and how few thanks it deserves. The knowledge that Manfred as neo-platonic magician had prided himself on having is here declared evil if possessed by mere creatures of clay. Cain, cut off from "those / Gardens which are his just inheritance" by a vengeful God, speaks to the "Master of Spirits," who is his own "immortal part which speaks within" him. Over and over in the play appear the words *divide* and *division*, for Cain, encouraged by that Lucifer who would have made men gods, commits the deed which had already occurred in the expulsion from Eden, dividing men from their original immortality. Cain's realization of the inalterable gap between men and gods makes him prefer death, "for to give birth to those / Who can but suffer many years, and die, / Methinks is merely propagating death, / And multiplying murder" (2.1.68–70). In this world the spirits whom Manfred summoned, if only to obliterate himself, do not hear; they are divided from men. There are no spells that will recall them to man's world and recall the living spiritual universe to fill the gap. The only spirit that might do so is falsely condemned as the author of man's death, when the real author sits on high wielding His harsh judgments. Cain's descent to the darkness where visions of the future dead spirits move in prophetic form before him, leads him to recognize "mortal nature's nothingness" (2.2. 422), to know that he and his kin are disinherited, and that Jehovah, in His blood-thirstiness, blesses those who give Him victims.

Byron pursues his attacks on the Judeo-Christian tyrant God in the unfinished *Heaven and Earth*. The jealous God more and more avidly separates mortals from immortals, forbidding relationships between them. He makes the spiritual world inaccessible. "The woman wailing for her demon lover"—the play's epigraph from "Kubla Khan"—points by contrast to the fact that the characters in this dramatic sequel to *Cain* are forbidden that communication with the spirits that was possible in a living universe such as Coleridge imagined in "The Rime of the Ancient Mariner," "Christabel," and "Kubla Khan" or in a living universe such as *Manfred's*, where "spirits hear what spirits tell." Under Jehovah's oppressive life-denying rule those who aspire to embrace the angels are condemned, partly because their families were preordained to die for being too assertive, partly because the life of the fiery independent spirit is threatening to a jealous god. In *Heaven and Earth* Byron tries to dramatize the end of the possibility of mingling natural and supernatural lives, at a time when some people had returned rebelliously to the pagan illusion that they could change their lives by incantations, before they learned that there was no future in these attempts. Taught by the angels who have defied God and entered the human world, they utter invocations and spells, and believe in powers that Jehovah declared false. For this belief they will be swept away by the waters. They invoke their spiritual lovers:

> Seraph!
> From thy sphere!
> Whatever star contain thy glory:
> In the eternal depths of heaven
> Albeit thou watchest with "the seven,"
> Though through space infinite and hoary
> Before thy bright wings worlds be driven,
> Yet hear!
> Oh! think of her who holds thee dear! (1.1.36–44)

Yet these invocations, however customary in an eclectic religion which allows human beings to love angels, are finally ineffectual. In these two Old Testament plays Byron dramatizes his rage at the biblical division of men from gods which makes these magical heretical communications fall dead and which forces us to accept an earthbound claylike existence, unilluminated by supernatural sparks, even if these supernatural sparks might lead us finally to solipsism and suicide. As illusory as these hopes for transcendence through magical incantation may be, they at least allow men to imagine conditions more inspired than those usually permitted to creatures of clay.

In the rarely discussed *Deformed Transformed* many of the problems which Byron encountered in *Manfred* in forcing his magical power onto supernatural beings come to the fore. The faults of the fragment and the fact that it is a fragment show these problems clearly. The first part of the drama is the most interesting because it combines elements from fairy tales, based, in Byron's words, "on the story of a novel called 'The Three Brothers', published many years ago, from which M. G. Lewis's 'Wood Demon' was also taken," with elements from Goethe's *Faust*, with painful allusions to Byron's own relations to his mother, and with a psychological intensification of the meaning of double personalities, here ambiguously changing shapes. The second part of the drama has little relation to the first; and in leading the transformed hero and his demonic double to fight with the Bourbons in Rome, Byron returns to the attacks on the horrors of war typical of cantos seven and eight of *Don Juan*.

In the first part Arnold's crippled body—hateful to himself and even to his mother—is transformed by magical spells into the shape of Achilles' body, and the discarded crippled body is invaded by a mysterious black man who rises at Arnold's wish out of a pool. Arnold's desire to escape from the limitations of himself is to be accomplished by magic. His mother, railing "Out, hunchback! . . . Out, / Thou Incubus, Thou Nightmare! Of seven Sons, / The sole Abortion!," teaches him to wish that he had never been born. Wounding himself while cutting wood, Arnold inadvertently voices the wish which the devil will answer:

Oh, that each drop which falls to earth
Would rise a snake to sting them, as they have stung me!
Or that the devil, to whom they liken me,
Would aid his likeness! If I must partake
His form, why not his power? Is it because
I have not his will too? For one kind word
From her who bore me would still reconcile me
Even to this hateful aspect.   (1.1.38–45)

Having uttered this dangerous wish to take on the devil's power with his shape, Arnold sees his own visage in a pool; far from falling in love with it as Narcissus had, he is sickened by it:

Hideous wretch
That I am! The very waters mock me with
My horrid shadow—like a demon placed
Deep in the fountain to scare back the cattle
From drinking therein.   (1.1.48–52)

Arnold sees his image in the water, names it demonic, and decides to kill "This wither'd slip of nature's nightshade— my / Vile form" (1.1.64–65), by letting the blood fill the pool where his demonic aspect lurked. In the act of killing himself, however, he catches sight of the water roiling:

The waters stir,
Not as with air, but by some subterrane
And rocking power of the internal world.
What's here? A mist! No more?—   (1.1.78–81)

The stage directions tell us that "a tall black man comes toward him." This double is to Arnold as the narrator of *Don Juan* would be to Harold, a pitiless mocker of Arnold's emotional excesses, and of his misshapen body, which he calls proper for a buffalo or camel. Arnold voices a second wish which will again come true:

Give me the strength then of the buffalo's foot,
When he spurs high the dust, beholding his

Near enemy; or let me have the long
And patient swiftness of the desert-ship,
The helmless dromedary!—and I'll bear
Thy fiendish sarcasm with a saintly patience.

(I.I.II3–I8)

The Stranger answers, "I will." The Stranger promises to change shapes, leaving the terms of the compact open. He takes Arnold's blood "to mingle with the magic of the waters / And make the charm effective" (I.I.I53–54).

Several long spells occupy the remainder of this first scene of the first part. The first spell, intoned over the elixir of Arnold's blood and the pool's water, begins:

Shadows of beauty!
  Shadows of power!
Rise to your duty—
  This is the hour!
Walk lovely and pliant
  From the depth of this fountain,
As the cloud-shapen giant
  Bestrides the Harz Mountain.
Come as ye were,
  That our eyes may behold
The model in air
  Of the form I would mould. . . .

(I.I.I57–68)

It is a spell for summoning forms in the air; Julius Caesar, Alcibiades, Anthony, Demetrius Polorcetes, and Achilles waft before them in response to it. Arnold, desiring beauty and love after suffering his mother's rebuffs, chooses Achilles' shape. Accordingly a second spell transforms a lump of earth into the shape of Achilles, and in a complicated transference invests this beautiful shape with the soul of the unconscious Arnold. The second spell begins:

Beautiful Shadow
  Of Thetis's boy!
Who sleeps in the meadow

> Whose grass grows o'er Troy:
> From the red earth, like Adam,
> Thy likeness I shape,
> As the being who made him,
> Whose actions I ape.   (1.1.381–88)

In a parody of divine creation, the Stranger speaks life into the earth; he ends this spell with lines describing how his magical power operates:

> Elements, near me,
>   Be mingled and stirr'd,
> Know me, and hear me,
>   And leap to my word!
> Sunbeams, awaken
>   This earth's animation!
> 'Tis done! He hath taken
>   His stand in creation!   (1.1.413–20)

The Stranger's vital presence animates the elements of nature, recombines them in the very language with which he describes them, and at the moment of his speaking, these elements leaping to his word accomplish their task. The new hollow man, inspired by the devil, is created. Arnold, arrogant and scornful in his new form, cries out, "I love, and I shall be beloved! O, life!" (1.1.421). By virtue of the devil's spells, or of the spells of that aspect of himself which might be thought demonic, Arnold has obliterated a self that he loathed. All the sorrows that his own limitations imposed upon him are miraculously banished without his having to submit to the slow process of character change, for change through magic is instantaneous.

The Stranger, the dark double self, chooses to assume the hunchbacked shape; he devises a third spell, explaining to Arnold that

> In a few moments
> I will be as you were, and you shall see
> Yourself for ever by you, as your shadow.
>
> (1.1.447–49)

This spell intoned over the late form of Arnold is less mellifluous than the other two; it is labored and theoretical:

> Clay! not dead, but soul-less!
>   Though no man would choose thee,
> An immortal no less
>   Deigns not to refuse thee.
> Clay thou art; and unto spirit
> All clay is of equal merit.
> Fire! *without* which nought can live;
> Fire! but *in* which nought can live,
>   Save the fabled salamander,
>   Or immortal souls which wander,
> Praying what doth not forgive,
> Howling for a drop of water,
>   Burning in a quenchless lot.   (1.1.453–65)

When the spell is over, a spark of flame *"flits through the wood and rests on the brow of the body. The Stranger disappears: the body rises."* Arnold shudders at the vision of his own form living, filled with the devil's power which he had originally wanted, and haunting him as a constant companion, the shadow of his former self.

Once Byron has accomplished this intricate exchange of bodies and souls, he seems to lose control over the structure of the play. Amid the flurry of battles, repartee among warring participants, and discussions about the vanity of human activity, the two transformed heroes—or parts of a single hero—can be seen flitting from one place to another, only occasionally referring to their recent transformations. For 122 lines spirits of the air sing a satirical song about war, and part 3 breaks off with a long chorus of peasants singing about the end of war. Not only is the action in the end of part 1 and in part 2 inconsequential, but the tone of Byron's characters is uncertain—sometimes sardonic, sometimes disgusted, sometimes earnestly dismayed. For some reason he fails to develop the psychological possibilities of the changes described in part 1: he does not tell what the terms of the bond will be; nor does he follow through with the ominous hints scattered throughout the fragment. He seems almost to have come too close to dealing with personal materials, the scorn of his mother, the shame of his deformity, the longing to be loved, the sardonic inner self rising from the pool's mirror in the form of a black man who despises the misshapen self and uses it as a mask to do evil (1.2.310–14). To escape from the implications of this fairy-tale material revealing psychological depths, he seems to flee into a chaos of motion and commotion and thus to abandon the loose ends of this curious series of wishes, spells, and magical renewals that permitted a hypothetical destruction and rearrangement of the self. It is possible that Byron abandoned this play because in part 1 it cut too close to the bone, and the foolishness of part 2 was too obviously covering over in agitation the revelations of part 1. I do not mean to insist upon a psychological reading of this blighted drama, but let me suggest that *The Deformed Transformed*, like *Manfred*, uses magic as a vocabulary for an otherwise unspeakable will to escape from oneself and to do so immediately, without having to undergo either pain or lasting awareness of such loss. By setting this will to self-destruction in magical terms, Byron is able not only to accomplish it but at the same time also to minimize its importance by making it seem like a fairy tale or a magic trick or some other form of mere play. He sets it away from himself in a fable that is a thin disguise, and he uses the magical apparatus to make the reader think that he knows that his desires are preposterous. Having left the reader with these unnerving tricks intended to abolish all trace of a loathed burden of himself, he dashes off into the thick of action, as if to pretend that this formless action were more important than the revealing introductory material.

Whatever his many private superstitions, Byron seems to be mocking his own speculative dramas or otherwise undercutting them. This mockery of himself is the result of the doubleness of his vision—one eye seeing "sincerely," the other satirically. It is difficult enough, as we saw in examining

Coleridge's and Shelley's magical poems, to suspend disbelief about the transforming power of magical spells; it is all the more difficult when a cold derisive eye is included within the narrative, commenting on its foolishness from a diabolical angle. This double vision was at work, as we have seen, in *The Deformed Transformed*, where the agony of shape-changing as a metaphor for personal growth was mocked by the skeptical eye of the debonair devil, whose viewpoint corresponds to that of the narrator of *Don Juan*. The devil in *The Deformed Transformed* can be seen as one eye of Byron's stereoscopic vision, looking askance as poor Arnold struggles to get out of his hated skin by means of the powers of spells and potions, powers which in any case turn out to be rhetorical and temporary. Even when one lands on the relatively stable terrain of *Manfred*, where it is possible to discern theme and structure that have been thought through, one is still haunted by a skeptical witty eye peering over the rim of the mountains. For Byron's other writings contradict *Manfred*, and they suggest that Manfred would have been an object of ridicule if he had been set in a later work, as Arnold is a Manfred transplanted into rakish mundanity. To find consistent belief seriously maintained, or even consistent use of the material as metaphor, one must concentrate on the early work and exclude the later work, or vice versa, as many of Byron's best commentators have done, choosing to see either *Don Juan* as a footnote to the authorial development of *Childe Harold* or *Childe Harold* as an exercise preparatory to the mature style of *Don Juan*.[4]

As John Wain has suggested in his "The Search for Identity,"[5] Byron may have failed to locate a central core from which his various personae could be seen to radiate. This failure gives to his postures a theatrical quality, easily translatable, fascinating, yet ungrounded. Because that usually unprofitable theme, insincerity, does finally affect the coherence of Byron's work by making one part of it cancel out the other, I have mentioned it here. The desire to use magical power to transcend the human clay, a desire fervently and consistently maintained in *Manfred*, is made to serve cosmetic purposes in *The Deformed Transformed*, with the unconscious underlying psychological symbolism of this eventually abandoned. Indeed the very assumptions about the accessibility of spirits to language are contradicted immediately after the composition of *Manfred* in *Cain* and *Heaven and Earth*, where natural and supernatural are sharply divided. Byron does not hesitate to sweep his own protestations into the hopper of his ridicule; whether he does so from fear of revealing himself, from disgust with himself and man, from brokenheartedness, or from boredom with earnestly held opinions cannot be determined. It is important to remember that Byron's views are undercut ironically and are open to question at every turn like a vast unconsciously arranged *Praise of Folly*. Therefore we cannot say what Byron means in his imagery from one work to another, for *Manfred* and canto 17 of *Don Juan* come from different aspects of his mind as from different worlds.

If in spite of the overlay of ironies we try to summarize the conclusions to be drawn from Byron's tetralogy on limits, we find that Byron combines both Wordsworthian and Coleridgean attitudes toward language and its changes. For Byron, as for Shelley, magic leads to freedom—from bodies, time, physical laws, and physical things. Wordsworth considers that this freedom is senseless and unrealistic, refusing to grant the reality of substantial things and the necessity of these for grounding character. Coleridge, on the other hand, considers it a creative freedom that confirms the supernatural origin of the imagination by demonstrating its power to make new beginnings. Wordsworth laments that words call up phantoms in place of things. Byron and Shelley, however, are glad to be released through magical incantations into a zone of ephemeral words and phantoms. They use magic deliberately to lead them out of natural forms: Prometheus, never a solid character, becomes more and more disembodied, disseminated into voices, and finally freed into free-floating song and feeling; Manfred, no longer attending to ordinary mortals, converses only with spirits, and then he sloughs off the burden of self by means of his spells. Their view on the areas to which magical metaphors apply may differ, but in general Shelley and Byron use magic to escape from the tedium of reality. Thus Wordsworth accurately foresees the life-denying qualities of magic, the annihilation of time and self in the desire for radical freedom; and in doing so he anticipates the criticisms levelled against the unreality and inhumanity of romanticism by such twentieth-century critics as Irving Babbitt and Jacques Barzun.

Shelley, hopeful that language would transform the reality, hoped not for annihilation but for a better life; his use of magic changed, as we saw, the original Coleridgean use by turning it outward toward pragmatic ends. Byron, too, asks the reader to accept imaginary cures for actual ills. Magic leads both poets to the verge of science fiction—luminous, fabulous, and willed. Paradoxically, then, in reacting against the universe of death, Coleridge, Shelley, and Byron use the magical metaphor to describe an ideal freedom but produce a fatal enthrallment. Magic obliterates the self that Coleridge had been trying to preserve as a spiritual entity and casts it back into nature, into death.

The very powers that were intended to lift men above nature allowed men to make themselves vanish either entirely, as in Manfred's case, or as specific individuals, as in Arnold's. Nevertheless, to be deprived of these possibilities, used for whatever fatal purposes, was to be oppressed by a tyrannical orthodoxy and to be deprived of private will. In the speculative dramas, then, magic was a way to resolve the complexities of personal character, pitting occult power against occult power and finally transcending human limitations altogether by abolishing them in a flash. Byron may have given no credence to these powers learned in the caves of death, but he exploited them to give creatures of clay a way out and a chance before going to shout wild and whirling words.

Many of these paradoxes emerge in Keats's work, but Keats

seems to have been consistently aware of the dangers that he was skirting, and he rejects them not, as Byron does, in the mockeries of the next poem but in the very poems where the magical enthrallment exerts its force. Keats, the Ovid of the romantic movement (as Byron may be thought its Juvenal), uses magic also as a means of escape from human limitations, as a metaphor for a circean transformation out of which men must struggle to be fully human.

Keats is concerned with the dangers of marginal beings who lure men from their human life into some closed world that they cannot escape. Recent scholars have demonstrated the importance to him of demonic powers, derived either from pre-Christian Hellenic mythology as relayed to Keats through Lemprière's *Classical Dictionary*[6] or from Celtic myths[7] or from Wieland's *Oberon*, the story of the demon king, itself inspired by the fairy lore of Shakespeare's *Midsummer Night's Dream*.[8] In these traditions the demon is interpreted as an otherworldly being who overtakes the poet in moments of inspiration or, in Celtic legend, as an otherworldly being who spirits the hero away, teaches him the secrets of the underworld, and sometimes, in exchange for this knowledge, prevents him from leaving. The demon is variously presented as a "daemon poesy," an image of imaginative absorption, or as a female demon, tantalizing but sinister, as an obsession, or as a completing power from a sphere beyond consciousness. It is therefore usually a power that enchants the victim or beneficiary away from the ordinary world of experience, into some invisible, irrational, even fatal world.

Keats extends this mythology to include the obsession with poetic creativity as an enthralling power. In *Endymion*, for instance, the poet longs, as did Manfred, to evaporate, but for different reasons. He calls for a "fellowship divine, / A fellowship with essence; till we shine, / Full alchemiz'd, and free of space" (1.778–80). In the intensity of feeling and sensing, we seem to have "stept / Into a sort of oneness, and our state / Is like a floating spirit's."

> But there are
> Richer entanglements, enthralments far
> More self-destroying, leading, by degrees,
> To the chief intensity: the crown of these
> Is made of love and friendship.   (1.795–801)

Endymion wishes to evaporate into essence, in the intensity of his feelings; he wishes a fellowship with essence cultivated through the physical senses rather than a fellowship with essence won as Manfred's was at the expense of physical sensation. There are "enthralments far / More self-destroying," for in the ecstasy, literally the standing outside oneself, of sound, smell, sight, and touch, experienced with gusto, the perceiver concentrates so intensely upon the object of perception that he blots out his consciousness of the burden of his private self. It is as if the sensation has cast a spell over the perceiver, filling him with the pulsations of that sensing experience, and making him dead to the reality in which he normally lives. In one sense this desire for a fellowship with essence comes to Endymion in reaction to the fear of real things in their ordinary dying condition; in another sense it is a dying of its own, either into a higher life or into a forgetfulness of life. It is not always certain which of these dyings is meant, or if one necessarily excludes the other. "O magic sleep!" cries Endymion of that "silvery enchantment" (1.450, 461) indicating that magical terms are applicable to all forms of self-forgetfulness.

In his search for self-destroying enthrallments, Endymion encounters Glaucus, an elusive figure who has been copiously interpreted as a poet, a wise man, a failure, or a figure of Endymion's future self. Glaucus, sitting in "the concave green of the sea," is an ancient magician wrapped in a cloak of blue

> O'erwrought with symbols by the deepest groans
> Of ambitious magic: every ocean-form
> Was woven in with black distinctness; storm
> And calm, and whispering, and hideous roar,
> Quicksand, and whirlpool, and deserted shore,
> Were emblem'd in the woof; with every shape

> That skims, or dives, or sleeps, 'twixt cape and cape.
> The gulphing whale was like a dot in the spell,
> Yet look upon it, and 'twould size and swell
> To its huge self.   (3.198–207)

His cloak depicts his now dormant protean powers to transform, by the use of symbols, the sizes and shapes and nature of
all created beings as the ocean brings forth forms and changes
them. Glaucus, with his pearly wand (3.213) and an entranc-
ing book (3.221) is silent and intent, so silent that it seems as if
he "had not from mid-life to utmost age / Eas'd in one accent
his o'er-burden'd soul, / Even to the trees" (3.228–30).
When he recognizes Endymion as the man who was prophe-
sied to redeem him, he pours out his long pent-up language,
telling the tale of his bewitchment at the hands of Circe. This
tale, derived from Ovid and from Milton's *Comus*, shows Circe
as the prototype of La Belle Dame sans Merci and of Lamia.
Her honey words (3.426), the dew of her rich speech (3.429),
tears, gestures of cradling, and charming syllables (3.444)
leave Glaucus a "tranced vassal" (3.460). Like La Belle Dame,
Circe reveals the cruelty hidden beneath the charm; she leaves
him sleeping, and is discovered fiercely transforming human
beings into beasts. She is shown "seated upon an uptorn forest
root,"

> And all around her shapes, wizard and brute,
> Laughing, and wailing, groveling, serpenting,
> Showing tooth, tusk, and venom-bag, and sting!
> O such deformities!   (3.499–503)

In a nightmarish passage these shrieking creatures begin "to
bloat, / And puff from the tail's end to stifled throat" (3.
525–26), until they suddenly vanish at her nod. She has
become a fierce witch, a curst magician (3.538, 555) denying
even the prayers of one lone elephant begging to be released,
not to his normal life and shape, but to the cold bleak air (3.
539–54). She turns her spells on Glaucus, and in potent
language she dooms him to an eternal old age. But her wicked

magic is countered by a rival magic rising strangely in the form of a miraculous hand from the sea, the source, as the cloak suggested, of benevolent transformations. An old man's hand passes Glaucus a wand and a scroll imprinted with the new magic. The new magic proclaims that if Glaucus "utterly"

> *Scans all the depths of magic, and expounds*
> *The meanings of all motions, shapes and sounds;*
> *If he explores all forms and substances*
> *Straight homeward to their symbol-essences;*
> *He shall not die.*   (3.697–701)

Once he has penetrated the depths of magic and the source of all changes in the core of forms, he will be joined by a youth who will be his twin and release him from Circe's spell. Glaucus can be seen to have close resemblances to the figure of the hermit in Shelley's *Revolt of Islam*. Like that hermit, who, we recall, taught Laon magical lore during his captivity and thereby gave to his already enchanting songs a foundation in magical knowledge, Glaucus teaches Endymion his magical knowledge. The relationship between Glaucus and Endymion is mutually releasing. Like Shelley's hermit, whose magical wisdom is fulfilled when embodied in songs, Glaucus is rejuvenated by finding the long expected poet whose songs will release him from the spell that has kept him silently paralyzed. With Endymion to sing for him, to be his voice, he becomes young and powerful enough to release all the loving pairs imprisoned with Scylla in the thralls of death. This task he accomplishes by sprinkling the now fulfilled words of the magical scroll over their corpses until the lovers rise—the opposite effect of the final words of "Lamia," where the true name shrivels and kills. In a ritual transference of power, Glaucus symbolically invests Endymion with his powers by giving him his magical cloak. He

> Began to tear his scroll in pieces small,
> Uttering the while some mumblings funeral.

He tore it into pieces small as snow
That drifts unfeather'd when bleak northerns blow;
And having done it, took his dark blue cloak
And bound it round Endymion: then struck
His wand against the empty air times nine.—
"What more there is to do, young man, is thine:
But first a little patience; first undo
This tangled thread, and wind it to a clue.
Ah, gentle! 'tis as weak as spider's skein;
And shouldst thou break it—What, is it done so clean?
A power overshadows thee! O, brave!
The spite of hell is tumbling to its grave.   (3.747–60)

When Endymion shows that he is able to unwind the thread
effortlessly, he proves that the combined powers of the scroll,
the mumbled incantations, the nine movements of the wand,
and the dark blue protean oceanic cloak have had their
effect—and that Endymion is now magically empowered as a
poet.

Endymion's poetic powers rise, then, through stages—first
of indifference to the real world, then of intense enthrallment
in sensation to the point of entering the center of sensation to
its essential core; then, with Glaucus, to the stage of accumulating the wisdom of the mysteries, incantations, and
perennially potent words, which reveal that essences are symbols. His final aim is to merge with the moon herself, symbol
of metamorphosis, who draws changes, transformations, and
transmutations after her, as the imagination hopes similarly
to do.

In the moment when Endymion temporarily evaporates, he
transmutes himself through the alchemical alembics of imagination to the full oneness with essence. He abandons the limits
in space that a physical body has, becoming pure vision. As
many critics have shown, Endymion rejects this kind of transmutation at the end of the poem, choosing instead to love a real
Peona, only to learn, in a choice reminiscent of the generous
choices in such fairy tales as the Loathly Lady, that he can love

both natural and supernatural lovers in one person at the same time—that the supernatural abides in the natural.

Magical metaphors represent a similar alternative in the "Ode to a Nightingale." In the "Ode to a Nightingale" the desire for a fellowship with essence triggered by the bird's song is more ringed by doubts and impossibilities than is the same desire in *Endymion*. At the central line "Already with thee!," however, Keats momentarily overcomes his doubts and accomplishes in words what he knows he cannot accomplish in reality. In stanza 4 he declares that he will reach the nightingale's timeless spaceless realm of essential song through "the viewless wings of Poesy" ("viewless" because they are "full alchemiz'd" and free of space, and hence impalpable and invisible). Immediately after this announcement of the means of flight, his wish is magically accomplished, and he is where he wants to be. The utterance "Already with thee!" can be read as itself a spell, like "Lo!" or "Let it be!" or "Rise!" that causes what it describes in the moment that it names it. Significantly this utterance occurs near the center of the poem (line 35 of eighty lines). Just when Keats has decided to join the nightingale through poetry, he discovers that, by some magical charm of his own words, he is there in the center of the poem that he hoped to write in order to wing beyond himself.

This magical world of words, which he enters suddenly, is a world of death. He enters a dark kingdom whose only colors and smells are those that he summons up when he magically names them. They exist in their names alone, as the white hawthorn, eglantine, violet, and musk-rose; but in their embalmed darkness are redolent of death, and they remind the poet once again, at this very moment of his magical power, that it will not last. He consoles himself that he, unlike the nightingale, is conscious and can invent the visions of those figures of many historical periods and social classes who may have heard the same indestructible song. He can invent by naming them the places where the nightingale cannot remember having visited—the magic casements, the perilous foam, and the fairy lands. This he does by his own magic. But he discovers that these fairy lands are finally forlorn and as empty of real life as the town on the Grecian urn. He must recognize at last that this second half of his poem is the work of a deceiving elf, who has cheated him for a while by her magical sleight-of-hand of naming things, summoning them, and leaving him dead to reality in their contemplation. She may well be the same merciless elf, or fairy's child, who leads the knight of "La Belle Dame sans Merci" to her elfin grot, enthralling him through her fairy's song and her sweet moans, and finally abandoning him in the midst of a blank moribund November, himself now clearly a youth who grows specter-thin and dies. "Adieu! the fancy cannot cheat so well / As she is fam'd to do, deceiving elf" ("Ode to a Nightingale," ll. 73–74); for magic keeps the poet from living in his real life, as Wordsworth had foretold, and abandons him on the cold hillside of reality, a pale, loitering, always unsatisfied figure, still dreaming of a magical world that he invented from language.

Keats's poems thus contain their own criticisms of the changes they embody, while Byron's self-loss in *Manfred* and *The Deformed Transformed* is criticized in the light of the results demonstrated in later works. While the noble Manfred is still defying the commonplace world at the end of his play, the knight of "La Belle Dame" wanes from his enchantment, fading and sickening along the sedge, a warning for other susceptible wanderers. The rejection of those self-fulfilling and self-absorbing involutions represented by magic is complete in Keats: enchantments are perilous; if the poet wishes to live and act, he must flee from them, with Wordsworth's warnings ringing in his ears. The alternatives of submerging oneself in a rich, succulent, hermetic world of fancy or of turning away from its charm toward effective action will become the choices open to the Victorians as luxuriance or experience, the lotos-eaters or Ulysses, art or life. Keats awakens just in time from the magical world of death.

Like Shelley, Byron and Keats first become enthralled by their powers and allow their words to carry them out of the limitations of time, space, mortality, and imperfection. Once they are thus transported, they no longer believe temporal and spatial limitations to be significant, since these are subsumed in words. They enter into an interior world made up of disembodied words, charms, songs, and wishes. This world has no physical extension and is easily manipulated by grammar. It is an interior world of metaphor, likeness, interchange, and symbolism, wherein one thing becomes another as immediately as words command such a change. However, either from fidelity to real events or from fear of self-revelation, as in Byron's case, or from a recognition of the airlessness and heartlessness of this otherworld, as in Keats's, both poets decisively reject it and emerge as advocates either of satire or of heroic epic, correcting or depicting action. Shelley, too, after longing to create perfection, comes despairingly to see the triumph of life.

No such brave rejection of the purely imagined and hence maddening world occurs in Beddoes, however, or in Poe and the French symbolists, who submerge themselves in it without thinking of its dangers. Thomas Lovell Beddoes in particular has no fear of the magical temptation itself, but he only laments that magic has no power over the reality of death. Like Keats a contributor to the renaissance revival, Beddoes borrows from *Dr. Faustus*, *The Tempest*, *A Midsummer Night's Dream*, and *Hamlet* for his *Death's Jest Book; or a Fool's Tragedy*.[9] This is a play even more frenzied in its transformations than Byron's *Deformed Transformed*. Two magicians, Homunculus Mandrake, "zany to a mountebanke," and Ziba, use their spells to try to surmount the ultimate magical changes of death. "A student of the black arts, a journeyman magician, a Rosicrucian," Mandrake transmutes himself to Egypt on the trail of Raymundo Lully and other "hoary magicians"; "son of the great Paracelsus," he aims "to bottle Eternity." Among sepulchres, nightshades, and hieroglyphia, victims and villains seek to defy death's metamorphoses. Ziba learns occult formulae:

> Upon this scroll
> Are written words, which read, even in a whisper,
> Would in the air create another star.   (3.3.514–16)

"Voices in the air" sing of the relentless compulsions of magic:

> As sudden thunder
>   Pierces night;
> As magic wonder,
>   Mad affright,
> Rives asunder
>   Men's delight:
> Our ghost, our corpse; and we
>   Rise to be.
> As flies the lizard
>   Serpent fell;
> As goblin vizard
>   At the spell
> Of pale wizard
>   Sinks to hell:
> Our life, our laugh, our lay
>   Pass away.   (1.4.204–19)

Finally it is the magic of death—that sudden transformation from being to not being anything at all—that triumphs. Athulf takes poison and cries

> O I am changing, changing,
> Dreadfully changing! Even here and now
> A transformation will o'er take me. Heark!
>   (4.3.372–74)

Like Circe's victims in Keats's *Endymion*, beings are de-created by magic: "The spell of my creation is read backward" (4.3.376), observes Athulf; "Now it is; / I break, I magnify, and lose my form" (4.3.391–92). *Death's Jest Book* tries to fend off the omnipresent threat with magic, only to find that death works its own, always more powerful, spells and that, unlike

Byron's Manfred, the magician cannot hope to be in control of these forces.

Thus Shelley, Byron, Keats, and Beddoes gradually change the meanings of magic as it refers to art. Where it had been a supernatural and vital power in Coleridge's interpretation, capable of animating nature and of corroborating the miracles of the spirit, it showed its debilitating aspects to Byron and Keats, who turned away from it in time. But symbolists of the late nineteenth century were unable to free themselves from the sinister spell of words in isolation from things and believed that these words guarded them from the mindless enchantments of nature. Poets such as Emerson in his "Merlin," Poe, Rimbaud, Verlaine, Mallarmé, and Valéry and French occult novelists such as Barrès, Huysmans, and Villiers de l'Isle-Adam continued to refer to their art as magical with varying degrees of seriousness, calling their verse "incantation," cultivating languid evocative meters, and avidly reading Eliphas Levi's *Dogme et rituel du haute magie.* Only in the early twentieth century did new critics show in their attacks on "word magic" that the decadents had performed a vanishing act on the world, leaving Coleridge's cautious modifications and larger purpose far behind.

8 • *Conclusion*

From an examination of several matters of significance in the period between 1740 and 1840, five conclusions emerge. First, the living powers of language, in all their complexity of source and effect, point to the inscrutability of the mind, as the ancients had traditionally imagined in their imagery of incantations. Second, a discernible rediscovery of these complexities—some irrational in spite of the prevailing stress on scientific verification and some empirically observable in the effects of poetic devices—occurs in the second half of the eighteenth century. Third, the conjunction of these rediscoveries about language and poetic powers with the wider need to prove that human beings are not mere organisms but possess spirit and miraculous will is explored within a theological context in the prose of Coleridge—and as a theurgical possibility in his poetry. Fourth, the dangers of such assertions of separateness to the stability of the moral being are evident in the substitution of words for things and in an obliviousness to steadying external realities, most clearly exemplified in Coleridge's condition as it is perceived by Wordsworth. Fifth, the lure of spiritual freedom inherent in the tradition that language is magical is imagined to have practical possibilities in political oratory, but its perhaps more sinister result is the obliteration of the self when the vital will paradoxically becomes a morbid airlessness, which is finally shunned by both Keats and Byron.

The development of these tendencies in later French symbolism and in the decadence of Oscar Wilde can be seen in a wavering genealogy from Coleridge to Poe to Baudelaire to Villiers de l'Isle-Adam, with influences from German romantic sorcery coming from Novalis through Nodier, with additional formulations by Victor Hugo, particularly in his preface to *Cromwell*. This labyrinth of influences is too intricate to trace here. It has been observed by Albert Béguin in *L'Ame romantique et le rêve*, by Gabriel Josipovici in *The World and the Book*, and by Jacques Maritain in *Creative Intuition in Art and Poetry*, which criticizes the surrealists for seeking an absolute magical knowledge. Neither these readings nor others on magical idealism in late-nineteenth-century symbolist literature recognize the struggles of earlier English romanticism as the matrix of this later development.

With these matters in mind, we can step back and see the period in perspective, as a spirit of the age that rises up in response to certain aridities felt to have existed in the preceding age and that works its way through intricate dialogue to an extreme position, where the will to power through language finally reaches a dead end. The metaphor of magic—as it applies to the workings of poetic language and as it applies by extension forward to the creation of imaginary words and by extension backward to the psychology of sudden and unaccountable creativity—corresponds to this rise and fall, because it had helped to release it or at least to provide a vocabulary for its release. For this vocabulary describes in a deliberately veiled and imprecise way unknown areas of language, poetic technique, faculties of perception and apprehension, powers of imagination, kinds of imaginary literature such as romance, and the often trancelike relations between speaker and audience, suspended in the flow of sound. In its very imprecision the vocabulary excites and inspires, arouses and provokes the mind to its creative possibilities.

It is significant that magical language was revived in a period when religion and politics were both exploring revolutionary forms. For both religion and politics could exploit the latent powers in magic: politics aimed to reform by verbal persuasion, and religion sought less and less orthodox varieties of the Word: both in different ways expected the Apocalypse. As the religious Word aims to include all time and the political word aims suddenly to abolish all the flawed time of the past and to establish with one declaration a timeless utopia, so the magical word, combining both aims, attempts also to cancel the merely human time which will bring the magician finally to death. It aims to catapult him into death and hence beyond it. The magician chants his spells to assert his supernatural origin and to assure himself that he is outside the generations that are begotten, born, and dying around him. He does not want to take his bodily form from any natural thing. If he can understand the processes of nature, he can command them, because he can reproduce these processes in the act of naming them. He thinks of himself as the hub of the universe, keeping things alive by the willed vibrations of his voice.

Coleridge combined these interests at their most balanced. He was concerned especially in later life with the Word which should mediate—the symbol which should coadunate—the disparate forces in the individual, in the state, and in the trinitarian structure of the universe; he wanted to find the word which would compress difference across space and time and yet miraculously would keep the difference there as well. His search for the unifying Word of God in theology and his search for the magical word in poetry encouraged Shelley's faith that things could be better owing to words. For both Shelley and Coleridge, despite their wonder at nature's beauty, things become shadowy, to be overshadowed and eventually replaced by the words that rendered them into ideas transporting them in the supernatural paradises of the mind.

Coleridge synthesized from occult studies, early romance literature, and primitivism a total vision of magic at work in the imagination and in verse, consequently determining the course of poetry after him. The poet whose work has been frequently the object of emotional responses ranging from pity to scorn to disgust (vide Carlyle) was in reality a triumphant figure. The scattered unsystematic nature of his prose writings and the slimness of his volumes of verse notwithstanding, he casts a giant shadow, and where we stand in this shadow is difficult to say. Only Wordsworth among the poets of the late eighteenth and nineteenth centuries warned against the heresies implicit in a magical theory of poetry. "Words, words, words," he seems to snort with Hamlet; but, whereas Hamlet was able to stop Polonius, Wordsworth was unable to stop the incantatory enthusiasm that his friend Coleridge bequeathed to the ensuing century. For Coleridge believed that words make worlds, and this was to be the magical password, the Open Sesame of the decades to come.

The dangers foreseen by Wordsworth appear not only in *The Magic Mountain* but also in Wallace Stevens's "Sea Surface Full of Clouds." Where in Mann's work, as we saw, the escape from time, relationship, and the state (in its emblem of war) into a timeless and therefore death-directed magical world is diseased, decadent, and narcissistic (the patients staring into x-ray images of themselves), in Stevens's poem all language is arbitrary. No word can render a thing or confront it. If there were not some contradictory signs in recent literature, we could see this poem as the last gasp of the incantatory tradition, and as a parody of it. Here the poet tosses up metaphors like a juggler keeping balls in motion over a void. Color succeeds color until we realize that there is no color but what the mind calls color. Not only the noticeable fluctuations of cloud and sea shapes, but also the primary reality of color turns out to be subject to the words which summon it to mind. The universe is verbal. Even a poet who writes at another time "Let's see the very thing and nothing else" is aware that our choices and our designations are solipsistic.

In the all-inclusive universe of the word the outer world is obliterated; when we live only among words, any assigning of names or transmuting through metaphor is an act of pure invention, having no need or ability to correspond accurately to what is. The poet assigning words becomes more and more frantic, and finally he falls prostrate before the inscrutable reality assumed to be beyond but invisible on the other side of a cloud of words. The universe of words is rich, lush, but diseased; no light comes from outside. There is no way of getting beyond the hermetically sealed world of the poem or of the word or sentence designating or describing the thing. This lofty self-limiting power makes the poet strangely exhilarated and giddy, as by thin mountain air; but it also transforms him into a shade moving among other shades. He is transfixed by the image of himself, motionless in his own fiction. The universe is one vast library, as Jorge Luis Borges, many of whose recent narrators are magicians, assures us, acknowledging in *Ficciones* the influence of Coleridge. Coleridge's magic isolates us in words, and, glorifying supernatural powers, eventually leads us out of life altogether.

Magic combines the romantic interest in language with its revival of neglected Renaissance themes; it allows the romantic poet to see his kinship with primitive, Greek, and oriental magicians, and thus to trust in the antiquity of his grand position. It inspires the romantics, and even presents them with actual forms in which they can assert the powers of mind and thus enforce the hopes introduced by opponents of Locke; but it also leads on to a swooning trance of self-loss. In addition the arcane and mysteriously arousing sounds of the spells introduced a poetry of secrecy working persuasively because its workings are not understood. To the extent that magic fortifies theories of the omnipotence of thought in the face of nature, it points forward to Yeats's belief that "all that flames upon the night, / Man's own resinous heart has fed," that all that exists is imagined and spun out of the imagination in words. At the same time it also points forward to the hieratic inscrutability of much symbolist verse. Wordsworth stood in opposition to this elitism, wishing instead to let poetry voice our common experience. The alternatives first presented to us by Coleridge and Wordsworth—alternatives of words and things, supernatural and natural, the magic of mind and the stability of assimilating what lies outside the mind, transformation and permanence, poetry of potentiality and poetry of existing realities, simultaneity and successiveness—still struggle for preeminence on aesthetic and moral grounds.

Notes

Introduction

1. Keith Thomas, *Religion and the Decline of Magic* (New York: Scribners, 1971), p. 643.

2. Ibid., pp. 650–63.

3. Ernst Cassirer, *The Philosophy of the Enlightenment* (Princeton: Princeton University Press, 1951).

4. Gershom Scholem, *Major Trends in Jewish Mysticism* (1941; reprint ed., New York: Schocken, 1972), p. 9.

5. John Locke, *An Essay Concerning Human Understanding*, ed. Alexander Campbell Frazer, 2 vols. (1894; reprint ed., New York: Dover, 1959), 2:4–6.

6. David Hartley, *Observations on Man* . . . (1749; reprint ed., Gainesville, Fla.: Scholar's Facsimile, 1966), chap. 3, sect. 2.

7. Hans Aarsleff, *The Study of Language in England 1770–1860* (Princeton: Princeton University Press, 1968), pp. 17–36; on Horne Tooke, see pp. 73–96.

8. Pedro Lain Entralgo, *The Therapy of the Word in Classical Antiquity*, trans. L. J. Rather and John M. Sharp (New Haven: Yale University Press, 1970).

9. Eric Havelock, *A Preface to Plato* (Cambridge: Harvard University Press, 1963), pp. 25, 26, 154, 159.

10. Karl Preisendanz, *Papyri Graecae Magicae*, 2 vols. (Leipzig: Teubner, 1928–31), 1: 118; quoted in E. M. Butler, *Ritual Magic* (Cambridge: At the University Press, 1949), p. 9.

11. *Mysteriously Meant: The Rediscovery of Pagan Symbolism and Allegorical Interpretation in the Renaissance* (Baltimore: Johns Hopkins University Press, 1970).

12. E. R. Dodds, *Pagan and Christian in an Age of Anxiety* (New York: Norton, 1965).

13. Origen, *Contra Celsum*, trans. Henry Chadwick (Cambridge: At the University Press, 1965), pp. 22–24.

14. For a close reading of the influence of Augustine on the

Renaissance, especially on George Herbert, see Mark Taylor, *The Soul in Paraphrase: George Herbert's Poetics* (The Hague: Mouton, 1974), pp. 30–68, 93–99. See also Jerome Mazzaro, *Transformations in the Renaissance Lyric* (Ithaca: Cornell University Press, 1973), chap. 1, for a survey of *res-verba* relations, Augustine's role in them, in the Renaissance, and for indications of the incantatory nature of Renaissance songs.

15. D. P. Walker, *Spiritual and Demonic Magic from Ficino to Campanella* (London: Warburg, 1958), pp. 69–70, 80, for Lazzarelli's theory of language and politics; Frances A. Yates, *Giordano Bruno and the Hermetic Tradition* (London: Routledge and Kegan Paul, 1964), pp. 125–27; and Wayne Shumaker, *The Occult Sciences in the Renaissance: A Study in Intellectual Patterns* (Berkeley: University of California Press, 1972), pp. 108–59.

16. Agrippa, *The Philosophy of Magic*, trans. Henry Morley (Chicago: de Laurence, Scott, 1913), pp. 211–16. See also Charles G. Nauert, *Agrippa and the Crisis of Renaissance Thought* (Urbana: Illinois Studies in the Social Sciences, 1955), for Agrippa's return to irrationality.

17. For magic in the poetic techniques of Renaissance poetry, see Kitty Scoular, *Natural Magic* (Oxford: Clarendon, 1965); for Shakespearean magic specifically, see D. G. James, *The Dream of Prospero* (London: Oxford University Press, 1967).

18. References to Plotinus are to *Plotini Opera Enneades* 4–5, ed. Paul Henry and Hans Rudolf Schwyzer (Paris and Brussels: Desclée de Brouwer, 1959), pp. 139–43; for Jacob Boehme, see *Six Theosophical Points*, trans. John P. Earle (Ann Arbor: University of Michigan Press, 1958), p. 130; and for clarification, see Alexandre Koyré, *La Philosophie de Jacob Boehme* (Paris: Vrin, 1929), pp. 348–447.

19. Eugene Susini in *Franz von Baader et le romantisme* (Paris: Vrin, 1942) describes a system similar to and derivative of Boehme's, emphasizing its magical aspects; Paul Kluckhohn's *Das Ideengut der Romantik* (Tübingen: Niemeyer, 1961) links Baader and Boehme as founders of German romantic thought, pp. 26–27.

20. Samuel Taylor Coleridge, *Shakespearean Criticism*, ed. Thomas Middleton Raysor, 2 vols. (London: Dutton, 1907), 2:74; see also 2:72, for his opposition to a view of language as the naming of facts.

1 · *An Eighteenth-Century Metaphor*

1. Albert J. Kuhn, "English Deism and Romantic Syncretism," *PMLA* 71 (1956): 1094–1116.

2. Sir William Jones, *The Letters*, ed. Garland Cannon (Oxford: Clarendon, 1970).

3. Kathleen Raine and George Mills Harper, *Thomas Taylor the Platonist* (Princeton: Princeton University Press, 1969), pp. 3–48.

4. Arthur Johnston, *The Enchanted Ground: The Study of Medieval Romance in the Eighteenth Century* (London: Athlone, 1964).

5. Geoffrey Hartman, "False Themes and Gentle Minds," *PQ* 47 (1969): 55–68. The eighteenth century, he writes, "knew only too well that great literature was magic and for that reason could only flee from it, as from an enchanter."

6. Patricia Meyer Spacks, *The Insistence of Horror: Aspects of the Supernatural in Eighteenth-Century Poetry* (Cambridge: Harvard University Press, 1962).

7. Northrop Frye, "Towards Defining an Age of Sensibility," *Fables of Identity: Studies in Poetic Mythology* (New York: Harcourt, 1963), pp. 130–37.

8. M. H. Abrams, *The Mirror and the Lamp: Romantic Theory and the Critical Tradition* (New York: Norton, 1958), p. 62. In Wordsworth's note to line 106 of "Tintern Abbey" he acknowledges his debt to Young's phrase "our senses . . . half-create." See *The Poetical Works of Wordsworth*, ed. Thomas Hutchinson and Ernest de Selincourt (1936; reprint ed., London: Oxford University Press, 1959), p. 165.

9. Auguste Viatte, *Les Sources occultes du romantisme* (Paris: Champion, 1928) and Jacques Roos, *Aspects littéraires du mysticisme philosophique et l'influence de Swedenborg au début du romantisme* (Strasbourg: Heitz, 1951) are among many other studies of this period.

10. Richard Hurd, *Moral and Political Dialogues, with Letters on Chivalry and Romance* (London: 1788), pp. 250–52.

11. Edward Young, *Conjectures on Original Composition, The Complete Works*, ed. James Nichols, 2 vols. (1854; reprint ed., Hildesheim: George Olms, 1968), 2: 551–67.

12. Sir Joshua Reynolds, "Discourse VI," *Discourses on Art with Selections from the Idler*, ed. Stephen O. Mitchell (Indianapolis: Bobbs Merrill, 1965), pp. 72–77.

13. Maurice Morgann, *Essay on the Dramatic Character of Falstaff*,

Shakespearian Criticism, ed. Daniel A. Fineman (Oxford: Clarendon, 1975), pp. 172–74.

14. Daniel Defoe, *Compleat System of Magick: or, The History of the Black Art* (London: 1727), pp. 35–36.

15. For other uses of the imagery in Scott see *The Complete Poetical Works of Sir Walter Scott* (Boston: Riverside, 1900), pp. 39–41, 440–42, 455. See Coleman O. Parsons, *Witchcraft and Demonology in Scott's Fiction with Chapters on the Supernatural in Scottish Literature* (Edinburgh: Oliver and Boyd, 1964).

16. Francis Barrett, *The Magus, or Celestial Intelligencer*, ed. Timothy d'Arch Smith (1801; reprint ed., New Hyde Park, N. Y.: University Books, 1967), p. 26.

17. Norman O. Brown, "Apocalypse: The Place of Mystery in the Life of the Mind," *Interpretation: The Poetry of Meaning*, ed. Stanley Romaine Hopper and David L. Miller (New York: Harcourt, Brace and World, 1967), p. 10.

2 · *Magical Language and Poetic Analogy*

1. Stephen Ullman, *Semantics: An Introduction to the Science of Meaning* (Oxford: Clarendon, 1970), p. 3. See also A. O. Lovejoy, "Monboddo and Rousseau," *Essays in the History of Ideas* (Baltimore: Johns Hopkins University Press, 1970), pp. 38–61. For an illuminating discussion of how these researches into the origins of language provoked difficult meditations for Wordsworth, see Frances Ferguson, *Wordsworth: Language as Counter-Spirit* (New Haven: Yale University Press, 1977), pp. 1–20.

2. H. M. and N. K. Chadwick, *The Growth of Literature*, 3 vols. (Cambridge: At the University Press, 1940), I: 474.

3. William Butler Yeats, "Magic," *Essays and Introductions* (New York: Macmillan, 1961), p. 43.

4. George Thomson, *Aeschylus and Athens* (New York: Grosset and Dunlap, 1968), p. 11.

5. Bronislaw Malinowski, "An Ethnographic Theory of the Magical Word," *Coral Gardens and their Magic: The Language of Magic and Gardening* (Bloomington: Indiana University Press, 1965), p. 216. See pp. 52–55 and 213–41 for the "effective change brought about by utterance" and for Malinowski's interesting concept of "the coefficient of weirdness."

6. Kenneth Burke, "Magic and Science," *Perspectives by Incongruity*, ed. Stanley Edgar Hyman (Bloomington: Indiana University Press, 1964), p. 119.

7. Ernst Cassirer, *Language and Myth*, trans. Susanne K. Langer (New York: Dover, 1956), p. 3.

8. Martin Heidegger, *On the Way to Language* (Evanston: Northwestern University Press, 1971), p. 62.

9. Thomson, p. 175.

10. "Magic, Animism, and Omnipotence of Thought," *Totem and Taboo, Basic Writings of Sigmund Freud*, ed. A. A. Brill (New York: Modern Library, 1938), pp. 872–83.

11. Ibid, p. 872.

12. Sir James Frazer, *The Golden Bough: A Study in Magic and Religion* (1951; reprint ed. New York: Macmillan, 1958), pp. 12–56.

13. Hazard Adams, *Blake and Yeats: The Contrary Vision* (Ithaca: Cornell University Press, 1955), p. 4.

14. In *Theory of Literature*, 2nd ed. (New York: Harcourt, Brace, 1956), René Wellek and Austin Warren discuss these two alternative kinds of metaphor, the animizing and the deanimizing. They indicate (p. 194) that there is some confusion over terms, for H. Pongs sees magical metaphor as abstracting and petrifying, whereas K. Vossler claims that magical metaphor brings every thing under its control, while mystical language rejects and breaks all form (p. 295, nn. 46–47).

15. Bronislaw Malinowski, *Magic, Science, and Religion* (Garden City: Doubleday, 1948), p. 73.

16. Thomas A. Sebeok, "Structure and Content of Cheremis Charms," *Language in Culture and Society*, ed. Dell Hymes (New York: Harper, 1964), pp. 357–71.

17. Winifred Nowottny in *The Language Poets Use* (London: Athlone, 1962), pp. 54–71, uses the helpful term *extremes* instead of the usual terms *tenor* and *vehicle*. In *The Burning Fountain: A Study in the Language of Symbolism* (Bloomington: Indiana University Press, 1964), pp. 175–76, Philip Wheelwright examines the magical structure of metaphor, saying that the action of both poetry and magic is "intended to work coercively upon nature and bring about specific desired effects by exploiting the sympathetic connection that

subsists between things that have once been joined or that are significantly similar."

18. William Empson, *Some Versions of Pastoral* (1935; reprint ed., Norfolk, Conn.: New Directions, 1960), p. 32.

19. *Magic, Science, and Religion*, pp. 79–81.

20. *Coral Gardens*, p. 229.

21. Claude Lévi-Strauss, "Magic and Religion," *Structural Anthropology*, trans. Claire Jacobsen and Brooke Grundfest Schoepf (Garden City: Doubleday, 1967), p. 162.

22. Ibid., p. 193.

23. Samuel Taylor Coleridge, *The Statesman's Manual, Lay Sermons*, ed. R. J. White in *Collected Works of Coleridge*, ed. Kathleen Coburn, 16 vols. (Princeton: Princeton University Press, 1972), 6: 30. In *Literature and the Irrational* (New York: Washington Square Press, 1966), pp. 102–4, Wayne Shumaker claims that Coleridge's definition really suggests the *pars pro toto* of primitive belief and is therefore closer to synecdoche than to symbol.

24. For the differences between symbols and signals, see Wheelwright, *The Burning Fountain*, pp. 19–48; see also William York Tindall, *The Literary Symbol* (New York: Columbia University Press, 1955), p. 5. Classing symbols and metaphors as subdivisions of analogy, Tindall believes that symbolism developed in conjunction with mid–nineteenth-century hermeticism as it stressed universal correspondences, pp. 50–66.

25. C. M. Bowra, *Primitive Song* (New York: New American Library, 1963), p. 82.

26. Victor Turner, "The Syntax of Symbolism in a Ndembu Ritual," *Structural Analysis of Oral Tradition*, ed. Pierre and Elli Köngäs Maranda (Philadelphia: University of Pennsylvania Press, 1971), pp. 125–36.

27. Northrop Frye, *Anatomy of Criticism: Four Essays* (Princeton: Princeton University Press, 1957), p. 278.

28. Ibid., p. 280.

29. For an examination of irrational possession as an aid to metrical composition see Nora K. Chadwick, *Poetry and Prophecy* (Cambridge: At the University Press, 1942), pp. 6–61. See also Mircea Eliade, *Shamanism: Archaic Techniques of Ecstasy*, trans. Willard Trask (New York: Pantheon, 1964); for classical en-

thusiasm, see Joseph Pieper, *Enthusiasm and Divine Madness: On the Platonic Dialogue Phaedrus*, trans. Richard and Clara Winston (New York: Pantheon, 1959), and E. R. Dodds, *The Greeks and the Irrational* (Berkeley: University of California Press, 1968), and Dodds's *Euripides' Bacchae* (Oxford: Clarendon, 1944).

30. W. K. Wimsatt and Monroe Beardsley, "The Concept of Meter: An Exercise in Abstraction," *Hateful Contraries* (Lexington: University of Kentucky Press, 1965), p. 120.

31. Felix Grendon, "The Anglo-Saxon Charms," *Journal of American Folklore* 22 (April–June 1909): 125.

32. J. Knight Bostock, *A Handbook of Old High German Literature* (Oxford: Clarendon, 1955), pp. 17–18:

> Once the women were seated on the ground,
> Here and there, one company
> bound a captive, one company
> hindered a host, one company
> picked at the fetters: 'Escape
> from the fetters; escape
> from the foes.'

33. *Macbeth*, ed. Kenneth Muir (1951; reprint ed., Cambridge: Harvard University Press, New Arden Edition, 1957), 4.1.12–19.

34. *PQ* 47 (1968): 5–18.

35. Ben Jonson, "The Masque of Queenes," *Ben Jonson*, ed. C. H. Herford and Percy and Evelyn Simpson, 10 vols. (Oxford: Clarendon, 1941), 7: 285. See varieties of spell meter, pp. 283–300.

36. Songs from "King Arthur" in *The Poems of John Dryden*, ed. James Kinsley (Oxford: Clarendon, 1958) 2: 564–78. Comus, too, pretends to be reasonable, and this veneer is part of his power, beneath which lurks the Macbethian "insane root."

3 · *Coleridge and the Magical Power of the Imagination*

1. Charles Lamb, "Christ's Hospital Five and Thirty Years Ago," *The Complete Works and Letters of Charles Lamb*, ed. Saxe Commins (New York: Random House, 1935), p. 21.

2. *Biographia Literaria*, ed. J. Shawcross, 2 vols. (London: Oxford University Press, 1907), 1: 93–94. M. H. Abrams, *Natural Supernaturalism: Tradition and Revolution in Romantic Literature* (New

York: Norton, 1971), pp. 141–95, discusses the contribution of these Neoplatonists and mystics to a distinctly romantic way of thinking of time in spiralling cycles, and of returning from mechanical divisiveness to a oneness learned from esoteric philosophies. An even more extensive appreciation of the importance of these philosophies for romanticism and for Coleridge in particular is shown by Elinor S. Shaffer in *"Kubla Khan" and the Fall of Jerusalem: The Mythological School in Biblical Criticism and Secular Literature 1770–1880* (Cambridge: At the University Press, 1975), pp. 62–188. Shaffer explains that from the researches involved in the higher criticism of the Bible a synthesis of pagan hermetic philosophies, Greek and Coptic gnosticism, Mohammedan and Hindu mythology resulted in new understanding of the Revelation of St. John, of inspiration, the bard, and the prophet, and of non-factual but nevertheless true readings of myth. The neoplatonic fusion of ideas seemed to Coleridge, according to Shaffer, the "real birth of European civilization," p. 37.

3. This and subsequent references are to *The Notebooks of Samuel Taylor Coleridge*, ed. Kathleen Coburn, 3 vols. (Princeton: Princeton University Press, 1957–73).

4. "Lectures on Revealed Religion," *Lectures 1795 on Politics and Religion*, ed. Lewis Patton and Peter Mann, in *The Collected Works of Samuel Taylor Coleridge*, ed. Kathleen Coburn, 16 vols. (Princeton: Princeton University Press, 1971), 1: 14.

5. All references to the letters are to *The Collected Letters of Samuel Taylor Coleridge*, ed. E. L. Griggs, 4 vols. (Oxford: Clarendon, 1956–71).

6. Section the second, essay 11, "Essays on the Principles of Method," *The Friend*, ed. Barbara E. Rooke, *The Collected Works* (Princeton: Princeton University Press, 1969), 4.1.514. Coleridge goes on, in a discussion which he later borrows for *The Statesman's Manual*, to say: "Not TO BE, then, is impossible: TO BE, incomprehensible. If thou hast mastered this intuition of absolute existence, thou wilt have learnt likewise, that it was this, and no other, which in the earliest ages seized the nobler minds, the elect among men, with a sort of sacred horror."

7. *The Statesman's Manual*, appendix C, *Lay Sermons*, ed. R. J. White in *The Collected Works* (Princeton: Princeton University Press, 1972), 6: 78.

8. *Table Talk, The Complete Works of Samuel Taylor Coleridge*, ed.

W. G. T. Shedd, 7 vols. (New York: Harper, 1853), 6: 398–99.

9. *The Philosophical Lectures of Samuel Taylor Coleridge*, ed. Kathleen Coburn (London: Pilot Press, 1949), p. 212. All subsequent references to the *Philosophical Lectures* will appear parenthetically within the text.

10. *Aids to Reflection, Complete Works*, ed. Shedd, 1: 154.

11. Ibid., p. 263.

12. "Death and the Grounds of Belief in a Future State," *Complete Works*, ed. Shedd, 5: 441.

13. *Aids to Reflection*, p. 264. In *The Romantic Will* (New Haven: Yale University Press, 1976), Michael G. Cooke, shifting the focus of critical attention from consciousness to willed action, sketches the contribution of will to Coleridge's theory of imagination (pp. 12–29), but repudiates its importance for the spiritual life (p. 227, n. 26).

14. Lecture on "Poesy or Art," *Biographia*, 2: 261.

15. Ibid., 2: 234.

16. *Shakespearean Criticism*, ed. Thomas Middleton Raysor, 2 vols. (London: Dutton, 1907), 1: 198.

17. Ibid., 1: 36, 60.

18. Ibid., 1: 119, 118.

19. August Wilhelm Schlegel, *Lectures on Dramatic Art and Literature*, trans. J. Black (London, 1846), p. 396.

20. *Complete Works*, ed. Shedd, 4: 232.

21. Lecture 3, *The Course of Lectures of 1818, Complete Works*, ed. Shedd, 4: 250; lecture 8, "Cervantes' Don Quixote," in *Coleridge's Miscellaneous Criticism*, ed. Thomas Middleton Raysor (Cambridge: Harvard University Press, 1936), p. 99.

22. "On Poesy or Art," *Biographia*, 2: 253–54 passim.

23. *Biographia*, 2: 64; for meter as a voluntary act, 2: 50.

24. *The Watchman*, ed. Lewis Patton, in *The Collected Works* (Princeton: Princeton University Press, 1970), 2: 91–92.

25. *Shakespearean Criticism*, 1: 116. See *Aids to Reflection, Complete Works*, ed. Shedd, 1: 355, for a late allegory of magical dreams under moonlight.

26. *Biographia*, 1: 202, 2: 6.

27. *Philosophical Lectures*, p. 244; *Biographia*, 1: 173.

28. "On Poesy or Art," *Biographia*, 2: 254.

29. *Biographia*, 2: 6.

30. "On the Principles of Genial Criticism," *Biographia*, 2: 239.

31. "On Poesy or Art," *Biographia*, 2: 254–55.

32. Letter to Godwin, September 22, 1800, *Collected Letters*, 1: 626.

33. *Biographia*, 1: 167.

34. Frank Kermode, *Romantic Image* (New York: Macmillan, 1957), p. 44.

4 · *Coleridge and the Potent Voice*

1. *The Poems of Samuel Taylor Coleridge*, ed. E. H. Coleridge (London: Oxford University Press, 1912), p. 101. Subsequent references to the poems will be to this edition, with pages and lines noted in the text.

2. As he later expresses it in the lecture "On Poesy or Art," *Biographia*, 2: 259.

3. Humphry House, *Coleridge* (London: Rupert Hart-Davis, 1953), p. 119. For a full discussion of the significance of Plato's *Ion* and other writings for Coleridge's depiction of a creativity beyond good and evil, see Charles I. Patterson, Jr., "The Daemonic in *Kubla Khan:* Toward Interpretation," *PMLA* 89 (1974): 1033–42.

4. Patricia Adair, *The Waking Dream: A Study of Coleridge's Poetry* (New York: Barnes and Noble, 1968), p. 78. See also James Volant Baker, *The Sacred River* (Baton Rouge: Louisiana State University Press, 1957), p. 68: "The *fons et origo* of Coleridge's vitalistic and dynamic theory of imagination is to be sought in Plato's *Ion*, the theory of inspiration as divine drunkenness, coupled with Plotinus."

5. See Mircea Eliade, *Shamanism: Archaic Techniques of Ecstasy* (New York: Pantheon, 1964), and Nora K. Chadwick, *Poetry and Prophesy* (Cambridge: At the University Press, 1942).

6. For an interpretation of Coleridge's theory of imagination stressing his interest in language see J. de R. Jackson's *Method and Imagination in Coleridge's Criticism* (Cambridge: Harvard University Press, 1969). In *Biographia*, 2: 39–40, Coleridge states that "the best part of human language, properly so called, is derived from reflection on the acts of the mind itself. It is formed by a voluntary appropriation of fixed symbols to internal acts, to processes and results of imagination, the greater part of which have no place in the consciousness of uneducated man."

7. E. R. Dodds, *The Greeks and the Irrational* (Berkeley: University of California Press, 1968).

8. Robert Penn Warren, "A Poem of Pure Imagination," *Selected Essays* (New York: Random House, 1958), pp. 198–305, and J. B. Beer, *Coleridge the Visionary* (New York: Collier, 1962).

9. Adair, p. 127.

10. *Table Talk, Complete Works,* ed. Shedd, 6: 421–25. For a biographical study of Scot, indicating that he in fact rejected black magic, see Lynn Thorndike, *Michael Scot* (London: Thomas Nelson, 1965), pp. 116–21.

11. For negative assessments of the poem see the analyses of E. E. Bostetter in *The Romantic Ventriloquists: Wordsworth, Coleridge, Keats, Shelley, Byron* (Seattle: University of Washington Press, 1963), pp. 82–135; and of Elizabeth Schneider in *Coleridge, Opium and Kubla Khan* (Chicago: University of Chicago Press, 1953), pp. 238–88.

12. House, *Coleridge*, p. 120.

13. For the parallels between aesthetic and religious mediation see Thomas McFarland, "The Trinitarian Resolution," *Coleridge and the Pantheist Tradition* (Oxford: Clarendon, 1969), pp. 191–255.

14. "Osorio," in *Complete Poetical Works,* ed. E. H. Coleridge (Oxford: Clarendon, 1962), 2: 518–98.

15. In the essay "On Poesy or Art" Coleridge observes that speech has always distinguished men from nature, which is mute or dumb. See *Biographia*, 2: 254.

16. George Whalley, *Coleridge and Sara Hutchinson and the Asra Poems* (Toronto: University of Toronto Press, 1955), pp. 5–7. Whalley believes that the poem was "composed (?) 1800–1; entered (?) Aug.–Sept. 1801."

17. *Biographia*, 2: 49–51.

18. Ibid., 2: 50. Coleridge criticizes Scott's use of magical meter in a letter to Wordsworth, *Collected Letters*, ed. E. L. Griggs, 4 vols. (Oxford: Clarendon, 1956–71), 3: 290–96.

5 · *Wordsworth's Arguments against Magical Words*

1. Stephen Maxfield Parrish, "The Wordsworth-Coleridge Controversy," *PMLA* 43 (1958): 367–74; William Heath, *Wordsworth and Coleridge: A Study of their Literary Relations in 1801–2* (Oxford: Clarendon, 1970); and Stephen Prickett, *Coleridge and Wordsworth:*

The Poetry of Growth (Cambridge: At the University Press, 1970). See also C. D. Thorpe, "The Imagination: Coleridge vs. Wordsworth," *PQ* 18 (1939): 1–18. H. M. Margoliouth's *Wordsworth and Coleridge 1795–1834* (Oxford: Clarendon, 1953) does not show these underlying tensions; but S. M. Parrish, in his chapter "Partnership" in *The Art of the Lyrical Ballads* (Cambridge: Harvard University Press, 1973) has explored them deeply and tactfully.

2. *Inquiring Spirit: A New Presentation of Coleridge from his Published and Unpublished Prose Writings*, ed. Kathleen Coburn (New York: Pantheon, 1951), entry 73, p. 101.

3. *Peter Bell, The Poetical Works of Wordsworth*, ed. Thomas Hutchinson and Ernest de Selincourt (London: Oxford University Press, 1959), p. 188. Subsequent references to *Peter Bell* will be from this edition. References to the *Prelude* will be to the 1805 version, unless otherwise specified, ed. Ernest de Selincourt and Helen Darbishire, 2nd ed. (Oxford: Clarendon, 1959), with lines noted in the text.

4. Arthur Beatty, *William Wordsworth: His Doctrine and Art in their Historical Relations* (1922; reprint ed., Madison: University of Wisconsin Press, 1962), p. 51.

5. Herbert Read, *The True Voice of Feeling* (New York: Pantheon, 1953), p. 178. In elucidating Hartley's beliefs, Basil Willey also suggests Wordsworth's debt to him: "Nature builds up for us 'the being that we are,' from sensation, through imagination to reflexion, . . . he is therefore a spiritual forerunner of Wordsworth." See *The Eighteenth Century Background: Studies on the Idea of Nature in the Thought of the Period* (New York: Macmillan, 1940), p. 137.

6. John Jones, *The Egotistical Sublime: A History of Wordsworth's Imagination* (London: Chatto and Windus, 1964), p. 43.

7. Melvin Rader, *Presiding Ideas in Wordsworth's Poetry* (Seattle: University of Washington Press, 1931); Newton Stallknecht, *Strange Seas of Thought: Studies of William Wordsworth's Philosophy of Man and Nature* (Bloomington: Indiana University Press, 1945).

8. "The Preface of 1802," *Literary Criticism of William Wordsworth*, ed. Paul M. Zall (Lincoln: University of Nebraska Press, 1966), pp. 50–51; Paul de Man, "Intentional Structure of the Romantic Image," in *Romanticism and Consciousness*, ed. Harold Bloom (New York: Norton, 1970), p. 70; "Preface of 1802," p. 49. Alan Grob, *The Philosophic Mind: A Study of Wordsworth's Poetry and*

Thought 1797–1805 (Columbus: Ohio University Press, 1973), p. x, suggests that criticism of Wordsworth has always fallen into these two camps, and that the two ways of thinking should be seen as phases in Wordsworth's development.

9. Alec King, *Wordsworth and the Artist's Vision: An Essay in Interpretation* (London: Oxford University Press, 1966), p. 17. Perhaps the most satisfactory way of viewing Wordsworth's career is to see him changing from associationism to something short of Platonism in the course of it. This is the solution offered in two recent books: Donald Wesling in *Wordsworth: The Adequacy of Landscape* (New York: Barnes and Noble, 1970) sees Wordsworth trying to correct the inadequacy of his earlier writing by moving from description to discourse, learning to blend sense with thought. Similarly James A. W. Heffernan in *Wordsworth's Theory of Poetry: The Transforming Imagination* (Ithaca: Cornell University Press, 1969) sees Wordsworth developing from a conception of poetry as transcription to one of poetry as transformation; though unfortunately the more Wordsworth advocates poetry as transformation, Heffernan argues, the weaker his poetry actually becomes.

10. Paul Sheats, *The Making of Wordsworth's Poetry 1785–1798* (Cambridge: Harvard University Press, 1973), pp. 16–30, considers the importance of substantial things; see p. 53 for Wordsworth's opposition to metaphor.

11. Geoffrey Hartman, *Wordsworth's Poetry 1787–1814* (New Haven: Yale University Press, 1971), p. xvi: Wordsworth "retains the genetic, matter-of-fact, earth-bound context. Things may be lost in each other, but they are not lost to each other."

12. José Ortega y Gasset, *The Dehumanization of Art* (Garden City: Doubleday, 1956), pp. 30–31.

13. Coleridge, "On Poesy or Art," *Biographia*, 2: 258.

14. "Preface of 1802," *Literary Criticism of William Wordsworth*, p. 53.

15. "Essay on Epitaphs," ibid., p. 126. But see Wordsworth's "Note to 'The Thorn' (1800)," ibid., pp. 13–14, where he praises repetition of words because of "the interest which the mind attaches to words, not only as symbols of the passion, but as *things*, active and efficient, which are of themselves part of the passion."

16. *The Quest for Permanence* (Cambridge: Harvard University Press, 1959), p. 88.

17. "Peter Bell the Third," *The Poetical Works of Shelley*, ed.

Thomas Hutchinson (1905; reprint ed., London: Oxford University Press, 1956), p. 353.

18. *The Letters of William and Dorothy Wordsworth*, ed. Ernest de Selincourt and Mary Moorman, 3 vols. (Oxford: Clarendon, 1968), 1, letters 207, 213, 220, 223, 227, 229, and following. The complaints increase in volume 2.

19. For the two newer interpretations, see Thomas A. Vogler, *Preludes to Vision: The Epic Venture in Blake, Wordsworth, Keats, and Hart Crane* (Berkeley: University of California Press, 1971), and Richard Onorato, *The Character of the Poet: Wordsworth in the Prelude* (Princeton: Princeton University Press, 1971).

20. For documentation of Coleridge's wandering in 1804–6, see Donald Sultana, *Samuel Taylor Coleridge in Malta and Italy* (Oxford: Basil Blackwell, 1969), though the work, like Norman Fruman's *Coleridge, the Damaged Archangel* (New York: Braziller, 1971), is unflattering. See E. K. Chambers, *Samuel Taylor Coleridge: A Biographical Study* (Oxford: Clarendon, 1938), pp. 6–12, for a sympathetic recounting of Coleridge's move to the city after the death of his father in October 1781.

21. *Literary Criticism of William Wordsworth*, p. 21. For an explanation of Wordsworth's stress on environment, see Willey, pp. 143–45. For Coleridge's opposition to this stress, see J. de R. Jackson, *Method and Imagination in Coleridge's Criticism* (Cambridge: Harvard University Press, 1969), pp. 139–40.

22. See Roger Sharrock, "Wordsworth's Revolt against Literature," *Essays in Criticism* 3 (1953): 396–412.

23. *Literary Criticism of William Wordsworth*, pp. 178–79.

24. Ibid., p. 149.

25. Ibid., p. 146.

26. William Hazlitt in "The Spirit of the Age" castigates Wordsworth's diction. See *The Complete Works of William Hazlitt*, ed. P. P. Howe, 21 vols. (Toronto: University of Toronto Press, 1930–34), 4: 270–79. Coleridge is outspoken in the *Biographia*, 2: 28–34, 2: 64. In his close investigation of Coleridge's "To William Wordsworth," Reeve Parker reveals that Coleridge, aware of Wordsworth's subtle disparagements, builds an equally subtle self-defense, with echoes of *Lycidas*. See *Coleridge's Meditative Art* (Ithaca: Cornell University Press, 1975), pp. 220–43.

27. In *The Collected Letters of Samuel Taylor Coleridge* E. L. Griggs explains the quarrel that began with Wordsworth's intervention

between Coleridge and Montague. His notes in the second half of volume 2, particularly on pp. 309–10 and 404–10, are disturbing. De Quincey, who suffered similar disdain from Wordsworth, believed that Wordsworth had been disloyal to Coleridge. He declared that "Wordsworth most assuredly drew such a picture of Coleridge and of his sensual effeminacy as ought not to have proceeded from the hands of a friend"; see *The Collected Writings of Thomas DeQuincey*, ed. David Masson, 14 vols. (London, 1896–97), 3: 203. See John E. Jordan, *DeQuincey to Wordsworth: A Biography of a Relationship, with the Letters of Thomas DeQuincey to the Wordsworth Family* (Berkeley: University of California Press, 1963), chap. 3.

6 · *Shelley's Political Enchantments*

1. Thomas Carlyle, *The Life of Sterling* (London, 1885), pp. 44–48. Wordsworth and Carlyle were not alone in describing Coleridge in terms of magical enchantments. Henry Crabbe Robinson wrote Mrs. Clarkson how Coleridge wandered from the topic of his Shakespeare lectures: "As you express it, 'an enchanter's spell seems to be upon him,' which takes from him the power of treating upon the only subject his hearers are anxious he should consider, while it leaves him infinite ability to riot and run wild on a variety of moral and religious themes. . . . Unhappily some demon whispered the name of Lancaster in his ear. . . . As if spell-bound, he cannot prepare himself for his lecture." See Coleridge, *Shakespearean Criticism*, 2: 178–79.

2. Newman Ivey White, *Shelley*, 2 vols. (New York: Knopf, 1940), 1: 18.

3. Letter 114 to William Godwin, January 10, 1812, *The Complete Works of Percy Bysshe Shelley*, ed. Roger Ingpen and Walter Peck, 10 vols. (New York: Gordion, 1965), 8: 239.

4. *The Apocalyptic Vision in the Poetry of Shelley* (Toronto: University of Toronto Press, 1964), p. 11.

5. *Complete Works*, 4: 353–96.

6. All further quotations from Shelley's poetry will be from *The Poetical Works of Shelley*, ed. Thomas Hutchinson (1905; reprint ed., London: Oxford University Press, 1956).

7. Ibid., pp. 35–37.

8. Neville Rogers, *Shelley at Work* (Oxford: Clarendon, 1967), pp. 72–77.

9. References to Plotinus are to *Plotini Opera Enneades* 4–5, ed. Paul Henry and Hans Rudolf Schwyzer (Paris and Brussels: Desclée de Brouwer, 1959), pp. 139–43.

10. Frances Amelia Yates, *Giordano Bruno and the Hermetic Tradition* (London: Routledge and Kegan Paul, 1964), pp. 126–27, where she also translates Ficino's rendering of the *Symposium.*

11. Giovanni Pico della Mirandola, *Oration on the Dignity of Man*, trans. A. Robert Capronegri (Chicago: University of Chicago Press, 1959), pp. 53 ff.

12. Yates, pp. 292–94.

13. Yeats, *Essays and Introductions* (New York: Macmillan, 1961), p. 78; Carl Grabo, *A Newton Among Poets* (1930; reprint ed., New York: Gordion, 1968), pp. x–xi, 5; James Rieger, *The Mutiny Within: The Heresies of Percy Bysshe Shelley* (New York: Braziller, 1967), p. 14; Ross Woodman, *Apocalyptic Vision*, p. ix.

14. Coleridge, *Inquiring Spirit*, ed. Kathleen Coburn, pp. 224–25.

15. D. P. Walker, *Spiritual and Demonic Magic from Ficino to Campanella* (London: Warburg, 1958), pp. 7–8. See p. 18 for music and the sun's power.

16. Letter 104 to Elizabeth Hitchener, October 18, 1811, *Complete Works*, 8: 160–61.

17. "Essay on Life," *Complete Works*, 6: 195–96.

18. See Donald Reiman's discussion of speed in terza rima in *Shelley's "Triumph of Life": A Critical Study* (Urbana: University of Illinois Press, 1965), pp. 87–94.

19. "A Defence of Poetry," *Complete Works*, 7: 137.

20. Carlos Baker speaks of the play as a "biography of an hour" in *Shelley's Major Poetry: The Fabric of a Vision* (1948; reprint ed., New York: Russell and Russell, 1961), p. 96. See also Milton Wilson's "This Far Goal of Time" in his *Shelley's Later Poetry* (New York: Columbia University Press, 1959), pp. 207–35.

21. Rogers, p. 334; see also 334–38.

22. "Defence," *Complete Works*, 7: 137.

7 · *Self-destroying Enthrallments: Byron and Keats*

1. *The Letters of John Keats 1812–1821*, ed. Hyder Edward Rollins, 2 vols. (Cambridge: Harvard University Press, 1958), 2: 67; for second letter, September 20, 1819, p. 200. References to the

poems will be to *Keats' Poetical Works*, ed. H. W. Garrod (Oxford: Clarendon, 1958).

2. All references to Byron's poems are from *The Poetical Works of Lord Byron* (London: Oxford University Press, 1945).

3. See Leslie Marchand, *Byron: A Biography* (New York: Knopf, 1957), 2: 516, 937–38.

4. For the first alternative see Jerome McGann, *Fiery Dust: Byron's Poetical Development* (Chicago: University of Chicago Press, 1968). For the second see George Ridenour, *The Style of Don Juan* (New Haven: Yale University Press, 1960).

5. John Wain, "The Search for Identity," in *Byron: A Collection of Critical Essays*, ed. Paul West (Englewood Cliffs, N.J.: Prentice Hall, 1963), p. 160.

6. See, for example, Charles I. Patterson, Jr., *The Daemonic in the Poetry of Keats* (Urbana: Illinois University Press, 1970).

7. Stuart Sperry, *Keats the Poet* (Princeton: Princeton University Press, 1973), pp. 232–41.

8. Werner William Beyer, *Keats and the Daemon King* (New York: Oxford University Press, 1947).

9. Thomas Lovell Beddoes, *Death's Jest Book*, *Works*, ed. H. W. Donner (London: Oxford University Press, 1935), pp. 321–498.

Index

105, 107, 114–15, 128; Wordsworth's opposition to assertion of,
142, 166, 172; in *Manfred*, 224, 226
Willey, Basil, 267 (n. 5)
Wilson, Milton, 208–9
Witches, 21, 80, 81, 215–18
Wizards, 20, 22–24, 27, 106, 121,
126, 170–72, 175
Woodman, Ross, 190
Words: mechanical theories of, 1–5;
power over things, 5, 8, 9, 10–12,
17, 38–42, 137–38, 196–201,
246–47, 253–55; Coleridge on, 13,
81–85, 97, 137–38; Wordsworth
on, 143–59, 163–69, 171; Shelley
on, 198–202, 211. *See also* Language
Wordsworth, Dorothy, 150–53 passim
Wordsworth, William: and supernatural fancies, 138–42, 161–70;
and words, 142–49, 172–76; and
things, 144–46; on metaphor,

145–46, 161–68; on growth,
145–55; on cities, 141, 156,
157–61, 173–74; on reason,
143–44, 170–74; and dismay over
Coleridge, 150–53, 155–60,
170–76; quarrel with Coleridge,
152, 175, 269–70 (n. 27); and
Shelley, 148–49, 181; and Byron,
228, 239, 240. Works: "Essay on
Epitaphs," 148; *Lyrical Ballads*, 150,
160; *Peter Bell*, 126, 138–44, 150,
163, 269–70; *Preface to the Lyrical
Ballads*, 144, 175; *The Prelude*,
146–49, 153–81; "Resolution and
Independence," 167, 224; "Strange
Fits of Passion," 55–56

Yates, Frances A., 9, 11, 188–89
Yeats, William Butler, 39, 53–55,
189–90, 226, 255
Young, Edward, 11, 17–18, 29–31